A CATHOLIC CONSCIOUSNESS

A Catholic Consciousness

Scripture, Theology, and the Church

LUKE TIMOTHY JOHNSON

Paulist Press
New York / Mahwah, NJ

Cover images: Geometric multicolored abstract pattern art by Pierre Cante / Shutterstock.com; background art by white snow / Shutterstock.com
Cover design by Sharyn Banks
Book design by Lynn Else

Library of Congress Cataloging-in-Publication Data
Names: Johnson, Luke Timothy, author.
Title: A Catholic consciousness : scripture, theology, and the church / Luke Timothy Johnson.
Description: New York / Mahwah, NJ : Paulist Press, 2021. | Summary: "A collection of talks and essays by scholar Luke Timothy Johnson on topics important to the contemporary Church"—Provided by publisher.
Identifiers: LCCN 2020037359 (print) | LCCN 2020037360 (ebook) | ISBN 9780809155422 (paperback) | ISBN 9781587689406 (ebook)
Subjects: LCSH: Church. | Catholic Church—Doctrines.
Classification: LCC BX1746 .J64 2021 (print) | LCC BX1746 (ebook) | DDC 282—dc23
LC record available at https://lccn.loc.gov/2020037359
LC ebook record available at https://lccn.loc.gov/2020037360

ISBN 978-0-8091-5542-2 (paperback)
ISBN 978-1-58768-940-6 (e-book)

Published by Paulist Press
997 Macarthur Boulevard
Mahwah, New Jersey 07430
www.paulistpress.com

Printed and bound in the
United States of America

CONTENTS

PREFACE

During a very long scholarly career, I have had the privilege and pleasure of writing and speaking in settings in which footnotes and other academic impedimenta were neither needed nor desired. The essays in this volume are a small portion of the hundreds of reviews, lectures, and articles I wrote for people who craved thought that was accessible as well as occasionally coherent or even stimulating. My goal, from the beginning of my career to its end, has been to be a scholar in service of the people of God. God's people include, to be sure, believers in many forms, and my public presence (if such it can be called), has been widely ecumenical. But when I think of church, I have in mind first and foremost my own Roman Catholic tradition, and all the essays in this volume reflect that Catholic consciousness.

Official Catholicism, to be sure, has managed to hobble along without my assistance. Indeed, for many years, the voice of an exmonk and expriest layperson was quite explicitly unwelcome in Catholic settings. Only in 1990, when Paul Baumann—a former student of mine at Yale Divinity School—asked me to review some books and then write some articles for *Commonweal* magazine, did I begin to inch my way into ecclesial visibility. And only after writing *The Real Jesus* in 1996 did I receive the first invitations to address Catholic audiences. Many of the essays in this volume appeared first in *Commonweal*, and my sense of gratitude to Paul and his colleagues at that journal is profound. The current editors have generously granted permission to publish pieces that appeared first in *Commonweal*. Similarly, permission to publish has been sought and received from the editors of *The Dartmouth Apologist*, *The Journal of Law and Religion*, and the book *Mentoring: Biblical, Theological, and Practical Perspectives* (2018). The details of original placement are indicated on the first page of each essay. I have not sought to update the essays in any fashion, not because I think they are timeless, but because I am not confident that fiddling with them will necessarily improve them.

In addition to expressing my thanks to Paulist Press for publishing these pieces, I must thank my former graduate students at Emory University who helped widely scattered pieces find a single home and—we hope—some coherent shape. I thank especially Christopher Holmes, David Carr, and Jarret Knight.

Luke Timothy Johnson
Atlanta, Georgia
June 11, 2020

INTRODUCTION

This introduction alters and substantially expands an essay called "It Started with Origen: The Commonweal *Catholic" that appeared in* Commonweal *in 2014.*

The essays collected here were written for a readership wider than the tiny professional guild of New Testament academics within which I plied my scholarly trade for some fifty years. For lack of a better term, they are a form of public theology, personal essays written from the heart, often in response to a specific moment within the larger culture. In them, I seek to locate and express what might be called a "Catholic Consciousness." They are not so bold or heroic to deserve the title "Catholic Conscience," but they do represent what I think is a distinctively Catholic approach to issues touching on Scripture, theology, and the life of the church.

Many of these essays first appeared in *Commonweal*, and my long association with that remarkable journal provides a convenient starting point for explaining what I mean by a "Catholic Consciousness." I have contributed to that publication for almost thirty years. I started (and continue) to serve as a book reviewer who has been allowed the widest latitude in my sometimes-idiosyncratic responses to books. But I have also contributed many essays on topical issues, so that my name has appeared as author or contributor nearly a hundred times over those years.

In a very real sense, then, my Catholic Consciousness means that I can be termed a "*Commonweal* Catholic," even though, as I will indicate a bit later, I have increasingly had qualms about some aspects of that magazine in recent years.

But first, the love story. From the first time I picked up a copy of *Commonweal* in the monastic library at Saint Joseph Abbey in Louisiana in the 1960s, I wanted to be the sort of writer whose work might appear in its pages. So many of my literary and spiritual heroes had written for it: Jacques Maritain and Thomas Merton, Daniel Berrigan and Michael Harrington, Wilfrid Sheed and Evelyn Waugh, Dorothy Day and G. K. Chesterton, and many more. These were people serious about the life of the mind and the condition of the world. They wrote passionately on war and peace, on Christian philosophy, on the hidden poor, and on art and literature as well.

Commonweal writers were, I thought, "Catholic" in the oldest and deepest sense of the word: they had a sensibility that was grounded in centuries of sacrament and spirituality. But they were not parochially "Roman Catholic." They were not apologists for the Vatican, nor did they shelter in a Catholic ghetto. Rather they engaged the pressing issues of the day with a bracing intelligence, freedom, and boldness; self-confidently Catholic, they wrote as citizens of the world. This combination of qualities was so fundamental to *Commonweal* that in 1999 Patrick Jordan and Paul Baumann summed them up in the subtitle of the magazine's seventy-fifth anniversary anthology, *Commonweal Confronts the Century: Liberal Convictions, Catholic Tradition*.

The heritage preserved and advanced by these writers can be traced all the way back to the greatest of early Christian theologians, Origen of Alexandria (184–254). Origen combined an unswerving embrace of the rule of faith with a willingness to subject obscure or undefined elements of that faith to critical examination. Origen was great not simply because of his astonishing learning and prodigious energy, but because, having devoted his heart to the gospel—he ultimately died following torture under persecution—he dedicated his mind to following the path of truth wherever it might lead. He was convinced that the tension between an unfettered intelligence and a heart committed to the tradition was creative; his sense of God's grandeur made him appreciate both the necessity for truth to be embodied in specific forms and words, and the reality that truth transcends all specific embodiments.

His is a heritage both precious and perilous for all who would seek to continue it. Origen himself, we might remember, was centuries later tarred with the brush of "Origenism" and lumped with the heretics. I do not by any means suggest that the combination of critical inquiry and Catholic sensibilities has ever been universally popular.

That Origen's heritage is so imperiled in today's church and society makes it even more precious. The space *Commonweal* (and its faithful readers) has sought to occupy is small and growing smaller. It is especially difficult to maintain in a world that insists that we either mindlessly adhere to received teachings or recklessly reject the wisdom of the past in the name of enlightenment.

In such a world, the notion that one can be "liberal" in some ways while "conservative" in others seems for many too difficult to grasp. But such a complex form of consciousness is not only healthy, it is downright therapeutic in today's First World context that expresses its "postmodernity" in a variety of returns to tribalism. The forces of bifurcation, to be sure, are not unique to Catholicism. All Christian denominations find themselves split between—for lack of better terms—fundamentalists and modernists. Judaism and Islam in their own ways are similarly divided. And current national politics is positively Manichaean in its refusal to acknowledge any gray areas between the light and darkness (however these are assigned).

On a wide range of pressing issues involving gender, sexuality, ecumenism, and authority, religious people tend (mostly unthinkingly) to an absolute adherence to the unquestionable authority of Scripture or the magisterium, or (mostly overthinkingly) advance a position that challenges tradition in wholesale fashion. Only a small but hardy minority attempts the art of theological tightrope walking between those extremes.

Meanwhile, the distance between liberals and conservatives—another inadequate but unavoidable distinction—inexorably grows, deepened by chronic misunderstanding and distrust. If the religiously liberal regard traditionalists as dumb sheep, the religiously conservative regard liberals as wolves seeking to ravage the flock. Mutual acceptance remains in our world difficult to find and almost impossible to sustain. The two ideologies (with all their respective splinter groups) drift ever further into separate self-righteous ghettos of indignation and contempt.

Catholics who espouse liberal convictions increasingly find themselves at the margins of the tradition they want to affirm. They tend to take refuge among more like-minded folk within the academy. They are more likely to view the Catholic center at the university as their spiritual home more than their local parish. The flight of Catholic intellectuals from the clergy and the parish has led to a dismaying divide in which the academy is celebrated as the place of the intellect and the church as the isolated repository of faith.

Such a division between the heart and the mind has had sorry consequences for both. The church and university alike have severed the link between critical thinking and faith. In Catholicism, as in almost all Christian denominations today, the tradition of the learned pastor is virtually dead. Rare is the bishop or parish priest who can hazard a genuinely critical reflection in a sermon or other public setting; the protectors of Catholic orthodoxy are vigilant, ever ready to identify—and report—such "freethinkers" as heretics.

On the other side, equally rare is the academic who can openly profess traditional Christian beliefs while retaining credibility as an intellectual. Hiding one's faith, or abandoning it altogether, is increasingly the price of citizenship in the world of (purportedly) free inquiry. Thus, in a university department of religion, it is a matter of pride for scholars to study religion rather than to practice it. Some professors of religious studies even understand their mission to be the demystifying of traditional beliefs and practices among their students.

One would like to think of institutions of higher learning that have an explicit religious affiliation as being an exception to such bifurcation, but in fact the pressures in such places are often even greater. In religious colleges and seminaries, many professors of theology become expert at practicing what I think of as a "higher fundamentalism." They camouflage a lack of genuine critical inquiry with an elaborate apparatus of scholarship. But behind their credentials and their impressive displays of footnotes, they are in truth little more than upper-level catechists, passing conventional wisdom on to the next generation. Scholars who actually try to bring critical acumen to the tradition, or who seek to expand the conversation beyond parochial boundaries, risk being censored or suppressed: the roll call of recent decades includes Charles Curran, Roger Haight, Elizabeth Johnson, and Margaret Farley. Spirited and passionate theology cannot thrive in such a context of fearful conformity.

At the same time, the supposedly liberal academy itself turns out to be repressive in its own fashion. Especially in the humanities, where free critical inquiry is the ostensible norm, varieties of progressive dogma exercise astonishing influence both in the classroom and in campus policy. On a great range of topics, one is hard pressed today to find any genuine diversity of political and social positions. *Political correctness* is an overused term, yet it accurately designates a complex set of academic "right thinking" that embraces an apocalyptic vision of climate change; the evils of tobacco (but not pot); the oppressive character of late capitalism; the malignancy of "europhallic" thought; the omnipresent infection of "white supremacy"; and the embrace of all forms of human diversity except those representing conservative and, above all, religious traditions. To take one glaring example, in recent years the *Chronicle of Higher Education* published an astonishingly ill-informed and illiberal essay ("The Great Accreditation Farce") by an Ivy League professor calling for the disaccreditation of religious institutions such as the academically demanding (but expressly evangelical) Wheaton College. As for politics, you are as likely to find a critic of Barack Obama in an English department as you are to find a Hillary Clinton fan in an Evangelical church.

In a convocation address to graduates of Harvard University, former New York mayor Michael Bloomberg—a great patron of Johns Hopkins University and late candidate for the presidency—lamented what he perceived to be a total lack of political diversity and social thought within the contemporary academy. A case in point from my former academic home: without question, the former Speaker of the House, political theorist, and historical novelist Newt Gingrich is among the most accomplished of Emory University's alumni. He is also a provocative and polarizing figure, whose worthiness for university recognition can be legitimately disputed. Yet so anathematic is he to the reigning university orthodoxy that it has been virtually impossible to put his name into consideration for an honorary degree from Emory. Even to suggest that he is as worthy of consideration for such a degree as, say, the CNN reporter Christiane Amanpour (who has received one), is to invite only an embarrassed silence.

Given such division, the ideal toward which *Commonweal* strove for nearly a hundred years is both rarer and more valuable than ever. The magazine was remarkable among Catholic publications for being from first to last entirely the work of laypeople. As such an expression of lay sensibility, it showed how authentic faith could support free inquiry. It insisted, and demonstrated, that rigorous thought is not alien to religious tradition, but rather is demanded by it. More than ever today, I think, the world needs a place where "liberal convictions" and the "Catholic tradition" are in conversation. For ninety years, *Commonweal* provided such a place, and I felt honored that my essays and reviews found a home there.

In one important respect, though, the past few years have made me less enthusiastic an apologist for the journal that I have so long loved. I find that its "liberal convictions," which ought not to mean a set of specific positions on matters liturgical, hierarchical, or political, but rather a conviction that the free engagement of serious thought from a variety of perspectives is necessary for healthy conversation, have tended to tilt in the last decade, especially in its editorial opinions, almost entirely toward one political platform rather than another.

The magazine has lately been in danger of embracing the McCarthyism of the religious and political left as consistently as it historically opposed the religious and political McCarthyism of the right. It may be a slight exaggeration, but especially during the Obama and Trump presidencies, the link between "Christian" and "Democrat" was virtually assumed. It would be better, I think, if *Commonweal*'s "liberal convictions" meant not that readers knew beforehand what views they would find in its pages, but that they could expect to engage vigorous and critical Catholic thought.

But if "liberal convictions" are difficult to maintain in a consistent and even-handed fashion, the other half of the equation, "Catholic tradition," has not been much easier. For the first half of *Commonweal*'s history, the magazine's editors and writers could address the non-Catholic world with the confidence of those who inhabited an unchanging, even unchangeable, tradition. But over the past fifty years that confidence has evaporated.

The Second Vatican Council, with its long and contested aftermath, has divided Catholics over the question of what constitutes authentic Catholic tradition, and the pages of *Commonweal* over these decades bear ample testimony to the ideological, moral, and political dimensions of the church's internal struggle. Because the reformist spirit of the council arose out of the critical inquiry of the great preconciliar theologians, who themselves experienced censorship and suppression for their efforts, it was natural for the magazine to applaud the effort to make the church more liturgically adequate, more ecumenically inclusive, and more institutionally responsive. Here "liberal convictions" seemed to correspond exactly with what seemed to be the new shape of the "Catholic tradition." That didn't last.

As we all know, forces within the Roman Catholic Church—as in other denominations—have pushed powerfully back against "reform" and openness to the world. In recent decades, champions of "tradition" have sought to mitigate and even reverse the reforms of the council—and have done so with the tacit and sometimes explicit support of the Vatican. Precisely in the name of the tradition, some have sought a return to a Tridentine church, which in their view means a church of absolute obedience to the magisterium, where critical thought is viewed as dangerous.

In this ideological struggle, *Commonweal* has done well, I think, in speaking boldly of a church large enough to embrace critical thinking and appropriate change. In such a battle about basics, one must take sides. It would not be possible for a magazine to be fair-minded to all positions, when one of those "positions" seeks to deny the legitimacy of any *other* position. Nevertheless, *Commonweal* has managed to include many less-than-liberal writers on religion in its pages and has continued to enunciate an understanding of the Catholic tradition that is much older, deeper, and wider than this contemporary fray. It has represented that deep tradition with its vigorous examination of Catholicism's historical sources in Scripture, in patristic authors, and in the writings of mystics and theologians through the centuries. As it was for the council, this sense of history is the necessary precursor to helping make the church more comfortable with a diversity of expression within its unity of faith.

What could my beloved journalistic home do better? I have a few ideas. With its Catholic sense of history and tradition, *Commonweal* could inquire more deeply and with greater empathy into the views of those who seek a return to a Tridentine church. What are the values they see as having been lost? What forms might best embody those values? Generous readings of positions hostile to one's own is the mark of genuine conversation within the church. Like few other fora, *Commonweal* could create such conversation among disputants through historically and theologically informed analysis.

Commonweal could also represent the Catholic tradition more comprehensively by devoting greater attention, not to the *ephemera* of political postures (whether civil or ecclesial), but to the demands of discipleship in the broadest sense: the moral entailments of the gospel, the shape of piety, the call to holiness. One way to do this is to engage with the prophetic lives of the saints of the past. Another is to elicit personal reflections on the path of sanctity from among the magazine's gifted and deeply committed writers.

Commonweal could continue to refuse identifying the Catholic tradition primarily with the Vatican or the papacy, instead (unlike so much of the media), giving more attention to many manifestations of the tradition in religious orders, monasteries, convents, and above all, local parishes. A lay Catholic journal, it would seem, ought to celebrate and illuminate what is precisely lay in the tradition. Thoughtful reportage on this larger and living tradition might help shift an unhealthy attention from a Catholicism that is defined by the Vatican to the Catholicism that lives vibrantly—or not so vibrantly—in parishes, convents, seminaries, and social ministries.

I only began writing for *Commonweal* in 1990 when I was already forty-seven years old, at first mostly book reviews at the invitation of my former student at Yale Divinity Student, Paul Baumann. Clearly, the roots of my own Catholic Consciousness were already old and deep by the time I became a "*Commonweal* Catholic." Since in the essays collected here I make fairly frequent allusion to some point or another in my past life, it may be helpful in this introduction to provide at least a sketch of the elements, positive and negative, that formed the kind of consciousness that I seem to inhabit and invariably think of as Catholic.

The positive elements begin at the beginning. The youngest child of a widowed mother (my father died when I was two months old) who herself died when I was eleven years old, the Catholicism I inherited and internalized in that tiny northern Wisconsin village had little if anything to do with doctrine or theology and everything to do with cycles of ritual and prayer that suffused all of life. My brother and I were pretty much the major part of the acolyte staff, and my sisters were the organist and half the choir. My mother was profoundly pious, even, as one of my sisters put it, a little "fey." I remember her saying the Jesus Prayer ("Lord Jesus Christ, have mercy on me a sinner") as she carried on her housework, ran my father's insurance agency, and served as town clerk. At the same time, she was a voracious reader, a lover of poetry and fine music who played the piano and sang beautifully, and read to her two youngest boys a wide range of books from Lewis Carroll's *Alice in Wonderland* to T. H. White's *Mistress Masham's Repose*, thereby ensuring that our material poverty was not without the compensating riches of culture. Intelligent conversation and quick wit were the gifts we children contributed to the meals she faithfully prepared for us.

Catholicism then meant blessed palms behind the picture of the Sacred Heart inscribed with all our names—palms handy for burning during terrible thunderstorms as we prayed the rosary together—as we also did as a family, kneeling here and there in the living room all during Lent. Catholicism meant CCD classes where the *Baltimore Catechism* (and the nine choirs of angels) was memorized, the weekly practice of fasting and confession and communion, blessings before meals and nightly prayers at bedside, benediction of the blessed sacrament and the stations of the cross, and the Legion of Decency. It was, in short, the very air we breathed. It was not an *aspect* of our lives, in a real sense, it *was* our lives.

When my mother died, I lost that seamless world with her, as we two youngest boys went to Jackson, Mississippi, to live with our oldest brother. For the first time, we attended a Catholic school, but also for the first time, we lived in an overwhelmingly Protestant (Southern Baptist) world and went from never having seen a person of color to inhabiting (and being bewildered by) the most solid fortress of Jim Crow. We arrived in Jackson about a year after Emmett Till was lynched, and I left Jackson for the monastery the summer Medgar Evers was assassinated.

Being taught by smart women like Joan Boone and Sister Paulinus Oakes at St. Peter's in Jackson sharpened my sense that a "Catholic Consciousness" was also a critical standpoint. They said flatly that our state-issued textbooks glorifying the racist Senator Theodore Bilbo were wrong, and that the segregation of the races was an evil. These intelligent and brave women showed me how being Catholic was not all the world but a specific and critical way of being in the world.

I went to the seminary in Covington, Louisiana, when I was thirteen years old, and several of my essays in this volume allude to my time at Saint Joseph Seminary. For fifteen years, first as a seminarian, and then as a Benedictine monk, I lived within the most intense formation of my Catholic Consciousness. Saint Ben's (as we all called it) continued my early childhood experience of total immersion in a specifically Catholic culture, but with the addition of explicit formation in liturgy, theology, the practices of prayer, and the voracious cultivation of the life of the mind, culminating in four years of theology at Saint Meinrad Archabbey in Indiana (1966–70). Fifty-two years after leaving the monastic life, I have discovered time and again that the experience of these fifteen years within the Benedictine world was far more formative of my Catholic Consciousness than I could possibly have been aware of at the time.

Now the negative. My lack of fit with the actual life of a monk, revealed simultaneously if unequally by hormones and Paul's Letter to the Romans, led to my leaving the monastic life and priesthood and marrying my dear wife, Joy, who was a divorced woman ten years my senior with six children from her first marriage. The rupture was catastrophic first for her, a profoundly devout Catholic and a leader in the Catholic charismatic movement, who had been a daily communicant since childhood and prayed more simply and directly than I ever could. Although I scarcely enjoyed being excommunicated, I was sufficiently sophisticated to be able to distinguish once and for all between the obedience owed to the Living God and the submission demanded by the institutional church. In hindsight, my life in the desert for over twenty years was an important and perhaps necessary step into full adulthood in the faith. Until Paul Baumann asked me to write a book review for *Commonweal* in 1990, I had spent nearly twenty-seven years outside the circle of Catholic culture, an exmonk and expriest who learned lay Catholicism from the edges of marginality.

I had already started PhD work in New Testament at Yale University in 1971 while still a monk. Here was another new and alien world, at once thoroughly Protestant in its sensibilities, and, especially in New Testament studies, unquestioningly committed to an Enlightenment epistemology expressed by the historical-critical method that then dominated the field. For the next three decades, I studied with teachers and students inhabiting this non-Catholic universe, taught in Protestant seminaries (YDS and Candler) and a state university (Indiana), lectured and preached at hundreds of Protestant churches and schools, but was not invited to speak at a Catholic institution until 1997, after I had written *The Real Jesus*. The result of this total ecumenical immersion, strangely, was not to make me less but more Catholic than ever. I grew to appreciate the distinctive strengths of the Lutheran, Episcopal, Methodist, and Presbyterian traditions, and was delighted to share Christian fellowship with them, but I also grew to understand and value more deeply than ever the profound riches of the tradition that was mine.

I hope this biographical sketch provides whatever context is needed for my random comments in the essays contained in this volume. If I were asked right now to define what I mean by a "Catholic Consciousness," I think I would say that it is a way of viewing the world that is deeply grounded in two-thousand year-old traditions (and therefore is capable of a long historical view of events), that is open to the work of God's Holy Spirit in the present (and therefore is able to be renewed in every age), and that combines the widest embrace of diverse cultures with the sharpest and most consistent use of human reason to test the cultures it embraces. But maybe these essays themselves show what I mean better than I can define what I mean.

Part I
SCRIPTURE

1

SCRIPTURE AND THE LIFE OF THE CHURCH

This small essay began as a presentation at Boston School of Theology and Ministry on the occasion of the new biblical commentary from Paulist Press, in October 2018. The dedication to Bill was part of the original talk, whose slight weight, I hope, is not taken as an adequate representation of my respect and affection toward him.

This essay is dedicated to Father William Stephen Kurz of the Society of Jesus, whose life of scholarship and service within the church has, as we all know, been exemplary. Bill and I were classmates in the New Testament doctoral program at Yale in the early 1970s, began our research together in Luke–Acts, and found our respective lives and study enlivened by the experience of the Catholic charismatic movement. Although circumstances have not allowed us to be together bodily as often as either of us would like, we have always felt close in the Spirit, never more so than when we worked together on the book *The Future of Catholic Scholarship* (Eerdmans, 2002). I have always been strengthened by the realization that my sense of Scripture and the life of the church is shared and convincingly lived by my brother in the faith.

I propose to approach the topic of Scripture for the life of the church under three headings: the historical, the theological, and the pastoral. The first two I regard as necessary preparation for my real interest in this essay, which is pastoral. I hope to focus on a longstanding and growing crisis, among Catholics, to be sure, but also within other families of Christians. On one side, the crisis consists of the church's loss of a living sense of Scripture, which is at once also a loss of its own life; on the other, the crisis consists of Scripture's loss of any real significance when it remains a vestigial organ analyzed dispassionately by scholars rather than embraced passionately by sinners and saints.

HISTORICAL

The church was not brought into existence through first-century people reading Scripture, but through the experience of the presence and power of the Living God in their lives that came, surprisingly and scandalously, through a crucified and raised Messiah. Because Jesus was exalted to a share in God's own presence and power, he became the "life-giving spirit" (1 Cor 15:45), who poured God's love into their hearts through the Holy Spirit (Rom 5:5). Because he was Lord, believers possessed the Holy Spirit; because they possessed the Holy Spirit, they could proclaim him as Lord (1 Cor 12:3; Rom 10:9; Phil 2:11).

This dramatic experience of empowerment through the crucified Jesus appeared at first to absolutely contradict the Torah, by whose norms Jesus's life could not be considered righteous, and in whose eyes his death was cursed (Gal 3:13; 1 Cor 12:3). In order to come to grips with their unexpected and overwhelming experience of God, the first believers began to reread the same Scriptures they shared with their fellow Jews, and found, above all in the prophets and the Psalms, the garments of Torah with which to clothe their experience and make it intelligible to themselves and others. They found a language for speaking about Jesus precisely in those places of Torah that revealed God's powerful and surprising presence among the poor, the weak, the rejected, the exiled, and the persecuted. In the Psalms, they found that a stone rejected by the builders could become the cornerstone; that a righteous man put to death by enemies could cry out as one forsaken. In the prophet Isaiah they found the vindication for an innocent servant who gave his life for the transgressions of others.

In the earliest letters and narratives composed for Christian readers, such Scripture texts played a key role in interpreting the identity, work, and significance of Jesus, showing how God was in Christ reconciling the world to himself (2 Cor 5:19). Scripture played an essential role in the shaping of the compositions we call the New Testament. In turn, through those Christian writings, that prior and formative Scripture, now called the Old Testament, underwent a fundamentally new interpretation, an interpretation governed precisely by the new experience of God gifted them through Jesus the crucified and raised Messiah.

Very quickly, because these distinctive Christian compositions—first the letters and then the Gospels—were read aloud in the worship assembly together with the writings of Torah, they also gained the authority of Scripture. By the late second century, the canons of the Old and New Testaments, what we Christians now designate as Scripture, was pretty much settled, with formal conciliar ratification taking place during the fourth century.

Although any number of factors went into the historical process of canonization, I want to stress a criterion that was more implicit than it was explicit, but perhaps was even more important as a result. I mean the criterion that can be termed the *sensus ecclesiae* (the sense of the church), which has both a formal and material element. Formally, the sense of the church means the process of use, discernment, and testing, which led to disparate communities exchanging, collecting, and selecting certain compositions and not others. Materially, the sense of the church means that the church perceived in these writings the distinctive capacity not only to express the experience of God in Christ that was the very life breath of the church, but also that these writing could bring into being, enliven, and guide the church in every age.

This is what we find in the lives of the saints whose stories—far more than doctrinal conflicts or institutional struggles—constitute the true history of the church. The church is most itself in the embodied witness of sanctity. And in a living tradition stretching from the apostles themselves, through the mothers and fathers of the desert, the monks, nuns, and mystics of the Middle Ages, down to the witnesses of our own age, the connection between a personal and passionate reading and praying of Scripture—above all the praying of the Psalms—and a prayerful and prophetic witness in the world, is clear and constant.

Because Augustine and Luther both read Paul as a script for their own experience, they at once enlivened the text of the Apostle and transformed their own lives. Because both Teresa of Avila and Teresa of Calcutta were reformed by the words of Scripture, they were also powerful reformers in the church. For the saints, that is, those who are fully and truly committed to the transformation of their lives according to the mind of Christ, Scripture is living and life giving, above all because it is read as if it speaks in all its parts to that process of transformation. The experience of the reader is identified and clarified even as that experience elicits the true telos of the text. The complex and challenging experiences of the church in every age and place are perceived through the symbols of Scripture, and in turn evoke readings of Scripture that are at once new and deeply continuous with earlier readings, paradoxically, most continuous perhaps when most new.

THEOLOGICAL

Such reading by the church past and present depends on a robust theological understanding of the canon. For two reasons, I return here to some thoughts on this subject that I first formulated some thirty-four years ago and have shamelessly repeated in print at least once. First, I finally grasp, at the age of seventy-five, that very few people have actually read anything I have written or remembered it if they did read it, and it is an extreme example of scholarly vanity to suppose that these particular thoughts are therefore repetitious. Second, I consider these ideas to be of such importance that they bear repeating any number of times. In their first iteration, I called these "canonical theses," and numbered them. Although I again use numbers for the sake of neatness, I prefer to call them, less sententiously, simply canonical principles, and I offer them now with a few significant modifications.

1. Canonicity is a statement of relevance. The church affirms with this unchanging and unchangeable list of books—note, not authors and not theologies, but books—that the particular and time-conditioned meaning of the texts is not their only meaning. They are not defined only by their historical context. They possess enduring authority. They can bring the church of every age into being and shape it according to the mind of Christ. A side note of some importance: when I speak of church, I refer first of all not to a worldwide organization, but the living organism of believers in every place who gather in the name of Jesus and call on the name of the Lord.
2. Relevance, however, is not the same for all times and places. This is why the entire collection of writings must be kept alive if the church in every time and place is to be alive in the Spirit. In times calling for renewal and change, the voice of Paul may be most pertinent, in times of moral lassitude, the Letter of James or the

Gospel of Matthew. The Book of Revelation is read quite differently in times of persecution than in circumstances of comfort. Not only times but also places differ. The universal church can exist in dramatically distinct circumstances simultaneously: here it enjoys position and prosperity, while there it is poor and persecuted. Here, it may require the voice of prophecy, and there, the comfort of promise. The canon must be able to address every time and place of church. This is why the Psalms play so unique a role within the canon. Praying the Psalms, the church, as Augustine understood, speaks directly to God out of every imaginable circumstance.

3. The relevance of the canonical writings is not found solely in how they speak individually; rather, it is as parts of a collection related dialectically to all the other parts of that collection. The way the writings work together to shape Christian identity is precisely what makes the canon such an important and intricate organ, and shows how the very idea of a "canon within the canon" reveals an arrogant assumption that we know for every age and place what documents possess relevance, and are willing to close the possibility that canonical witnesses other than the ones we now prefer might testify to other realizations of the church.
4. The canon can be regarded as the church's working bibliography. Whatever else individual Christians read on their own, these are the compositions to which the church as such turns for discerning, debating, and defining its identity. These are the public documents of the church. Public, first because they are read aloud in worship in the hearing of all; public, second, because they offer themselves to the entire community, providing the basis for discernment and debate among all believers as they encounter new issues and new experiences.
5. The canon is more than the residue of a historical process. It requires a commitment by the church in every age and place. The acceptance of these specific writings

for liturgical reading and public debate is the most fundamental identity decision made by communities. The decision rejects any writings from the present that would contend for equal recognition and asserts continuity with the tradition that handed on these compositions from generation to generation as the most consistent and visible thread of Christian identity through all its long history. Simultaneously, the decision assumes responsibility for transmitting that same measure to generations that follow us.

6. The canon and the church are correlative entities. The canon establishes certain writings from the past as the church's Sacred Scripture, a term that bears a weight different than *the Bible*, which only designates a set of books, not its role for the church. As the church stands under the norm of Scripture in every age—finding meaning and life in its prayerful reading—so do those ancient writings gain the recognition as Scripture by being read and prayed by a community, age after age, as the measure of its life and meaning.
7. It is essential that the canon be closed, for its stability enables it to mediate a specific identity through the successive ages of the church. Because the church today reads the very same writings as were read by Polycarp, Augustine, Aquinas, Luther, and Rahner, it remains identifiably the same community. If a lost letter of Paul should be discovered and shown to be authentic, it would cause great excitement but it should not enlarge the canon, for such a letter, from the time of its composition until the present, has not shaped the identity of the church catholic.
8. Indeed, it is because the canon is closed and exclusive that it is capable of being truly catholic, having universal and enduring pertinence. This is only an apparent paradox. A measure that can be altered by addition or subtraction at any time or place, cannot have the capacity to address every time and place. The closed nature

of the canon is what enables and encourages an open process of interpretation.

9. The acceptance of the normative role of the canon is what distinguishes theology from the history of ideas and the study of literature. For history and literature as such, the concept of canon is meaningless, except as a useful classification for a certain group of writings that for a certain period achieved classical status. But that recognition does not necessarily bear with it the distinctive interrelationship between texts and a living community over an extended period into the present, which is essential to the notion of canon.
10. The ecclesial decision to consider these writings as Scripture carries with it the acknowledgement that they have a peculiar and powerful claim on the lives of individuals and of the community as a whole. Believers assert that they do not control these writings so much as the writings exercise control over them, by providing the distinctive and indispensable framework for their self-understanding. The questions that readers pose to the texts are, in this recognition, far less significant than the questions that the texts put to readers.
11. Implicit in the recognition of the canonical writings as Scripture is the conviction that they speak not only in the voices of their many human authors, but also speak for God. Scripture speaks prophetically to every age, not only the age of its composition, and essential to the very concept of prophecy is the speaking of God's word. These texts do not contain revelation so much as they continue to participate in God's self-disclosure in every age.
12. The conviction that within the time-conditioned words and symbols of Scripture reflecting the perspective of many authors across many centuries, from the Yahwist to the seer on Patmos, there speaks as well the single word of God, finds expression in the phrase *divine inspiration*. To speak of the word of God is, by implication,

to speak as well of the work of God's Holy Spirit. Theological accounts of scriptural inspiration vary widely, as we might expect; but for the life of the church, such explanations are of far less significance than the truth that God's presence and power through the Spirit is at work in the process both of producing these texts and in the process of interpreting them among the faithful who faithfully read.

13. If the writings of Scripture arose as responses to God's presence and power, first in the experience of the people of Israel and then in the death and resurrection of Jesus, and if the history of the saints through the ages shows that Scripture was read as the essential frame and former of the experience of God, and if the nature of the canon is such as to invite the reading of these same Scriptures as concerning, above all, the experience of God among readers in every age, then it would seem to follow that the phrase *Scripture for the life of the church* ought to be a tautology—what else could it be?

PASTORAL

The hard pastoral reality, I think you will agree, is that for most Catholics and most Catholic parishes, this positive and enlivening relationship between Scripture and the life of the church is at best tenuous, and at worst, absent. The fond desire of Vatican II that a renewal of Scripture in the life of the church might follow from accessible and annotated translations, better catechesis, liturgy and hymnals in the vernacular, and vigorous biblical scholarship, have largely gone unrealized.

Catholic laypeople remain mostly ignorant of Scripture but seem less embarrassed by their ignorance since their mainstream Protestant friends don't seem to know much more than they do. Indeed, Catholics are as susceptible to the fads of academic reductionism as are members of other denominations, so that the bits of Scripture of which they become aware are approached with suspicion. The hermeneutics of suspicion has done its work, even among those who cannot pronounce the term.

The main point of contact with Scripture for most Catholics is Sunday Mass, where preaching on the lectionary—when it occurs—seldom if ever reveals either the complex and exciting intertextual possibilities of those fragments of texts or the way engaging them might illuminate and in turn be illuminated by, the experiences of God within their community.

This situation needs no belaboring. Nor is it entirely new. We ought not romanticize the relationship between Scripture and the church in the past. The ideal I have sketched as the history of the saints and the premises of canonicity was never universally realized, and often was found only among a few. Nor should we waste valuable time seeking to place blame for the present situation. Certainly, the academic captivity of biblical scholarship in its uncritical embrace of the historical-critical perspective has not helped. Even if one were to grant the adequacy of that approach, the scriptural education of clergy remains, even within that alarmingly superficial paradigm. Ministers with only a basic knowledge "about" the Bible find that knowledge insufficiently integrated with the loving use of Scripture in theology, preaching, and spirituality. Adult study programs of various stripes have the same tendency to be content with knowledge about Scripture more than being transformed by Scripture.

Let us grant that we cannot and do not want to return to the past. Let us admit that many of us bear at least some responsibility for the present. The question facing all of us is how to enable the future life of the church by restoring the proper role of Scripture within that life. How can we at least begin to move from the Bible as a strange book locked in the past to a Scripture that speaks powerfully to the world in the present? Let me propose a way.

First, let us recognize that what is required of us is massively difficult. It cannot be accomplished quickly or easily. We seek through the power of the Holy Spirit a transformation of our own minds and hearts, or, as Richard Hays felicitously phrases it, a conversion of our imagination. The answer is not one that you and I already have and can easily peddle to others. The answer is one that we ourselves are seeking. If you and I are not in the process of being transformed, then neither can we credibly invite anyone else to the process of transformation.

Let us acknowledge, second, that we make bold to challenge and subvert the hold that secular modes of knowing and valuing have on us all, making us all double-minded as we try at once to affirm the truths of our religion, while at the same time we measure our religion and all else by the canons of modernity rather than the canon of Scripture, so that the distinct perceptions and diction of faith appear strange and even false when we dare to express them.

I want to make clear at this point that a certain kind of double consciousness and bilingualism is required of believers in today's world. I am not interested in hammering the Enlightenment, which has brought many good things to the world, not only through science and technology, but also in bringing to consciousness the need for human rights for all, toleration of others, and governance by the consent of the governed. But modernity's epistemology is severely limited in what it can do. It is totally inept when it comes to what is properly human, the realms of art and music, of dance and poetry, of literature, and of mysticism—all the areas in which spirit and mystery are at play—all the areas that Scripture addresses with great competence. But the church—including you and me—has increasingly become fluent in modernity's outlook and language and has failed to cultivate the symbolic world and diction that makes sense of their gathering together in the first place.

Third, let us realize that such transformation will not happen through the publication of books, however fine, by study

Bibles, however well annotated, or biblical commentaries, no matter how sensitive, or by any catechetical guides, no matter how carefully crafted. The change we need will happen only if we bring our bodies together in the same space so the Spirit can have a place to dwell and to work. We must realize church to be made church. We ourselves must show up. We must embrace a ministry of personal presence rather than a manic commitment to ministry through program. We cannot turn this over to professionals, cannot outsource or farm out. Our embodied presence is essential to the process. But even if we should grant all these things, we still have not yet moved out of our private into a more public place, we still have given our assent only in our heads and have not yet assented with our bodies.

I have spoken elsewhere at some length of the elements of transformation, and for the sake of brevity I will only summarize here because I want to stress above all that this curriculum can only be realized through embodied practices that express and teach it.

1. The first is the most fundamental and is Copernican in its implications. We must learn once more to imagine the world that Scripture imagines. Within the life of the church, our concern ought to be entirely, not with what world produced the Bible, but with what world Scripture produces. We should ask not how history explains why ancient people thought and spoke this way, but we ask what would happen if we thought and spoke this way. The imaginative world of democracy becomes empirically realized when people vote and officeholders leave office when they receive fewer votes. The imaginative world of education becomes empirically realized when teachers actually teach and students actually learn. The imaginative world of astrophysics becomes empirically realized when humans stand on the moon. The imaginative world of Scripture, which proposes, all empirical

evidence to the contrary, that humans are created in the image of God, becomes empirically realized when all humans actually regard and treat each other as bearers of God's image.

2. We must recover a robust sense of creation, by which I mean a sense of God's bringing the visible world into existence at every moment through God's unseen power, renews the earth every morning, and brings new and surprising things into being, suffusing all of creation with God's presence and power every day. This sense is recovered from imaging the world imagined by Scripture, not from the reading of the first chapters of Genesis alone, but especially through reading the Psalms and the prophets, which speak of what God does in the present and will do in the lives of God's people. In the New Testament, we learn this sense of God's presence and power in creation especially in the letters of Paul, which speak of those in Christ as a new creation and a new humanity. But above all, we learn this sense in our hearts and bones through praying the Psalms, because in them we speak directly to this ever-creating God, we enter into the world imagined by Scripture, and slowly, slowly, begin to see our world as Scripture sees it, as radiant with God's glory, that is, as shot through with God's presence and power.
3. The third element in the conversion of the imagination is to reverse the Enlightenment's elevation of the general law over individual experience and learn once more to appreciate personal embodied experience as the privileged—indeed indispensable—source of revelation concerning God's activity in creation, and to cultivate ways such experience might be communicated in a disciplined fashion and also heard and discerned by a church that understands that if the Living God is at work here and now, then we need to learn what God is doing now through hearing and attending to the narratives of personal testimony. So it was with Moses, so

with David, so with Isaiah, so with Jesus, so with Paul. In the ocean of mystery that is our existence, we do not survive through scientific navigation, but are saved through the truths of personal witness.

4. Finally, the church must seek to recover the distinctive truth-telling capacities of myth, which alone can express the deepest realities of the mystery in which we find ourselves. If we are to make real sense of Scripture or be fully attentive to our own lives, then we must recognize that what is most important in both cannot be reduced to the impoverished categories of Enlightenment epistemology. Far from fleeing mythic discourse, we must embrace it, for without such embrace we shall forever remain alienated both from Scripture, which declares, "in Christ God was reconciling the world to himself" (2 Cor 5:19) and from the Creed, which declares both that "he descended from heaven" and "he ascended into heaven."

A MODEST PROPOSAL

This is, I gladly admit, an ambitious educative program. It surely will be difficult to realize. And it is impossible to implement through our usual mechanisms of reform: meetings, books, pamphlets, lectures, debate. It might, however, be worth trying simple communal practices that have a proven track record for accomplishing such transformation, not with each element dealt with separately, but as is the way with embodied practice, all at once. Let me conclude by suggesting two such practices.

The first practice is for small intentional groups to gather in prayer to read Scripture precisely as a means of perceiving and interpreting the experience of God in the lives of participants. I understand Catholics have tried again and again to organize faith-sharing groups, with greater or lesser success. But I am not convinced that an experience-based reading of Scripture was ever fully the focus of such groups. Here are several practical suggestions about this practice:

1. Start small. Better to start with three who truly gather in Jesus's name than with thirty who grudgingly cooperate with another new program. And when more than three want to join, form another group of three.
2. Ministers must be present, but as facilitators and participants rather than as instructors.
3. Never descend from such transformative reading to Bible study. This cannot be an academic exercise in pursuing knowledge about an ancient text. That knowledge can be pursued in other venues. This reading must remain a spiritual practice that seeks wisdom about our lives.
4. Persevere. Transformation above all takes time and persistent attention.
5. Pray constantly, whenever the Spirit moves among you. The work is the Spirit's work. We form a body that the Holy Spirit can enliven. Prayer is the way the Spirit can do that work.
6. Start, and perhaps stay, with the scriptural texts that speak most directly to life before God in the present: the Psalms, the prophets, the Apostle Paul. And in the Gospels, focus above all on the liberating acts of Jesus as windows for the liberating acts of the resurrected One in our lives.

The second practice is to introduce the praying of the Psalms together in every parish. I am convinced that there is a direct correlation between the collapse of such praying of the Psalms in common, and our inability to imagine the world that Scripture imagines. Because in the Psalms we already address God directly, we acknowledge God's presence and power among us as we praise, lament, petition, and rejoice. How can we do these things concerning our everyday life if we do not have the words and dispositions that make them possible? Praying the Psalms opens our hearts and minds to God, but also opens our eyes to the creation in which God makes everything new at every moment. A few practical notes on this practice:

1. Find a time when as many as possible can take part—note the contrast to the other practice—say, for example, ten minutes before every Mass.
2. Recite or chant alternate verses, so that speaking and hearing alternate for participants.
3. Encourage, and set the example for, speaking or chanting in full voice rather than muttering.
4. Conclude each psalm with the *Gloria Patri*—why not connect our practice with that of the saints over some 1500 years?
5. Pray the Psalter from beginning to end, just as in the first practice we should read books from beginning to end. The lectionary has done enough butchery of Scripture; let the people experience the full grandeur of the complete Psalter.

This program and these practices may appear utopian and banal, obvious and undoable. Perhaps they are. Many among you can perhaps do better. But I do think that unless we begin to imagine a way forward that has intellectual coherence and make that way forward embodied by actual communities, the topic of Scripture for the life of the church will remain a subject about which theologians might rhapsodize but no pastor could describe.

2

ON TAKING THE BIBLE SERIOUSLY

Originally published in The Dartmouth Apologist 5, *no. 1 (2011): 10–14.*

These days, among religion's educated (and semieducated) despisers, the charge that someone "takes the Bible seriously" is enough to remove the person from serious intellectual consideration. The pious reading of the Bible is considered to be pretty much on a par with studying tea leaves, analyzing astrological tables, or even reciting the Qur'an—a form of intellectual stagnation or emotional regression. Surely only stupidity or superstitious fear could allow people to take seriously the shabby pretensions of these ancient writings that have repeatedly been shown to be historically inaccurate, cosmologically ignorant, and morally deficient.

How, they ask, could people in the early twenty-first century who routinely floss their teeth, use the internet, and take vitamins, look for personal and societal norms in stories, laws, and poetry composed for people who lived in tents, thought moss was leprosy, and spared no rod lest they spoil a child—compositions, by the way, that prescribed for these advanced readers that they kill witches, adulterers, and children who curse their parents? For the educated elite, "taking the Bible seriously" means not to be taken seriously.

From the opposite side and in neat symmetry, fundamentalist Christians use the charge of "not taking the Bible seriously" as a way of dismissing the claim of others to be Christian while not agreeing with the fundamentalists' particular construal of religion. Serious Christianity, such believers claim, is biblical Christianity. The Bible is not only the inspired word of God—in every jot and tittle—but normative for every aspect of life. It is, furthermore, a perspicuous norm: what it demands of humans is plainly stated and requires no interpretation, only the obedient will to do it.

People who want to pass as Christians—who consider themselves liberal Christians and appeal to other norms such as experience and intellect—are *poseurs* who do not "take the Bible seriously" as guides for their life. They are actually more dangerous than Christianity's public detractors, for they sap the faith from within.

There is some clear inconsistency on both sides. The cultured despisers reject taking the Bible seriously as a norm for life, but they take is very seriously indeed as a threat to their own vision of a religion-free, or at least, Christianity-free universe. The Bible-thumping Christians, in turn, claim to take the Bible with utter seriousness as a guide to life, but in practice rely much less on the careful reading of the Bible than on general appeals to its authority—and their lives starkly fail to reflect some central biblical norms.

More remarkably, though, biblical defenders and detractors have more in common than they might think. They share, for example, a narrow referential understanding of truth: if an ancient narrative does not correspond to the historical facts, it is false and unworthy of consideration; if an ancient mandate is not carried out in practice, it loses all value. The biblicist, to be sure, insists that such nonverification does not apply, and that therefore the Bible is "true," whereas the critic delights in pointing out the many ways in which the Bible errs in its description of the world and human events, concluding that it is therefore "untrue."

Both parties are also selective in what they choose to read: the defenders of the Bible focus only on its positive aspects and suppress all the embarrassments presented by the ancient writings, while the critics fixate on the toxic elements in the text, ignoring all the ways the Bible has been life enhancing. Neither side assesses the whole range of biblical evidence when considering what it might have to say about any subject. Neither side weighs the implications of the disparity between contemporary concern and ancient witness: biblicists obsess over the relatively small amount of attention the Bible gives to sex but conveniently ignore (or distort) the abundant testimony it provides with regard to the use of material possessions; intellectual critics, oddly, share the same obsessive attention to the issues of sexuality. Neither side ponders the even more interesting fact that the Bible does not directly address many of the questions that readers would like to put to it.

Finally, corresponding to the narrow understanding of truth, both sides share a manner of reading that might be termed primitively and resolutely literalistic: the text is read in its English translation as a set of propositions or declarations and little or no attention is given to the original context or to the function of statements within that context. By original context, I mean not only the historical and social circumstances addressed by the compositions, but at an even more basic level, the linguistic constraints of the ancient languages of composition, the literary context of statements in their narrative or discursive settings, and the conventions of ancient rhetoric and poetics. As a result, metaphors are literalized (and killed), argument is ignored, and the subtleties of ancient narrative techniques are missed entirely.

In short, neither those today who are dismissive of the Bible as intellectually serious while fearful of it as religiously toxic, nor those today who embrace the Bible as religiously true and morally uplifting, are actually serious readers of the Bible. They resemble lovers and despisers of Shakespeare who quote lines at random—completely removed from Elizabethan culture and literary conventions—to show how the Bard is either good or bad as an influence on culture today. What is lacking in the conversation is a sense of "taking the Bible seriously" that has any real intellectual rigor.

Because the extreme positions are so sharply and shrilly stated, they draw attention to themselves and (much to the delight of the ideologues advancing them) manage to appear as the only available options. But they are not. In fact, there has been a long tradition of intellectually rigorous reading of the Bible within Christianity—a tradition that long predates the phenomenon of fundamentalism (which is actually a reaction to modernism defined by its terms). It extends from Origen of Alexandria in the third century up to Rudolf Bultmann in the twentieth century, and embraces such figures as Augustine, Theodore of Mopsuestia, John Chrysostom, Thomas Aquinas, Erasmus, Luther, and Calvin. It continues today especially in schools of theology, where the highest standards of critical thinking and the deepest loyalty to the voice of Scripture are not thought to be incompatible but rather mutually dependent.

This ancient and continuing tradition is distinguished from Christianity's cultured despisers by its positive embrace of Scripture as authoritative but shares with the intellectual critics the conviction that the Bible requires as rigorous an intellectual examination as any other cultural claimant. It is distinguished from fundamentalism by its willingness to read all the Bible's texts with intellectual honesty and appreciation for context, but it shares with biblicists the conviction that, especially when read so rigorously, the Bible continues to enhance more than hurt the minds and hearts of readers. In contrast to both the extremes, this tradition of reading is above all a tradition of serious and sustained *reading*, and it is precisely in the seriousness of that endeavor that it "takes the Bible seriously."

The first great figure in this tradition exemplifies its characteristics. Origen of Alexandria (184–254) was raised Christian during a time of persecution (his father was a martyr and he himself died as a result of torture) in the most intellectually alive and culturally diverse city of antiquity. Alexandria, with its great library and museum, was the home of philosophers, scientists, mathematicians, and artists. Several schools of ancient philosophy competed for attention and allegiance. In addition to the still-thriving forms of Greco-Roman religion, Alexandria was home to a large Jewish community—that produced the Greek translation of the Hebrew Bible in 250 BCE and an extensive apologetic literature based on that translation—as well as several competing versions of Christianity, including Valentinian Gnosticism.

Origen grew up with the best available education in philosophy and rhetoric, and his writings show wide reading and firsthand knowledge of the writings of philosophers such as Plato. Origen's fierce devotion to his Christian faith was joined to a first-rate mind that was also remarkably fearless and open to the truth however it might make itself known. He once declared that it mattered little whether a truth was spoken by Jesus or the apostles or Moses or one of the philosophers. If it was true, it was true, no matter its source.

As a teacher in the catechetical school at Alexandria, Origen found himself in the middle of competing currents that are not entirely dissimilar to those swirling around present-day Christianity. Within the Alexandrian church, there was a sharp division between the intellectual sophistication of the Gnostics who despised simple believers and sought higher truths for the enlightened, and those simple believers who clung to a literalism that led them to believe things of God, Origen saw, that they would not have attributed to a wicked human being. And outside the community, Origen felt the still-vibrant tug of Judaism and Greco-Roman religion, the appeal from each still strong, and more convincing than the claims of the upstart and already divided Christian movement. Most challenging was the attack on Christianity by a leading intellectual, the philosopher Celsus, who shortly before Origen's birth wrote a sustained polemic (*The True Word*) against a sect that he saw as intellectually inferior, superstitious, and attractive mainly to the dregs of society who didn't know better. Sound familiar?

The greatest portion of Origen's astonishing literary output has been lost, but what remains, above all his apology *Against Celsus*, his *First Principles* (the pioneering effort at Christian theology that contains his explicit hermeneutical reflections), and a number of smaller treatises and sermons, are enough to show how fruitful was his distinctive combination of heart and mind, a steadfast commitment to the faith of the church (including the conviction that Scripture was divinely inspired), and an equally strong commitment to the most stringent sort of critical thought, turned precisely on that faith and that Scripture.

Regarding the faith, for example, Origen affirmed the shape of the Creed that came from the apostles. But he saw that the Creed left much undefined, and that the role of philosophical inquiry was to examine and extend those areas. From this starting point, Origen developed one of the most adventurous and intellectually ambitious visions of how the interplay of human freedom and God's goodness might interact with the origin and destiny of souls to bring about a final triumph over evil and the restoration of all things in God. The fact that lesser minds and smaller spirits later condemned him for this vision does not detract from the greatness of mind and heart it reveals, or from the fact that Origen set the table for all subsequent systematic theology.

Origen's influence is most powerful, however, on those who have sought to bring both faith and intelligence to the reading of the Bible, for no interpreter has ever exhibited both qualities so emphatically or dialectically. On one side, Origen was convinced not only that the Bible was divinely inspired but that God spoke to humans through these texts in the present as well as in the past. On the other side, he saw the actual texts of the Bible as far from perspicuous. As human compositions of the past, they present complex difficulties to the one trying to discern in them what God wanted to say. The task of reading is therefore impelled by faith but demands of the reader every critical skill available. The urgency of reading is connected to the desire to attend to what God speaks; the need to read critically is connected to the specific difficulties presented to specific texts. What makes Origen the model for all faithful biblical interpretation is his refusal ever to take the easy way out, his insistence on reading the texts as they were in all their difficulty and ambiguity in order to ferret out the meaning that God may have intended.

Origen himself displayed a formidable array of critical abilities. He brought to the text of the Old Testament the science of textual criticism learned from the interpreters of Homer, in order to establish the original text as closely as possible. All subsequent textual criticism of the Old and New Testaments simply elaborates and refines the steps first taken by Origen. He practiced a form of literary criticism, demonstrating in detail, for example, the differences among the Gospel accounts concerning Jesus. He displayed an acute linguistic sensitivity; page after page of his commentary on the Gospel of John is devoted to a consideration of the multiple meanings available for the phrase with which John begins, namely, "in the beginning." Origen is remarkably modern in his appreciation for the limits of historical knowledge. Indeed, he comes close to a postmodern position in his insistence that what really counts is not "what happened" but "what is written" in Scripture: it is the text that is the subject of inquiry and God's instrument for transforming readers. Origen regarded a quest for the actual events behind the texts as fruitless and foolish.

Above all, Origen brought a critical perspective to the religious and moral adequacy of the biblical compositions. Schooled both by the moral sensitivity of Greco-Roman philosophy and the religious perspective given by developed Jewish interpretation of the Bible as a whole—not to mention his immersion in the Gospels and letters of Paul—Origen saw clearly that, when taken literally, the Bible makes statements that are impossible, improbable, and morally objectionable. An important aspect of his serious reading of the Bible, then, was working through such textual *aporiae*, seeking to discover the wisdom that God might have hidden within the scandal of the all-too-human text. Origen's development of anagogical ("transposed") readings was a function of the seriousness with which he took the task of reading; if the literal sense of the text was historical, cosmological, moral, or religious nonsense, then the text must be made to yield a meaning consonant with the nature of the God who seeks the salvation not the destruction of the human soul. The point of reading for Origen was not information but transformation, a process that required of the reader an intellectual and moral effort consistent with the urgency of engaging the word of the Living God.

Not all of Origen's successors have had his great learning, his acute intelligence, his moral integrity, or his clear conception of the interpretive task. But there has been within Christianity from Origen's time to our own a continuous tradition of readers who have shared his loyalty to the faith and his willingness to engage it critically. I have already mentioned names who would appear on any "hit parade" of great theological interpreters, but it is important to recognize that their practice was not exceptional so much as illustrative. They stood within a deep and broad stream of critical interpretation that both affirmed the power of the Bible and recognized its potential for harm as well as for good.

Such readers have understood that neither a simplistic affirmation nor a simplistic rejection of the Bible is intellectually responsible, and only a vigorous and critical engagement with the specific language of the ancient compositions in all their specificity will enable readers to resist what was (and remains) toxic within them as well as celebrate what was (and remains) positively transforming in them.

It is a great pity that the skills and insights of this reading tradition are so little known or appreciated by those whose shrill voices dominate contemporary polemics. Who is to blame? Those who practice these skills today may be criticized for restricting their efforts mostly to the safe world of the academy, leaving public discourse on such matters to the charlatans who are all too willing to parody true scholarship in their "shocking" publications. Even more deserving of criticism, though, are the Christians who claim to revere the Bible, yet have waged war against the use of critical intelligence in the interpretation of the Bible, fearfully and ferociously purging seminary faculties and pulpits alike of anything that looks suspiciously like brilliance or imagination. Their insistence on reading the Bible as though it were as transparent as a daily newspaper is a form of childishness; their willful ignoring of the long history of faithful readers who struggled with the intellectual and moral challenges of Scripture before them reveals a desperate religious immaturity.

Most depressing, perhaps, is the abysmal ignorance of religion generally, of Christianity specifically, and of the Bible monumentally, exhibited by the noisy contemporary critics of all three. Present-day members of the cultured elite are remarkable for the superficiality of their knowledge of religious wisdom in any form. At least the ancient critic Celsus made the effort to know something about what he criticized and wrote from a coherent philosophical perspective. In terms of genuine learning, rigorous argument, and moral passion, both Celsus and Origen make present-day disputants on the Bible appear as mere children whose moral obtuseness, sadly, is matched, by ignorance.

3

HOW IS THE BIBLE TRUE?

First presented as the Thomas Verner Moore Lecture at the Catholic University of America in 2008 and published in Commonweal *136, no 10 (2009): 12–16.*

The title of this essay is meant to provoke thought, by complicating the relation of truth to the Bible. Surprisingly, perhaps, for a scripture scholar, I am not trying to complicate the Bible. For the purposes of this exercise, I understand by the term *Bible* the collection of compositions that make up the Christian Scriptures. I further assume that Christians read these compositions in the search for truth. We do not read these ancient texts simply as a source of neutral and arcane information that might be required should we be asked to play *Jeopardy*. We read them because the Bible has something to do with the truth of our lives.

My premise is that, like the character in the song who is "looking for love in all the wrong places," readers of the Bible, particularly in America, have been looking for truth in all the wrong places, specifically, that they have been looking for the truth of the Bible either in the past or in the future. Those who seek the truth in the past would seem to be opposed to those who seek it in the future; we are all familiar with the culture wars that pit critically trained academics against the advocates of Armageddon. I want to show that their extreme positions share more than is at first obvious. Then I want to develop my argument: that a more complicated understanding of truth leads to a richer and more satisfying way of asking how the Bible is true.

LOOKING FOR TRUTH IN THE PAST

I will begin with the apparently conflicting ways of reading the Bible that characterize the American culture wars. The first is the dominant paradigm for reading the Bible found among educated Americans, the so-called historical-critical method. It is dominant because its assumptions are shared by all those who are taught Bible in college religion classes, all clergy taught in seminaries, and all laity shaped by such education. I call it a paradigm because it assumes the truth of the Bible is to be found in its character as a historical document: not only that it is written in an alien culture and must be understood within its own symbolism, but that the truth of what it asserts is to be found in the accuracy of its historical assertions.

Such a presupposition concerning the truthfulness of biblical narratives was, to be sure, shared by all Christian readers up to the time of the European Enlightenment. They simply assumed that things happened the way the stories said they did. While patristic commentators acknowledged elements of disagreement and even conflict among accounts, they always tilted toward trusting the divine author not to lie in matters of fundamental importance. What changed in the sixteenth–seventeenth centuries was that world exploration discovered peoples and cultures never imagined by the biblical story—Augustine's *City of God* was the last credible attempt to subsume all empires into the framework of biblical chronology—and the development of natural and historical sciences exposed the factual character of the ancient stories to withering criticism.

As a result, the time from the eighteenth century to the present has seen a constant running battle between Christianity's cultured despisers—a surprising number of them also Christian—and Christianity's beleaguered defenders over the truth of the Bible, defined precisely in terms of its historical reliability. The historical credibility and with it the supposed truthfulness and worthiness of the biblical narrative weakened with each blow of the critical hammers: the Mosaic authorship of Torah, creation in seven days, the parting of the Red Sea, the conquest of the land, the Davidic kingdom—all had to be abandoned in the face of inexorable criticism.

The quest for the historical Jesus, which across these same centuries was governed by these precise presuppositions concerning truth and history and in its most recent iteration drew such attention to itself for its supposed debunking of Christian claims concerning Jesus, is the supreme manifestation of the historical-critical paradigm. Rejecting the church's christological doctrine as a falsification of "the real Jesus," it searches for a more accurate historical representation of him based on the deconstruction of the canonical Gospels and the reshuffling of the credible pieces that can be salvaged from them. One can have the "truth about Jesus," it says, only at the cost of the "truth of the Gospels."

The battle over the Bible and the truth about the past continues today. American Christianity remains deeply divided by modernist and fundamentalist. For the academics who make up the Jesus Seminar, televangelists are the enemy; for many evangelicals, academic biblical scholars are apostates from the faith. Yet the most dramatic result of these centuries of conflict has been that most Christians simply bypass serious engagement with biblical truth, mostly by avoiding any sustained engagement with the specific texts of the Bible. Liberal Christians are content with broad principles that they consider generally derived from Scripture, but they pay little attention to the actual texts, which so seldom actually conform to those principles. Perhaps surprisingly, conservative Christians are even more selective in what they choose to read: the most fervent or vocal defenders of biblical truth avoid consideration of passages that give rise to genuine critical questions. The contemporary argument about the resurrection of Jesus, for example, focuses on the historicity of the event rather than the historical accuracy of the Gospel accounts. And for liberal or conservative, history is made the measure of truth. Thus N. T. Wright, no friend of the Jesus Seminar, states in the beginning of his treatment of the historical Jesus that if Reimarus—the epitome of Enlightenment skepticism—had been correct in his historical reconstruction, then Christianity would be required to reconsider its teaching concerning Jesus. If the Bible gets history wrong, then its truth is in question.

LOOKING FOR TRUTH IN THE FUTURE

Some American Christians have sought relief from historical criticism by seeking the truth of the Bible in the future. The Bible's authority and truthfulness rests in its capacity to predict the events leading to the end of the world. It is not the Bible as history of the past but the Bible as prophecy concerning the future—indeed, the very near future—that commands attention. The historical-critical approach focuses on narratives. The millenarian approach focuses on the prophets: in the Old Testament, Isaiah, Zechariah, and above all, Daniel; in the New Testament, the prophetic portions of the Gospels and Paul, but supremely, the Book of Revelation. For those expecting the rapture of the saints from cosmic catastrophe and a thousand-year reign of the

Messiah on earth, the Book of Revelation is the supreme repository of biblical truth. I have heard one televangelist declare that all the other writings of the Bible were written for the past; only Revelation remains open as a prophetic word to the present.

The millenarian reading of the Bible has some significant antecedents—elements of it can be found in the apocalyptic expectations associated with Joachim of Flores and with the radical reformer Thomas Leyden—but it has acquired greater prominence among conservative Christians today as an apparently secure refuge from the attacks of intellectual critics. Those of us of a certain age remember how Hal Lindsey's *The Late Great Planet Earth* was required reading for anyone hoping to know the religious minds of undergraduates between 1970 and 1980, but few could have been prepared for the astonishing success of the Left Behind series by Tim Lehay and Jerry Jenkins, whose novelistic rendering of millenarian theology found millions of excited readers. It is not necessary to read books to learn the basics of this approach; on cable TV, religion channels regularly display preachers mixing predictions of the imminent end with grand plans for satellite expansion, whose visual aids include a map of the Near East and smudged newspaper articles concerning global warfare.

The hermeneutic of millenarianism is simple: Scripture is read as a prophecy concerning the future. Its precise meaning, however, was veiled from the prophets of old and remains veiled in the present unless its meaning is unlocked through correspondence to contemporary events—thus the maps and the headlines. The mysterious predictions of Revelation concerning the great beast and the reign of the Messiah emerge with startling clarity when aligned with the news of the day concerning the oppression of the saints. The beauty of this method is its resistance to fact. The number of persons identified as the wearer of 666 through the centuries is impressive: Nero, Frederick the Great, Hitler, Stalin,

Idi Amin, Gorbachev, Saddam Hussein, Osama bin Laden, and assorted popes.

No matter that the expected end never arrives as it is constantly predicted; the fault lies not in the method but in the mistaken reading of the headlines. This sort of prophecy cannot be disconfirmed: when one candidate fails, another immediately is nominated. The entire system is brilliantly evoked by the old "Beyond the Fringe" skit, with the long pause following the solemn countdown to the end, and then the resigned, "Not quite the conflagration we had anticipated," and then the chipper, "Oh well, better luck next time."

THE ENDS MEET IN THE MIDDLE

A new element in the millenarian approach is its recent warm embrace of conservative—some would say reactionary—social values and political activism. The mental agility required to balance a near expectation of the end-time and the pleasures of capitalism is impressive, but recent elections have demonstrated that awaiting Armageddon and voting Republican are not as irreconcilable as might be thought. Those who seek the truth of the Bible in future prophecy therefore neatly occupy one extreme in our contemporary culture wars. The other extreme is represented by the academic critics of the Bible who deny its historical truth and with it any relevance to political decisions. We all know that it is as difficult to find a Republican in academia (at least in the liberal arts) as it is to find a Democrat in the local Holiness church.

More interesting than the way in which these approaches to biblical truth get distributed politically is the way in which they can be shown to share the same presuppositions concerning truth. Both approaches work with a correspondence theory of truth, that is, truth is found in the correspondence between propositions and nonlinguistic realities (such as things and events). The meaning of a text is found in propositions that point outside themselves, and the truth of a text is to be found in the way its propositions match external reality. For the historical approach, this means how accurately the Bible describes the past; for the millenarian approach, it means how accurately the Bible predicts the future.

Verification—testing for truth—is therefore a matter of correspondence. Did this happen in the past or not? If it did not, then the biblical narrative is reduced to legend or myth, that is, "untrue" in historical terms, however attractive it might otherwise be. If the event did happen, then the Bible is "true," even though the implications of that truth are not clear for the present. Again, will this happen in the future, or not? The advantage of the futurist perspective, I have suggested, is that it cannot truly be disconfirmed. But verified or not, neither does the Bible's truth about the future necessarily guide human existence here and now.

Both approaches, furthermore, ignore the literary dimensions of the Bible. The text as literary composition is irrelevant and dispensable, valuable only insofar as it tells us something outside the text. For the historical approach, the literary features of narratives (including the Gospels) are an obstacle to accurate historical reconstruction because they "interpret." The millenarian approach equally ignores the literary character of prophecy. Taking the Book of Revelation as a unique prophecy about the future, for example, ignores the fact that Revelation is written in a literary genre (apocalyptic) that was common in the first century and shared certain well-established conventions. In short, both approaches literalize the poetry of the biblical text. And neither approach knows what to do with the biblical literature that is properly poetic—such as the Psalms and Wisdom writings—and has stirred the imagination and piety of countless readers. Both approaches are deaf to metaphor. For both, the Bible can only be true by ceasing to be literarily beautiful, metaphorically powerful.

THE BIBLE AND LITERARY IMAGINATION

I should like to propose another approach to the truth of the Bible, in and through literary imagination, as a way toward complicating the notion of how the Bible is true. I should begin by stating that I am by no means denying the importance of history and prophecy as aspects of such literary imagination. The Bible does in fact serve as a not-insignificant source for ancient history, even though it is severely limited in the amount of real history it provides and creates considerable problems for historical reconstruction. Likewise, the Bible is an indispensable source for prophecy, when prophecy is understood not in terms of prediction of the future but in terms of speaking to other humans on behalf of God. But granting these, I still want to insist that the question of how the Bible is true ought not to be attached primarily, much less exclusively, to either.

Instead, I ask you to consider not the world that created the Bible or the world that the Bible (might or might not) predict, but the world that the Bible itself creates. We can approach the Bible, not as an anthology of compositions locked in the past, but as a word that unlocks every present; not as a set of sources for describing reality, but as a set of witnesses prescribing reality; not as a set of propositions about the world, but as an imaginative construction of a world. In every age and in every circumstance, it is possible to read the Bible as creating an imaginative world in which humans can choose to live.

In each and every one of its parts and as a whole, the Bible imagines a world as created by and ordered to, cared for and saved by, a God who is at once infinitely powerful and infinitely personal; a world in which God creates humans in God's own image, with capacities for knowledge and love, pleasure and freedom; a world that is a garden that God plants for humans to enjoy and cultivate. Nothing about the imagined world is empirically verifiable, yet by imagining the world in this fashion, the Bible also reveals reality, and by revealing it, opens as well the possibility of humans living in it as though real. By imagining the world that the Bible imagines, humans can imagine—construct—their world as a new creation.

I am recommending with respect to the Bible what we recognize as axiomatic about the human project: we do not simply find a world, we together construct worlds on the basis of shared imagination and engage in practices that serve to make what we imagine seem natural. Because we can imagine a world called "education," we willingly attend classes and take exams, or teach and grade papers, and by doing these practices, we make the world of education become real. Because we can imagine a world called "democracy," we gladly petition and vote or campaign and serve, and by performing such practices we make a government by the people, of the people, and for the people something more than a figment of imagination. People really do learn things in education and change the face of society; people really do leave office when they have received fewer votes and thereby confirm the imaginative world of free citizens.

These examples do not seem strange to us because to some extent we have all become students of Thomas Luckmann and Peter Berger and recognize that the world in which humans live is by no means simply given or found, but is constructed through social activity and social imagination. We are comfortable, indeed, even in thinking about science in terms of such social construction: we recognize that before space travel was possible, humans needed to imagine the world in a new way, more like Copernicus and less like Ptolemy, more like Einstein and less like Newton. Once they imagined the possibility of standing on the moon and viewing the earth as a big blue marble, the practices of rocket engineering and space aeronautics made that world real by embodying what the imagination first conceived. Copernicus and Einstein were great scientists, not because they were great bench researchers but because they were great dreamers.

Imagining the world that the Bible imagines is an equivalent Copernican revolution. Our reluctance to embrace this shift in perspective is connected, at least in part to the epistemological reduction of all knowledge in the Enlightenment. When truth can be connected only to propositions that are empirically verifiable—through critical history or natural science—then imagination appears as epistemologically unserious. The Enlightenment in fact banished imagination and fantasy to the epistemological basement. Yet it is certainly the case that all great history and all great science is a matter of fantasy and imagination long before it is a matter of test tubes and text criticism, just as every interesting human life is driven by fantasy and imagination more than by sets of facts. But as children of the Enlightenment, we are not comfortable thinking about the truth of the Bible in terms of imagination.

There is also a moral factor in our reluctance to embrace such a reading, for it demands that we put into practice the world thus imagined by the Bible. If the Bible is "true" as description or prediction, it demands nothing of us but intellectual assent; its truth is like that of a weather report or a mathematical theorem. But if the Bible is true as prescription, then everything is demanded of us: we are called to embody that imagination, bring it into physical existence by the patterns of our lives. We are understandably reluctant to commit ourselves so willingly to that which is simply "imaginative." It would be like people voting even if their candidate might not be elected, it would be like men and women strapping themselves into jump seats inside space capsules with no guarantee of return.

The great advantage of this approach to the Bible is that it allows, indeed demands, the closest possible attention to the literary shape of its compositions, and above all its metaphors. The truth is sought not in propositions alone but above all in those powerful images that construct a vision of reality. Such images are constructed by the literary art of each composition and by the effect of all the compositions read together. I have mentioned the image of the garden that God planted for humans to preserve and tend. What a world it conjures! What a distinctive sense of the human place and vocation—tending the earth as a garden. Such an imaginative apprehension of the text demands of us not that we read faster but that we read slower, that we learn to savor, to taste, the poetry of this ancient literature.

COMPLICATING THE NOTION OF TRUTH

Approaching the Bible in terms of imagination already complicates the question of how the Bible is true. It already represents a shift from a pure correspondence theory of truth to a constructive model.

Here I am extending the definition of *truth* by Thomas Aquinas to encompass a broader range of possibilities. Aquinas spoke of truth in terms of an *adequatio rei et intellectus*, which sounds at first like the purest form of correspondence—the correspondence of a thing and a mind. For Aquinas, however, this was not at all simply a matter of human propositions and their correspondence to empirical facts. Thomas thought in terms of a mind (*intellectus*) and reality (*res*) in several dimensions. There is first the created world as the *res* that expresses the design of the divine *intellectus*. By this, Thomas meant the truth about the world as expressed in the biblical and creedal affirmation that all existence derived from, shows forth, and is ordered, to its maker. Second, there is the truth found in the apprehension by the human *intellectus* of the reality that God thus creates at every moment, the *res* we call God's world. And finally, Thomas applied truth to the exercise of human understanding (*intellectus*) in moral discernment and action—the *res* that we bring into being through our freedom—in alignment with the divine mind as revealed through the created order. We best follow in Thomas's footsteps, then, when we recognize that there are multiple ways of knowing reality and multiple ways of thinking about the *adequatio* of mind and reality. When we consider the discrete ways of knowing reality displayed respectively by art, literature, mathematics, dance, and music, we recognize the need to think flexibly about what "truth" in each such discourse might mean. We can go further and recognize similar complex dimensions of the meaning of truth in the discourses concerning personal relationships, morality, and religion.

When it comes to religious literature such as we find in the Bible, a constructive understanding of truth thinks in terms of a complex conversation among texts, readers, and the worlds they mutually construct through such conversation. Truth is not something outside us to which we need only assent; rather, truth is something in which we participate and for which we must take responsibility. There are at least three ways we can, from this perspective, think of how the Bible might be true.

1. We could ask, first, does the Bible imagine a true world? But as soon as we ask that simple question, we see what complexities it hides. We might mean, "Is the Bible true when it imagines a three-decker universe consisting of the heavens, the earth, and the netherworld," and, with the Russian cosmonauts and Rudolph Bultmann, declare that science has shown such an image to be false. But readers both ancient and modern have used such biblical language to understand not just the vertical physical arrangement of the universe but the issue of the material world's depth: Is there simply the surface that we can see and touch, or is that surface a veil, behind which is a deeper and more powerful sort of being? The language of heaven and earth enable readers to imagine a world that does not simply offer itself to immediate examination but rather that discloses itself slowly to those who are

open to the mystery that lies beneath the surface. In fact, we can reverse the question: Without a language that enables us to imagine inner and outer dimensions to human existence, or a sense of height and depth in being, is not our understanding of reality necessarily forced into flatness?

We can pose another sort of question: Is Scripture true when it imagines that the world is created by God and that humans are created in God's image? Certainly the two propositions are impossible to verify—and for most people as much evidence argues against them as for them—but choosing to live within such imaginative statements makes a profound difference in the way the world is construed and engaged. I think we can agree that little in our experience of human beings demands the conclusion that they bear a divine impress; yet when humans deal with each other as though they bore God's image, they discover that a truth that cannot be empirically derived can be empirically embodied.

Such questions push us to ask what criteria should be used to determine the truthfulness of the world that the Bible imagines. We are led directly back to my earlier point that a claim to truth is relative to the discourses within which it is made. Scarcely anyone wants to measure the truthfulness of the Bible on criteria derived from natural science anymore. Certainly the nutcases marching under the banner of creation science have nothing to do with real natural science. Some genuine scientists, like John Polkinghorne, continue to argue for the compatibility of biblical and scientific discourses, but such efforts have an extremely limited range. Natural science, however, is not the only or even the most interesting discourse about reality. We could also ask about the truth of the Bible within philosophical discourse: Are its statements capable of being engaged by reason, and do the mythic dimensions of the Bible raise and respond to questions of being? We can ask within moral discourse: Does the Bible create humans who are evil or who are good, does it suppress a full humanity or enhance it? And we can pose the question of truth within religious discourse: Does the Bible enable an adequate apprehension of God?

The question whether the Bible imagines a true world is complicated not only by the number of discourses—each with its own criterion of truth—within which the question can be posed, but equally by the plain fact that the Bible does not speak in a single voice on any subject, but speaks rather through multiple literary compositions that not only make meaning in diverse ways but respond to the questions readers might put (from within any discourse) from distinct perspectives and sometimes in flatly contradictory ways. I promised at the beginning of this presentation that I would not seek to complicate the Bible, but the awareness of the Bible's literary, perspectival, and thematic diversity is necessary to keep constantly in mind whenever we ask, on any point, whether the Bible imagines a true world.

2. It is therefore equally important that we always ask a second question concerning the truth of the Bible, namely, do we read the Bible truly? This question is all too seldom asked either by those who blithely assert or by those who confidently deny the Bible's truthfulness; they both assume that the Bible's meaning is familiar and easy to grasp. In fact, the meaning of these ancient texts is more often alien and difficult to grasp. In order to read the Bible truly, to be sure, it is first necessary to be reading it. Far too often claims concerning the truth of the Bible manage to avoid any actual reading of the texts themselves. But to be true, our reading must also be responsible. We must be responsible to the text of the Bible itself, which demands of us that we recognize its otherness in language and culture, and struggle with the very specific difficulties presented by the grammar and syntax of the text. It demands that we respect and consider the diversity of the Bible's literary form and expression, as well as the plurality of the compositions' perspectives on many points.

True reading also means being responsible to a community of other readers, past and present, part of our culture and apart from it. True reading yields open interpretations openly arrived at, it embraces exposure of such interpretations to the readings of others, it enters a process of mutual correction and growth in insight. Reading that is simply private cannot claim to be true reading; reading that is simply sectarian (whether denominational or academic) cannot claim to be true reading. Exposure to the review of other competent readers, whether through academic review or discernment of spirits, is a necessary component of true reading.

3. We can ask about the truthfulness of our reading in still another way, namely, do we act truly as readers of the Bible? This question addresses not our intellectual but our moral posture as readers. Are we fit to engage the world that the Bible imagines if we live in a manner totally inconsistent with its vision? There are again at least two aspects of this form of truthfulness—or its lack—to consider. The first is whether we are morally competent to read. This aspect is pressed by Stanley Hauerwas when he declares that only someone committed to nonviolence can truly read Jesus's Sermon on the Mount. This statement, as so often with Hauerwas, goes too far, but it goes in the right direction: a reader with a fixed disposition toward violence will always find a way of mitigating the prophetic power of Jesus's words on the necessity of turning the other cheek. In the same way, Paul cannot be read truly by those committed to racism or sexism. I must not overstate the point, because the texts of Scripture have repeatedly shown their ability to challenge and even change such presuppositions. Augustine was neither the first nor the last to hear the words of the Apostle directed to his twisted heart and begin the process of change within.

The second aspect of moral truthfulness with respect to the Bible concerns the specific ethics of our reading, a point pressed especially by Elizabeth Schüssler-Fiorenza. If we read the Bible above all to establish the correctness of our own ideology or the security of our own manner of life, we are not reading truly. If we read primarily to demolish the positions of others and to demonstrate that they are in error, perhaps even unloved by God, then we are not reading truly. It is impossible to lay claim to the law of love if the purpose of our reading is to place burdens on others rather than to help bear their burdens, to destroy others rather than save them. To read the Bible truly one must be in the process of being transformed by the world that Scripture imagines; in order to speak truly about Jesus, one must be in the process of being transformed into his image.

CONCLUSION

I conclude by proposing that the question of how the Bible is true is enriched and made more pertinent to our lives when we begin by cultivating that neglected organ, the imagination; when we seek to imagine the world that Scripture imagines—the world that Scripture creates through its literary art, rather than the world it describes or predicts; when we ask what is the shape of that world and its rules and how we might embody it; when in that quest we read both passionately and carefully; and when we are willing to complicate the question of truth, asking not only whether Scripture imagines a true world, but do we read truly, and do we as readers act in the truth.

The Bible is the sacred book of the Christian church. It is also deeply formative and informing of our national culture. Taken as a whole, the Bible deserves to be taken with the utmost seriousness by the most serious people. It is far too important and powerful a collection of texts to be dismissed as irrelevant by those whose own measure for truth is adequate only to small slivers of reality. The Bible has capacities for good and evil. In the hands of those who ascribe absolute truth to it without taking the care to investigate how it might be true, the Bible can become a harmful instrument bringing ugliness and evil into our common life. But in the hands of those who are willing to discover the richness of biblical truth, and begin by taking responsibility for the truthfulness of their own reading and moral actions, the Bible can still, as it has so often in the past, enliven hearts, expand minds, and energize the efforts of those seeking to serve the world's best future.

Part 2
THEOLOGY

4

HAPPINESS AND THE RESTLESS HEART

An Augustinian Perspective

Published in the Journal of Law and Religion *29 (2014): 67–75.*

In 397 CE, ten years after his baptism, Saint Augustine began his *Confessions* by directly addressing the God to whom he had devoted his life, using the words of Psalm 95:4: "Great art thou, O Lord, and greatly to be praised; great is thy power, and of thy wisdom there is no number." He continues, "This tiny part of all that Thou hast created desires to praise Thee. Thou dost so excite him that to praise Thee is his joy. For Thou hast made us for Thyself and our hearts are restless until they rest in Thee."

I am not sure how Frank Sheed's sturdy translation of Augustine's classic reached me when I was fourteen years old—I was in minor seminary then, and I think it was a seminary prefect who handed the book to me for spiritual reading. Nor am I any longer certain, so many years removed from the moment when I first read them, just what in these words so moved me at that stage of my life. Certainly I was not then an auspicious example of happiness or joy, or at least not by any ordinary measure. I was an orphan, I had been transplanted to an alien culture, and I was intensely lonely. I ended up in the seminary mostly because my confused aspirations to holiness (fantasies spurred by reading the lives of saints) were translated by well-meaning teachers into a vocation to the priesthood, and therefore into an adolescence spent in a seminary across Lake Pontchartrain from New Orleans taught by Benedictine monks. But at that point, I had no idea what being a priest meant, or that I would within a few years spend a not-inconsiderable portion of my life as one of those monks. What I knew then for certain was that I was among strangers who spoke strangely, that I had no real home to which to return, and that books offered the best company available to me. Perhaps it is all too obvious what moved me in Augustine's words.

In any case, despite my then-limited grasp of Latin, I located and then memorized the last words of the above citation: *quia fecisti nos ad te domine et inquietum cor nostrum donec requiescat in te* ("for hast made us for thyself O Lord, and our hearts are restless until they rest in thee"). Unlike other tags and snippets that I committed to memory in those days of intellectual energy and ambition, this line not only stuck in my mind, I found myself over the years returning to it and reciting it to myself on all sorts of occasions. It had clearly become something like a mantra, a statement that spoke to my life directly and consistently, without any necessary reference to its original setting. It was a wisdom that I recognized as addressed to me through which I could understand my own existence. Remarkably, though, as I carried this Augustinian line through the years, I did not remember how Augustine himself had connected his praise of God to the experience of joy or happiness: "to praise you is his joy" (*ut laudare te delectet*). But there is the distinct possibility that, as I called this text to mind repeatedly over the years, I was, consciously or not, also reminding myself of the basis of true happiness.

In this essay, I adopt that generous construal of my own experience with Augustine's text, and use it to examine some of the ways in which someone who wishes to be a Christian thinks about the elusive yet all-important dimension of human existence we call happiness—or (more often for Christians) joy. I am no longer a lonely adolescent boy, no longer either a priest or a monk, but a simple Catholic layperson who is also a husband, father, grandfather, great-grandfather, and by some estimations, a scholar and teacher. And, at my age, I dare to call myself reasonably if not ecstatically happy.

Before parsing Augustine's statement as a guide to one Catholic's conception of true happiness, I must note that Catholic Christianity is heir—as Augustine himself emphatically was—to the classical culture of Greece and Rome, in which philosophers considered happiness among the most serious of philosophical topics and gave it their best attention. Although the philosophers disagreed on many points, such as the relation of happiness to pleasure or to political engagement, they agreed on certain fundamental things. They all agreed that happiness was supremely important and supremely to be desired. They agreed that happiness could not be reduced to something external, momentary, or accidental: happiness, therefore, was not a fine house, or a splendid wedding, or winning a sweepstakes. Instead, they all regarded happiness as an abiding condition specific to the human construction of the self, a consequence of human choice and disposition—not the choice between this thing and that, as the colors for a carpet, but the habitual choice between good (virtue) and bad (vice). It was a matter of character. In one fashion or another, the pagan philosophers also connected happiness to the divine, for the gods could be called, simply, "the happy ones."

Like the Greek and Roman philosophers before him, Augustine gave serious thought to happiness. Even before his baptism, he wrote *De Beata Vita* ("On the Happy Life"). He agreed with the philosophers that "all persons want to be happy, and no person is happy who does not have what he wants" (2.10). He agreed that genuine happiness must consist, then, in something that is truly within the grasp of humans ("something that can be had when it is wanted," 2.11), rather than something external, temporary, or accidental. He agreed with them, finally, that happiness must derive from the divine (2.11).

For Augustine, however, the divine was neither Greco-Roman polytheism (which he regarded as idolatry), nor the philosophically refined and impersonal divine principle that was the best that philosophy could reach through critical refinement of polytheism. Augustine's divine was the Living God of the Old and New Testament, the God of Israel, and the Father of the Lord Jesus Christ. His conception of true happiness was correspondingly shaped by the ways in which the Living God revealed himself through the act of creation, through the giving of the law, through the shaping of a people, and above all, through the life, death, and resurrection of Jesus of Nazareth. From the words of Jesus on happiness ("the Beatitudes," Matt 5:3–12), Augustine understood that happiness involved meekness, lowliness, and purity of heart. From those same statements, and above all from the experience of the crucified Messiah, Augustine learned the paradoxical truth that happiness ("blessedness") was compatible with intense suffering and persecution. The purity of heart that Jesus stated as the premise for "seeing God" was demonstrated by Jesus in his unswerving and constant commitment of his human heart in obedience to his Father, even through his shameful death by crucifixion.

TO PRAISE THEE IS HIS JOY

It was during those early years in seminary that I discovered I was a religious person. I don't mean that I am a good person or a holy person. I am simply someone who delights in the worship of God, who finds the most significant activity in his life to be that centered in God. It was this above all that drew me to the monastic life—while candor forces me to acknowledge a bit of fear of the world's seductive power as well. As a young seminarian, my favorite moments were at the weekly vespers and benediction of the blessed sacrament that we shared with the monks who taught us: the stately sounds of the Gregorian chant, the solemn movement of monks in procession as they profoundly bowed before the altar as they entered choir in ranks; the prostrations and bows at the recitation of the Gloria Patri, the dramatic vestments, all the rhythm of liturgy carried out by people who had dedicated themselves to this "work of God." Surely some of the attraction all this had for me was aesthetic: the winter evening, the incense-filled church, the candles on the altar, and the golden monstrance glittering in the candlelight. But why draw a hard distinction between the aesthetic and the religious in an adolescent boy, when each intoxicated him in a way no human contact did. One impulse fed the other, and together, they delighted in praising the Lord. The monastic liturgy combined aesthetics and religious ritual in such measure as to delight a heart starved for a sense of deep communion.

I followed this longing into the cloister and spent nine years as a Benedictine monk. The delight I felt in praising God was fed by a way of life constructed around precisely such praise. In the Divine Office—the round of choir prayer throughout the day—I found the rhythm of chant and movement deeply satisfying. The best moment of every day was when the entire choir of monks chanted the words of Psalm 95:6 (the psalm immediately preceding the one quoted at the start of the *Confessions*):

> Come, let us bow down in worship;
>   let us kneel before the God who made us.
> For he is our God,
>   and we are the people he shepherds,
>   the flock he guides.

As we chanted these words, we genuflected in the presence of the invisible God. At this moment every evening, I had the sense of being rightly aligned with the order of things: God was our God, we were his creatures, and the body language of submission and awe was the perfect expression of that truth.

What I experienced in the communal prayer of the Divine Office—even in its discordant moments, even when at 5:00 a.m. aesthetics was as absent as consistent pitch in the chant—was an obscure awareness of participation in something larger and greater than myself: not merely the larger body of the choir engaged in joint effort (it is work, this "work of God"), but as part of that choir, linked to the very source of my existence and the existence of all things. Such awareness was made even more explicit and more acute when, after my ordination as a priest, I was able to celebrate the Eucharist. In no other action have I ever had an equivalent awareness of being in precisely the right place and time, reciting the right words and making the right gestures, as in the great Eucharistic Prayer, when, in the presence of and for all the people present, I was able to stand before the Lord in praise and petition, in thanksgiving and awe, with words not my own but fashioned centuries before me and recited for centuries before me by other priests standing in precisely the right place and time before the Lord. Such was my sense of delight, my sense of joy or contentment during my years as a seminarian, monk, and priest. It was located exactly in the act of praise.

FOR THOU MADE US FOR THYSELF

Augustine supplies the reason why the praise of God is a source of happiness to humans, "this tiny bit of all that you created": humans find happiness in the praise of God because they are creatures, and it is natural for creatures to honor their makers. Augustine's statement corresponds perfectly with the vision of the world that is imagined and expressed by Scripture. But it also corresponds perfectly—and this is even more critical—to the deepest instincts of the human heart when they are not otherwise distorted. In this understanding, human happiness (or joy, or contentment) is a consequence of being rightly related to an objective state of affairs, namely, the order of creation. The objective state of affairs for humans is the condition of creatureliness; happiness depends on the subjective apprehension and acceptance of this condition.

Three distinct but interrelated aspects of Augustine's pithy formulation deserve attention. The first is that each one of us is created by God: "Thou made us." Here we catch a glimpse of the basic drama concerning human existence that is played out in Scripture, the drama of faith and idolatry. Both begin in the same place, the realization by humans of their contingency, of the nonnecessity of their existence. Humans cannot account for themselves or ensure even an additional moment of their fragile existence. We are here in the world, yet we are neither the makers of the world nor of ourselves, and just as the world passes away before our eyes even as it comes into being, so also do we experience ourselves as passing away even as we are coming into being.

The terror of nonexistence that threatens them at every moment can drive humans to idolatry, which for Scripture is not a matter of paying homage to the wrong deity but a disease of human freedom by which it rejects the very conditions of existence and seeks to establish security in being through its own efforts. Idolatry is treating that which is not ultimate as though it were ultimate, making something that is not God into a functional god for the sake of human security. Whether it be pleasure or possessions or power—the basic options are drearily few and predictable—the thing made ultimate by the frenzied and fearful human spirit is itself merely a creature and cannot bear the weight of worship; it exists as god only through the homage of the human desperate to escape the truth of his existence: that he is utterly and always dependent and needy. The idolatrous impulse is the perfect existential expression of the "restlessness" of which Augustine speaks. Refusing to "rest" in the truth of creatureliness, the idolater is driven to seek anywhere and everywhere a place of rest in some other created thing that can be treated as though ultimate. The sadness and misery inherent in such restlessness is clear.

Just as for Scripture, idolatry is not wrong belief but displaced freedom, so for Scripture faith is not the confession of the right god but the proper disposition of freedom. Faith begins in the same realization as does idolatry: human existence is nonnecessary, derivative, contingent, and frighteningly fragile. But rather than be driven by anxiety to the compulsive search for security through the acquisition of pleasure, possessions, or power (treated as ultimate), faith regards contingent existence itself as a gracious gift, freely bestowed by the power that brings the human into existence at every moment and presently sustains him. Not by means of elaborate scientific theories or by means of complex philosophical arguments, but by the simple leap of the human heart toward truth, faith accepts that the human presence in the world is not a simple derivative of a self-contained worldly process, nor a cosmic accident, but rather the result of fashioning by the source of all that is in the world, the one who can be addressed as "thou" by the creature made to perceive and greet the one infinitely more powerful, intelligent, and loving than himself: "Thou made us." And in this truth, faith rejoices.

The second aspect of Augustine's formulation "Thou hast made us" is the use of the pronoun "us." Humans do not stand alone as God's creatures, but as only a "tiny bit of all that you created." Part of the deeply humbling realization of creatureliness is that each person is but a small piece of humanity, that God's purposes for humans as a whole are not likely to be restricted or contained exclusively in any single human—certainly not me—and that in the last analysis, each human story is in its basics the same. We may be born as natural narcissists, convinced that we are the center of the universe, and our parents may collude in that fantasy by convincing us that we are indeed special, but if we are fortunate, the process of life itself will reveal the truth that we are not, any one of us, much more than neighbor or stranger when it comes to brains or beauty or balletic grace. What is sometimes called the "mid-life crisis" is actually the intimation of the truth that our youthful vigor and the power of fantasy has prevented us from seeing: that we have one and *only one* life to live, and in all important respects, it is like every other human life ever lived. We are, as my wife quietly reminds me, merely "common clay," and our common walk toward death confirms that truth.

The other side of this truth, to be sure, is that each human has an indispensable role to play within the drama of idolatry and faith. Even as I am reminded by the great crush of common humanity of my smallness, I am reminded by the realization that "you have made us" of my distinctive and inalienable dignity as a human. No one can say yes or no to my Maker for me. It is entirely my responsibility to affirm or deny for "this tiny bit of all you have made" within the world, "you have made me." Each human carries the obligation to bear witness within a very specific body and a completely arbitrary placement within the world, to the truth of his or her creatureliness, a witness that each human exercises in behalf of every other human: "we are his creatures and the sheep of his flock." The capacity and obligation to speak the truth of human creatureliness is the basis of both priesthood and prophecy. It is carried out, moreover, not only in behalf of all other humans, but as well in concert with all other creatures, each in its own implicit way expressive of the Creator's intelligence and will but needing the explicit witness of the human voice to join the chorus of the Creator's praise.

The final phrase in Augustine's statement is most significant: God made humans "for himself." The Latin phrase is *ad te*, literally, "toward you." The phrase has a strong directional sense: humans are intrinsically, by their very fashioning, directed toward

God. God is the proper human telos. Once more, two aspects of this remarkable statement command attention. The first is that God has created humans precisely to be in relationship with him. God desires from humans a response commensurate with the gift of their fashioning. God craves from this creature what God cannot expect from any other creature, a dedication of human freedom to fellowship with God. Second, as Augustine would argue in another place, true human freedom is located not in the ability to choose this thing rather than that (*librium arbitrium*) but is located precisely in their relationship with the true goal of their existence (*libertas*). The implication is that the end of humans cannot be the world or any part of the world, but only the maker of the world and every part of it.

But here precisely is the difficulty for the disposition of human freedom, which so naturally tends toward idolatry, toward the location of the ultimate in something within the world that cannot be ultimate, and because it is chosen as ultimate, both distorts human freedom and is distorted by freedom's idolatrous choice. The difficulty is that God makes us for himself, yet God is not anything within the world, stands apart from the world as its Maker, as the implicit presence within and behind everything that is explicitly present. How can human freedom find its goal in the Maker when the Maker never explicitly appears in what is made, but remains the unthematic premise of what is made? If nothing that presents itself to us in the world can be God, how can we direct our freedom to God so long as we are in the world?

OUR HEARTS ARE RESTLESS UNTIL THEY REST IN THEE

I have already spoken of the restlessness of the heart that leads to idolatry: refusing to rest in the reality of creatureliness with all its dependence and inadequacy, the idolater rushes from thing to thing in the search for something that can serve as a surrogate for the divine. But there is also a restlessness—a "lack of quiet" (*inquietum*) in our hearts—of a more positive character, which is consequent upon the fact that God cannot be identified with any object in the world, yet our hearts are so constructed as to seek the face of God. There is a sense in which the person of authentic faith must have as restless a heart as the idolater, although the result of this restlessness is quite different. The idolater seeks to rest as quickly as possible in any object that can serve as the stabilizer of his existence and worth. The person of faith pushes past any temporary resting place in order to seek the one whose presence in creation is not to be identified with any specific thing within creation.

The difficulty for the disposition of the actual human heart is that it is not at all easy to distinguish authentic faith from idolatry through the course of a life with its concrete decisions and choices.

How should I evaluate—or how would Augustine evaluate—the restlessness that drove me to leave the monastic life and the priesthood in my late twenties, leaving the sacred precincts to marry a divorced woman with six children and to pursue a life of scholarship and teaching as a university career rather than a monastic or priestly ministry? The story can be made more complex, but in its essence, I left the place where my delight was the praise of God to inhabit a world almost completely devoid of the explicit devotion that was mine in the monastery. Was mine the restlessness of an idolater who abandoned the presence of the Living God in the round of daily monastic worship for the surrogates of pleasure, possessions, and power? Or was mine the restlessness of an authentic faith in the Living God that, despite error and even sin in the process, sought to respond to the Living God?

At this distance, it is hard for me to sort out the components of my heart's restlessness during my last years in the monastery, even as I am aware that my sorting out is both less significant and more prone to distortion than the steady gaze of God into my heart both then and now. I was restless emotionally because it was becoming clearer to me that the sense of communion I experienced in monastic worship and fellowship was not enough to satisfy the hunger for personal intimacy that I had acquired over years of oh-so-slow psychosexual growth between the ages of thirteen and twenty-six. The older longing for a home—that in part brought me to the monastic life—was now complicated by the more recent urging of hormones. My restlessness in my (ever-faithful) observance of the monastic life was fueled by a strong charge of emotional frustration, as I can see now, though at the time my tendency to specialize in intellectualization would have led me to deny any such influence. In any case, my heart no longer found the praise of God in the monastic ritual the adequate vehicle of happiness. That which appeared at the beginning to be the perfect explicit embodiment of God's praise (and of joy) now began to appear as inadequate to contain all that praise of God (and joy) entailed.

I do not want to minimize the role of hormones, for in the end they probably proved decisive, but there were other elements to my growing restlessness in the monastery that led me increasingly to regard it not as the place of my heart's rest (and happiness), but as an important but nonultimate stage in the journey to the rest that can be found in God alone. First, my education in philosophy and theology gave me a greater sense of self-confidence concerning my ability to play within a larger arena. Students at Notre Dame Seminary (where I did philosophy), at Saint Meinrad Archabbey (where I studied theology for four years), and then at Indiana University (where I did religious studies) were not so far above me that I could not hold my own. The fantasy of being a scholar in the real world seemed increasingly less fantastic. So, the ambition to exercise gifts of which previously I had only a vague notion played a role. Second, my theological education also made me acutely conscious of the ways in which the monastic life and I were not a lasting fit. I grew worried that the monastic life was for me too safe and comfortable, lacking the component of risk: understanding the response of faith in God in terms of obedience to rule and abbot seemed, I thought, to leave out a lot. I also discovered from the reading of Paul's Letter to the Romans that my performance as a monk fit perfectly the pattern of fearful compulsiveness that can be called works righteousness. What was meant to be the expression of faith in the Living God turned out to be for me a means of measuring my performance against that of others. Finally, as an ordained priest, I experienced the same tension with the teaching office of the church as did many other young theologians with the publication of Paul VI's *Humanae Vitae*. I could no longer in good conscience impose penance on those confessing the practice of birth control, since I regarded the church's position on the matter as both formally and materially in error. Yes, I was deeply restless, and the result was predictable: I left the monastery, married, took on the care of seven children, became a professor, and spent the next forty years in public trying to remain loyal to my Catholic heritage while at the same time serving as a critical voice within the church.

Despite the ways in which my restlessness was less than "divine discontent," with huge amounts of human frailty and folly intermixed, I have in the end considered my departure from the monastery more an act of faith than of idolatry. First, there was nothing in my new future that promised anything that idols characteristically offer: suffering, poverty, and powerlessness were the immediate outcome of my risky decision more than pleasure, possessions, and power—with the lagniappe of disapproval from family, friends, fellow monks, and the Vatican. Second, I see now that if I had stayed in the monastery despite the restlessness that (I am convinced now) God placed in my heart, that would have been idolatrous: the choice of the representation of God rather than the Living God.

UNTIL THEY REST IN THEE

The last part of Augustine's cryptic formulation continues to challenge me at this late stage of my life. What does "until they rest in Thee" really mean? An obvious interpretation is that of traditional Christian eschatology. If humans have been made "toward God," as Augustine claims, then only with their participation in God's "Sabbath rest" will their hearts also find a resting place. In this reading, restlessness—both the negative and positive sorts I have described—is ingredient to human existence, and satisfaction for that restlessness can be found only after death in the future life. A corollary would be that genuine happiness also is exclusively an eschatological reality, when humans hear Jesus say, "Well done, good and faithful servant, enter into the joy of your master" (Matt 25:21). I have no difficulty with this understanding: certainly the fullness of joy must be understood in eschatological terms, for it is only when human participation in the divine life is complete that the striving of human freedom can fully rest.

My experience over the past forty years of worldly endeavor, however, has given me a glimpse of another possible understanding of "until they rest in Thee," one that sees the possibility of a genuine if relative happiness through active engagement with the world that God draws into existence at every moment. Certainly, when I compare my activities over these years to those in the monastery, they can be characterized as restless. They have at least been both multiple and demanding. I have committed myself to spouse and children and discovered the circles of care to steadily expand rather than contract. I have dedicated myself to the role of the teacher within universities and seminaries and have found former students to be as needy and demanding as present ones. I have written many books and articles and reviews and have found that publications beget invitations. I have traveled as a lecturer in an ever-widening world of expectation and have spent more time than I desired before one sort of camera or another. And, in my fashion, I have continued to worship in my parish as a Catholic layperson, teaching adult education there and in other local churches. Amid all these activities, I have discovered something about happiness and the restless heart. I have begun to understand how resting in the Lord is not a matter of finding some single spot in the world or some specific activity and making it absolute, but a matter of allowing any place and any practice, in all its relativity, to be the means of resting in the Lord, who cannot be defined by any time or place or practice, but remains the invisible premise of every time and place and practice. If the heart is centered in the invisible God, then it is freed to engage any manifestation of God's world in all its partiality without making that manifestation idolatrous. The restlessness is on the surface, and shows itself in me as it does for others, in fatigue and irritability and even occasional depression; the rest (and happiness) is deeper and less accessible, recoverable mainly through those moments of silent reflection when what lies beneath the surface has time to make itself known.

I have come to appreciate the oscillation in my own life between faith and idolatry that I tried to describe in an early book (*Faith's Freedom*). When I am engaged in any one of these "projects" of mine—spouse, parent, teacher, writer—I experience something of the joy I first felt in the experience of monastic worship: I am caught up in a sense of being engaged with something large and important that demands my best efforts, and that engages others as well. My wife assures me that I am a better and more contented person when I am writing a large book, which consumes great amounts of my attention for great periods of time. My passion in each such endeavor tilts naturally and almost inevitably toward idolatry: I seek to make it absolute, seek to be the "best" parent, teacher, scholar possible, to make that activity defining of myself and my happiness. But the multiplicity of commitments has also meant that each project is challenged and rendered relative by the other projects: the demands of family keep scholarship from becoming an absolute; the needs of students prevent writing from being an exclusive commitment. Being thus jolted from my temporary serenity and contentment in a single project, I naturally experience dismay and a sense of loss. Only slowly have I come to understand how God thus keeps me off balance and therefore in a constant state of faithful response rather than idolatrous repose. Even more slowly have I come to appreciate that "resting in the Lord" is not only an eschatological hope, it can be a condition of present human existence to the degree that my response in every circumstance is to the God who has placed me in this circumstance and reliably will pull me out of it the moment I make it rather than God my place of rest.

I am grateful that early in my life, for whatever reason, I was given the gift of this text from Augustine, and have, throughout my life, found his statement to provide a guide to my own desire for happiness. As I grow ever closer to a return to the "common clay" that we are reminded each Ash Wednesday is the inevitable end to our mortal human existence, I am ever more content to tend the ever-more-limited part of God's world that is given to my care. In the quiet round of life with my wife and in the small accomplishments of the teacher and scholar, I do not despair at the passing of all human endeavor or the insignificance of all human achievement, but regard this time and place in God's world to be precisely the right time and place, and await gladly (but not restlessly) the possibility of exchanging notes with Augustine himself on happiness, if we both should find ourselves called to the joy of our master.

5

SPEAKING OF THE DEVIL

Originally published as "Powers and Principalities: The Devil Is No Joke," Commonweal *138, no. 17 (2011): 14–17.*

In the seventh of the *Screwtape Letters* (1942), C. S. Lewis nicely captures the modern view of the devil. The mentor Screwtape writes to his apprentice Wormwood that

> our policy for the moment, is to conceal ourselves.... The fact that devils are predominantly comic figures in the modern imagination will help you. If any faint suspicion of your existence begins to arise in his mind, suggest to him a picture of something in red tights, and persuade him that since he cannot believe in that (it is an old textbook way of confusing them) he therefore cannot believe in you.

By portraying the demonic realm in such individualistic and anthropomorphic terms, unfortunately, Lewis himself perpetuated the caricature; Screwtape is oddly attractive and his correspondence is downright cozy. As a friend recently observed, "Who doesn't like Screwtape?"

For that matter, who doesn't like Meryl Streep? In *The Devil Wears Prada*, her representation of the dark side is stylish, witty, and, well, attractive. Yielding to her seduction means losing for a time the right boy and indulging in some distracting sophistication, but the only real harm the devil does involves advancement and retreat in the small war of corporate competition. As in other movies and novels where the devil makes an appearance since the dalliances of Dr. Faust, the personification of evil appears less as a cosmic power battling God for sovereignty than as a small-time dealer in individual favors, and the source of humorous mischief: the cross-dressing comic Flip Wilson's character Geraldine invariably caused gales of laughter when she coyly declared, "The devil made me do it."

THE LANGUAGE OF THE NEW TESTAMENT

The perceptions of the first Christians were far grimmer. The New Testament's extensive language concerning malevolent spiritual forces is never humorous. The terminology varies: texts speak of the devil (Matt 4:1–11) or Satan (Luke 17:18), of demons or unclean spirits (Mark 5:1–20), of powers and principalities (Col 1:16), of elements of the universe (Gal 4:9), the ruler of the power of the air (Eph 2:2), the dragon and ancient serpent (Rev 20:2). The terms appear separately and in combination; together, they point to a conviction broadly shared by the writers of the New Testament that a cosmic power—lesser than God but greater than humans alone—inhabited the world and worked against human good in a manner that was anything but comic or quaint.

Paul speaks of Satan in personal terms as a constant threat lying outside the community (1 Cor 5:5; 1 Tim 1:20; 5:15) and capable of damaging action even within the community (Rom 16:20; 2 Cor 12:7; 1 Thess 2:18; 2 Tim 2:26). At a more cosmic level, Paul envisages the "powers and principalities" conquered by the death and exaltation of Christ (Col 1:13–23; 2:20) still capable of opposing believers, who must continue to do battle against "not flesh and blood, but against the rulers, against the authorities, against the cosmic powers of this present darkness, against the spiritual forces of evil in the heavenly places" (Eph 6:12). Similarly, Peter pictures the devil as a ravening beast able to destroy unwary believers: "Be sober and watch, because your adversary the devil goes about like a roaring lion seeking whom he may devour" (1 Pet 5:8). Luke–Acts envisages Satan (the devil) as the arrogant ruler of a counterkingdom to God's own (Luke 11:17–23), capable of granting great power to those willing to worship him (Luke 4:1–13) and in charge of a vast army of demonic spirits (Luke 11:17–26). John declares that "the whole world lies under the power of the evil one" (1 John 5:19). Finally, the Book of Revelation imagines the servants who continue the prophetic witness of Jesus in the world caught in a cosmic battle between Christ and Satan. The great beast wages ceaseless war against the saints in unholy alliance with the corrupt power of an empire that buys and sells human lives and brands them with its mark (Rev 12:7–12, 17; 13:16–18; 17:7—18:24).

Language about evil spiritual forces is not restricted to a single New Testament composition, or to the perception of a single author. It is found in rhetorically crafted letters (such as 2 Corinthians) as well as in realistic narratives (such as Mark), in the most apocalyptic (Revelation) and in the most Hellenistic of writings (Hebrews), in arguably the earliest (1 Thess 2:18) as well as probably the latest (2 Pet 2:4) canonical composition. The language manifestly arises from the shared convictions of the ancient writers and seeks to express realities that for them cannot be described in other terms.

If this language cannot be dismissed as a single author's eccentric vision, or as the literary mode of a specific genre, or as a primitive stage of religious evolution, then serious consideration must be given to the New Testament's powerful and pervasive language about the satanic realm and to the question of why, if it meant something to those ancient writers and readers, it no longer speaks to us of something real or important. Is this another example of cultural baggage that must be jettisoned if Scripture is to remain afloat in modernity's choppy waters—like the New Testament's language about men and women or slaves and masters?

At one level, the time-conditioned character of the language is clear. In the ancient world, the New Testament is not exceptional in its use of language about demons and evil spirits. Both Greco-Roman and Jewish literature, in popular writings (such as novels) and in specialized writing (in philosophy and religion) used such language fluently. As the third-century Christian philosopher Origen remarked to his Epicurean opponent, "It is not we alone who speak of wicked demons, but almost all who acknowledge the existence of demons" (*Against Celsus* VII, 69). But the New Testament's language is not "prescientific" in the sense that it seeks to explain phenomena that later was more adequately captured by natural science: it is not employed for earthquakes, storms, or celestial phenomena; it is not invoked to account for the collapse of buildings or the appearance of leprosy. Instead, the language of the New Testament concerns power at work among specifically human and social realities. Because it seeks to describe that which is both human and more than human, which is intricately connected to the disposition of human freedom in the empirical world yet has a "plus factor" that the choices of individual human freedom cannot explain, the language of personification is not only appropriate but necessary. Is it possible, then, that the New Testament's language about the demonic is true in ways that are important for us to relearn? The question can be approached indirectly by examining first the functions of demonic language within the New Testament, then the ways in which such language became corrupted within Christianity, and last, whether it is worth trying to repristinate. Does the language say what needs saying in a way no other language can?

WHAT THE LANGUAGE EXPRESSES

The narrative of Luke–Acts provides a sense of how the devil was perceived to work among humans. In the Gospel narrative, we observe that Jesus encounters the devil not only in his personal testing in the wilderness (Luke 4:1–13), but at the time of his passion and death; the narrator identifies Satan as the one who enters the heart of Judas and leads him to betray Jesus (22:3) and who "sifts like wheat" Peter and the other disciples who will deny and abandon Jesus (22:31). In his ministry, Jesus encounters a series of persons whose lives have been ravaged by being possessed by unclean spirits—the minions of Satan. They are portrayed as in bondage (8:29; 11:20–22; 13:16); they are subject to violence (4:35; 8:28; 9:36); their condition alienates them from themselves and from their community (8:26–33; 9:37–43). Those possessed are not unlike those who suffer physical ailments such as leprosy, fever, or hemorrhage within Luke's narrative: sickness also stigmatizes and segregates those afflicted from a full participation in the common life.

Luke portrays Jesus's prophetic ministry, in turn, as one of liberation. His first public words declare that the Spirit has anointed him to proclaim good news to the poor, and to "proclaim release to the captives," and "to let the oppressed go free" (4:18). Luke shows this promise enacted in Jesus's acts of healing, which always terminate in the restoration of the sick to their community (4:39; 5:24–25; 7:15; 8:40–56; 13:11–12; 17:11–19;

18:35–43), and above all in acts of exorcism, which free those captive to unclean spirits and enable them to live once more in the human community (see esp. 8:34–39), so that Jesus's inner circle in Galilee included with the Twelve, "some women who had been cured of evil spirits and infirmities: Mary, called Magdalene, from whom seven spirits had gone out...and many others" (8:2–3). That Luke understands Jesus's ministry of liberation in just such terms is shown by his summary of that ministry in Acts 10:38: Peter declares that "God anointed Jesus of Nazareth with the Holy Spirit and with power...he went about doing good and healing all who were oppressed by the devil, for God was with him."

In the narrative of Acts, Luke shows Satan at work in both subtler and more systemic ways. Satan "fills the heart" of Ananias and Sapphira to counterfeit the impulse of the Holy Spirit and hold back a share of what they own from the community possessions (Acts 5:3), and the "gall of bitterness and chains of wickedness" lead Simon Magus to seek to purchase a share in the Spirit (8:23). When the magician Bar-Jesus opposes Paul, the apostle calls him "son of the devil, the enemy of all righteousness, full of all deceit and villainy, who makes crooked the straight paths of the Lord" (13:10). Paul drives out from the slave girl in Philippi the spirit that enabled her to prophesy for pay (16:16–18). In Ephesus, the mere touch of Paul's garments cause diseases to leave the afflicted and "evil spirit came out of them," so that the practitioners of magic in the city publicly burned their books of spells (19:11–20).

As the gospel revealed a power of evil at work in human misery that caused those physically and mentally afflicted to be oppressed not merely by their individual suffering but by the social dynamics of alienation and exclusion, so does Acts display within magic and religious practices profound patterns of greed and deception whose power transcends yet works within the human choices of those captive to them. In the gospel, the Holy Spirit at work in Jesus liberates those oppressed through the prophet's word and touch; in Acts, the same Holy Spirit is the power necessary for the disciples to name and tame Satan's oppressive rule over humans. Luke–Acts lacks the apocalyptic urgency and imagery that characterize Paul and the Book of Revelation, but its sane and sophisticated narrative is no less certain that within the oppressive expressions of human culture there is at work a darker and more malevolent force than can be accounted for simply through individual wickedness. Nor is this familiar and congenial composition less certain that the battle to which disciples are summoned through the power of the Holy Spirit is against that evil power: when the seventy disciples sent out by Jesus to heal and proclaim God's rule return to him and report, "Lord, in your name even the demons submit to us," he responds, "I watched Satan fall from heaven like a flash of lightning" (Luke 10:17).

Like the other New Testament writings, Luke–Acts does not use language about Satan, the devil, and unclean spirits to deflect responsibility away from individual human freedom but to express the manner in which the freedom of individuals can be deceived, distorted, and even held captive by social structures and dynamics whose energy and force transcend the capacities of individual humans. Such language is, to be sure, mythic. But mythic language as used by anthropologists and increasingly by philosophers and theologians does not denote a form of falsehood or error. Myth as used in these discourses designates a register of language—often but not necessarily in the form of narrative—that is essential for the expression of what is most profound—both positive and negative—in the human experience of the world. In this instance, mythic languages speak the truth that evil is far more extensive and powerful and far more systemically effective than can be spoken through ordinary scientific analysis or the jargons of sociology and psychology.

THE CORRUPTION OF LANGUAGE

The New Testament's language about the devil and the satanic realm was corrupted over time by misapplication, overextension, and trivialization. The misapplication began at once with Paul's statement in 1 Corinthians 10:20 that Gentile sacrifice and religious meals amounted to fellowship with demons. Christian apologists subsequently ascribed the entire system of pagan worship to Satan; thus, the vow to "renounce Satan" in the baptismal ritual of Christians in the patristic period was spelled out as a rejection of all forms of Greco-Roman religious practice. What was lost in the specificity of this attribution was the New Testament's sense of the demonic power as operative in realms other than the specifically cultic. That social sensibility disappeared, as the charge of demon possession extended over time to include Jews, Christian heretics and schismatics, Muhammad, assorted witches, and in the full flourishing of missionary fervor, all pagan babies of Asia and Africa. When anything alien or threatening is automatically designated as the work of the devil, the credibility of such language diminishes. The suspicion that religious language is being used manipulatively is almost unavoidable when pastors of megachurches caught with their pants down or when ecclesiastics subject to press scrutiny conjure their mild opposition as the work of the devil seeking to destroy God's elect.

Overextension of speech about the devil leads, in turn, inevitably to its trivialization. When Satan's power is portrayed in terms of individual temptation and seduction rather than in terms of systemic evil and social oppression, when the cosmic battle between the angels of Michael and the angels of Satan pictured by Revelation is reduced to "my guardian angel" and a corresponding imp competing for a moral victory in my choice between candy and fruit, the way is cleared for devil jokes and (for the little ones) devil Halloween costumes. When the scariest thing about Satan comes from the special effects in movies like

The Exorcist, the collapse of myth into cartoon is complete. The loss, however, is not simply to language; the loss is to the ability to perceive and express the dark side of human existence in the world.

Children of the Enlightenment delight in the dismissal of superfluous cosmic entities, good or bad, rejoice at the purging of the supernatural from the conversation of the educated elite, celebrate the triumph of the so-called social sciences in providing all the language ever needed to define humans and their social interactions. But if the children of the Enlightenment are at all alert, they also find that the language of the social sciences fails to account for the puzzling persistence of behaviors that are at once malevolent, irrational, and systemic. Why does racial hostility triumph over civil rights laws? Why do mobs gather and explode seemingly without cause and without point? Why do highly educated people dedicate themselves to self-destruction through addiction to drugs or gambling? Why do nations destroy each other over oil and honor?

The rational discourse offered by the social sciences cannot describe much less comprehend the horrors of the past century—the Shoah under Hitler, the Gulag archipelago under Stalin, the Cambodian genocide under Pot Pol, to name only the best known and most visible. These massive and systemic exercises in oppression began in deception and led to the captivity and destruction of the innocent. Not the virtue or vice of Eichmann nor the innocence or malice of Malenkov—not even the megalomaniacal pretensions of the dictators themselves adequately account for the human and more than human passion and energy for destruction generated among the thousands of functionaries through which evil was unleashed on others. This must be a somber conclusion drawn from our common experience of life: there exist powers at work in humans and through humans, but with a superhuman blind energy, that do not work for the good but rather for the destruction of humans and with them all human beauty and grace. Such powers can adequately be named not by the language of social description but only by the language of myth. It is important to be able to speak of the devil.

SPEAKING OF THE DEVIL

If Christians are to speak of the devil—and all the realm of evil represented by Satan and demons—then they must begin by eschewing their history of linguistic misapplication, overextension, and trivialization. The way toward rehabilitation must pass through reticence and linguistic discipline. Christians need to refrain from designating every temptation to which individuals are subject, every trouble caused in the community, everything that is alien and threatening, as demonic. Even in the face of those who use this language with respect to them, they must resist the impulse to retaliate in kind. Instead, they should begin to use such language primarily to name and engage those systems of social alienation and oppression that the New Testament itself addresses when it speaks of the devil and his kingdom.

Christians do not need to seek out another holocaust, gulag, or genocide in order to identify the deceitful, captivating, and oppressive patterns characteristic of Satan. Such patterns are evident all around us. They manifest themselves in systems of addiction—to drink, drugs, gambling, sex—that literally enslave people in our culture, bring ruin to them, and destroy their families. The power at work in sustaining such patterns of addiction are clearly both personal and systemic: pushers and enablers and pimps represent a system of enslavement—in the case of prostitution, literally an enslavement—that transcends the intentions and acts even of the individuals caught up in such systems. The church is able to extend the liberating ministry of Jesus through exorcism when in the power of the Holy Spirit it names such systems as demonic, refuses to enable them in its own common life, and provides an alternative mode of life characterized by the freedom of faith within the community. To speak of the devil in such contexts of communal exorcism is to speak properly.

Similarly, liberation theologians have properly identified the "powers and principalities" at work in patterns of social behavior that systematically deceive, enslave, and oppress those who are "other" and vulnerable. Linguistic purists may shudder at the multiplication of "isms" that are identified by critical analysis. But racism, sexism, ageism, and homophobia are real and powerful in their capacity to damage and even destroy others even as they corrupt those who practice them. The demonic character of these systems is revealed particularly by the corrupt forms of speech they sponsor. Those who claim, "Some of my best friends are [fill in the blank]" or "Personally, I admire [fill in the blank]," while participating without protest in social systems that marginalize, exclude, and even destroy the lives of those who are other in age, gender, sexual makeup, race, or class—an increasingly important category—simply reveal how little such malevolent systems are a matter of individual taste or sincerity. The systems hold just as much captive those who oppress as it does those who are oppressed, deceive those who act on behalf of the evil spirits even more than they deceive those who are victims of evil doing.

The church's call to exorcize such demonic systems is clear. Once more, the act of liberation begins with naming such systems for what they are: the work of powers and principalities—the devil's work—to hurt God by harming humans. Naming is a beginning rather than an end. The church must also in the power of the Holy Spirit reject and repudiate such demonic systems within its own common life. So long as sexism and homophobia and racism are practiced within the community that claims allegiance to Christ, the church simply colludes, in a profoundly corrupt fashion, with the devil's work of hurting God by harming humans.

Does this mean that language about the demonic is never appropriately used for the trials and testing of individuals? No, but it must, at least for a time, until we learn to get this language right once more, be used much more circumspectly and precisely. To speak of those caught in the webs of deceit and destruction spun by the agents of addiction and social alienation as "tormented by the devil" is to speak in a manner consonant with the language of the Gospels. But just as language about God's activity is trivialized and emptied when associated with successful free-throw shooting, so is language about the devil corrupted when attached to such quotidian impulses as profane speech or irritability. The Letter of James sorts it well when it speaks of the patterns of envy that cause murder and war to come from a "wisdom from below" that is "devilish" (James 3:15), but refrains from such language when speaking of garden-variety temptation: "One is tempted by one's own desire, being lured and enticed by it" (1:14).

Finally, the church as the Body of Christ must seek to provide a community that directly opposes the life-destroying social dynamics that are properly called demonic. The church that lives by the vision of the prophet Jesus and the Holy Spirit bestowed by Jesus is called to embrace more than to exclude, to reconcile more than to alienate, to cultivate the reciprocity of diverse gifts within the Body of Christ more than the suppression of gifts in the name of good order, to enable the full participation in the life of the community precisely for those who in the devil's counterkingdom are rejected from such full participation. This is not easy work, for as Paul declares, "our struggle is not against blood and flesh, but against the rulers, against the authorities, against the cosmic powers of this present darkness, against the spiritual forces of evil in the heavenly places"—but it is serious and necessary work, for whatever else he may be, the devil is no joke.

6

HUMAN AND DIVINE

Did Jesus Have Faith?

Published in slightly altered form in Commonweal *135, no. 2 (2008): 10–12 and 14–16.*

On November 26, 2006, the Congregation for the Doctrine of the Faith (CDF) issued a Notification concerning certain elements in the theological works of Jan Sobrino, SJ. Apart from his "methodological presuppositions," the complaints all centered on Christology. The Congregation found Father Sobrino's teaching inadequate regarding the divinity of Jesus Christ, the incarnation of the Son of God, Jesus Christ and the kingdom of God, the self-consciousness of Jesus, and the salvific value of Jesus's death.

The issue of Christology is not trivial. Getting Jesus right is at the heart of Christian identity. But both substance and the style of the Congregation's composition reveal a troubling tension in contemporary Catholic theology. On one side are those like Sobrino whose thought is forged with explicit attention to specific cultural contexts and who claim their teaching about Jesus is faithful to Scripture; on the other side are the ecclesiastical officers who also claim to interpret Jesus faithfully to Scripture, precisely because they do so within the framework of the doctrinal tradition of the great councils and the popes.

It is not troubling that there should be criticism and response among theologians or that there should be question and answer between theological teachers and representatives of the church's magisterium. Such exchanges are part of the healthy functioning of the Body of Christ, in which the different gifts are exercised as the Spirit gives direction. It is the theologian's task to inquire critically into received teaching in light of culture and science; it is the magisterium's task to test whether such critical inquiry stands within the creedal framework of the church and builds the Body of Christ in faith and love. What is troubling is when, in place of a mutually informing conversation, there are mutually excluding claims, and when the participants in the exchange do not seem to recognize that they are, quite literally, talking past each other.

In this essay, I focus on one point of caution in the Notification, concerning Father Sobrino's statements on the faith of Jesus in *Jesus the Liberator* that are based on Hebrews 12:2, such as, "Jesus was an extraordinary believer and had faith," and, "With regard to faith, Jesus in his life is presented as a believer like ourselves," and, "He is the model, the one on whom we have to keep our eyes fixed in order to live out our own faith." The Congregation's response is framed in terms of Jesus's "filial and messianic consciousness" that is the "direct consequence of his ontology as Son of God made man," which makes it impossible for him to be "a believer like ourselves," because then "he would not be able to be a true revealer showing us the face of the Father." Before addressing the substance of this issue—the faith of Jesus Christ—and why the expression of the issue both by Sobrino and the Vatican is unsatisfying, I need to make a few preliminary points.

THE DIFFICULT TRUTH

The identity of Jesus Christ is a mystery in the proper sense of the term: even when it is disclosed, it remains beyond human grasp: neither human reason nor human speech can adequately comprehend or express the truth that Paul states succinctly as "in Christ God was reconciling the world to himself" (2 Cor 5:19). Christians never had trouble professing "Jesus is Lord" (1 Cor 12:3), or recognizing at the experiential level that the Holy Spirit at work among them came from the exalted Lord Jesus (2 Cor 3: 17–18) or praying to God through Jesus Christ (Rom 16:27). From the beginning as well, believers affirmed both that "God sent his Son" and that Jesus was "born of a woman, born under the law" (Gal 4:4). The Nicene Creed was consistent with the earliest experiences and convictions concerning Jesus when it affirmed both that the one who was "God from God" was also the one who was "born of the Virgin Mary, suffered under Pontius Pilate."

The difficulty for the first Christians, as for us, is not at the level of experience or profession or prayer, it is at the level of thought. The rule for prayer is the rule for faith (*lex orandi, lex credendi*), without doubt, but theology is more than faith: it is the attempt to critically assess and express what is prayed and believed. For those whose most basic convictions were monotheistic, the Christian claims about Jesus appeared dangerously close to polytheism. To affirm both divinity and humanity simultaneously and with equal emphasis more than challenges the ordinary categories of thought, it confounds them. There was, however, no escaping the obligation to think, even in the face of absurdity, for the alternative was to admit that Christianity was no more than a superstition, as its opponents claimed, that it had no place in the realm of the intellect.

The thinking we call Christology was, from very early on, impelled by two distinct imperatives: the first is the desire to have the mystery that is Jesus respond to the demands of rationality, such as they were defined age by age; the second is the need to think about Jesus in a manner that corresponds to believers' experience, profession, and prayer. And since that experience, profession, and prayer is given normative expression in the writings of the New Testament, thinking about Jesus has always been required to find a basis in these normative texts.

PENDULUM SWINGS

The measure of rationality in the first six centuries was that of Greek philosophy, especially pertaining to questions of being or ontology. Such philosophical language was a splendid and supple instrument to express the mythic dimension of the Christian faith: God entered the frame of human existence and elevated it to a participation in God's own life. And since challenges to the traditional faith were posed in terms of ontology—as was the case throughout the long Arian crisis—the language of orthodox defense that eventually found its way into the creeds also necessarily employed the same idiom. It does, however, have certain built-in limitations.

The first limitation is that it is better at abstractions than at particulars, better at the level of "humanity" than at the level of a specific human life. The second is that it aligns only awkwardly with the language of the New Testament, which is more often narrative in character than ontological. For those schooled in philosophical idiom, there was a natural tendency to privilege the parts of the New Testament that sounded like ontology—such as the "I am" language in the Gospel of John—and to reduce the complexity and diversity of the New Testament's language about Jesus in service of a few, if essential, abstract assertions concerning divinity and humanity.

The centuries of christological controversy leading up to the Council of Chalcedon in 451 showed how difficult it was to maintain an equal and simultaneous emphasis on both divinity and humanity. Theologians in Alexandria tended to emphasize divinity: their *logos-sarx* ("word/flesh") Christology drew heavily on John's Gospel and was driven by the conviction that only God can save humans. In its extreme form, this Christology took the form of monophysitism ("one nature") because it eliminated the full humanity of Jesus. Antiochean theologians, in contrast, tended to emphasize the humanity of Jesus: their *logos-anthropos* ("word/human") Christology was driven by the conviction that only what was assumed by the divine could be saved. Christ must therefore be human in every respect apart from sin. In its extreme form, this Christology took the form of Nestorianism, which minimized the force of the conviction that "God was in Christ." Stimulated by the *Tome* of Pope Leo the Great (in 449), which sought a compromise that respected the strength of both positions, the Council of Chalcedon (451) finally reached the formula that has defined all subsequent orthodox Christology: in Christ is one person in two natures; he is fully human and fully divine, without separation or mixture. The Chalcedonian formula was successful both in its fidelity to the complex witness of the New Testament, and in its ability to define the limits of reflection without privileging one emphasis over another.

It must be recognized, however, that in subsequent centuries the strength of much Christian piety and the influence of Alexandrian theology tended to favor the affirmation of Christ's divinity over his full humanity. Although monophysitism had been condemned at Chalcedon, it continued to dominate some eastern traditions, and despite its condemnation, remained the default form of "orthodoxy" for many Christians. A variant of monophysitism that is of immediate pertinence to the current issue, in fact, was called monotheletism ("one will"), which taught that there was only one divine "energy" or "will" at work in Christ—he lacked a true human will. After a long and bitter struggle, this teaching was finally condemned by the Council of Constantinople in 680.

The residual power of monophysitism is found in the peculiar principle called *communicatio idiomatum* ("exchange of characteristics"), which serves to compromise the "unmixedness" of the two natures in Christ by asserting the legitimacy of ascribing the characteristic of one nature to another. But while all would recognize the value of asserting that Mary is the "Mother of God"—the first and most important instance of the principle—it is, in fact, a principle that can be dangerous when used carelessly, as, for example, if one would assert, without careful qualification, that God was born in Nazareth or that Jesus created heaven and earth. Is such language appropriate to the exuberance of prayer and piety? Yes, but sober theological discourse requires greater circumspection.

Such assertions are dangerous to the degree that they suppress the full humanity of Jesus, making of him simply a docetic "god in human form." It should be noted that the Vatican composition criticizes Sobrino for being insufficiently expansive in his use of this principle. Sobrino had defined the principle in this fashion: "the limited human is predicated of God, but the unlimited divine is not predicated of Jesus." The Vatican responds that the principle works equally in both directions: "the human is predicated of God and the divine of man," so that, "in Christian terminology, it is possible to say that Jesus is God, who is creator and omnipotent."

The CDF places itself in self-conscious continuity with the theological heritage of earlier centuries. It thinks of "faith" primarily in terms of "belief," that is, as a cognitive more than a volitional response. It privileges ontological categories for expressing Christian confession. It is fond of traditional formulas that can be treated as axioms from which one can argue deductively. Its understanding of truth tends toward the propositional, and it is suspicious of theological wording that does not replicate the accepted propositions precisely. And although it pays lip service to the critical study of Scripture, its use of the Gospels in particular is resolutely precritical. It reads the New Testament exclusively through the lens of developed doctrine and uses the New Testament exclusively as a repository of propositional support for doctrinal propositions. In a word, it continues as though nothing in the theological world has changed. But much has changed.

THE CHANGED SITUATION

Two factors in particular have changed the context for Christology today. The first is the development of diverse discourses concerning humans. The categories of Greek philosophy are little learned nor deeply understood by many contemporary theologians. I do not regard this as a positive, but an unfortunate deprivation. The language of ontology, as I have suggested above, is not only legitimate, it addresses with distinct authority the mythic dimension of Christianity: the drama of the human and the divine at its most profound and essential level. The loss of this language represents a potentially tragic gap in tradition.

The development of other discourses that can be used for conversation about Jesus is, however, positive. The emergence of critical historiography since the Enlightenment enables us to focus on the particulars of human experience and action in the past—including that of Jesus—and not simply on the abstractions of being and essence. Within philosophy, a number of idioms, notably that of phenomenology (embraced by John Paul II himself), enable ways of engaging the specifics of human experience in the world. The social sciences also, above all psychology, sociology, and anthropology, have had a dramatic impact on our understanding of what it means to be human, not only in the present but in the past, not only in our culture but in other cultures as well. The study of literature has allowed an appreciation for the multiple ways in which texts mean: how narratives read as a whole convey meaning that no single part of them can convey and how the actions of characters in narratives can disclose the structures of existence, how discourses use rhetoric to shape arguments in which each part depends on all the other parts, how truth can be expressed more powerfully if more allusively through metaphor than through proposition. It is safe to say that our understanding of what it means to be a human being in this world has been enhanced by these ways of seeing and speaking.

The second factor is a changed way of reading Scripture. Once more, the development of historical consciousness is important. With respect to theology, however, I stand by the position I have taken frequently in recent years, namely that the so-called quest for the historical Jesus has not, as a whole, turned out to be either the right direction for Christology, or the most significant contribution of a historical-critical perspective. I agree that the embrace of the historical Jesus approach by some forms of theology—including several liberation theologians—has indeed led, however inadvertently, to a reduction of the mystery of Jesus in the New Testament.

More important is the way that historical analysis has enabled a more complex appreciation of the process by which New Testament compositions came into existence and their character as witnesses and interpretations of the mystery that is Jesus Christ. We have come to understand that the Gospels, for example, are far from straightforward records of Jesus's sayings and deeds that give direct access to Jesus's self-understanding. They are, rather, literary compositions that combine genuine memories of Jesus selected and shaped by the communities believing in him as the raised and powerfully present Lord and given specific form by the literary and religious intentions of the evangelists. In this light, we recognize that each of the Synoptic Gospels is as theologically sophisticated and profound as John, just as we recognize that John has the same mixture of fact and interpretation as the Synoptics. We have, therefore, come to appreciate the diversity in the Gospel accounts not as a scandal that must be eliminated by means of either historical reduction or theological harmonization, but as a Spirit-guided set of portraits that invite contemplation of the person whose identity could not be captured by any single rendering. And we have begun to realize that a responsible reading of the Gospels—or any of the New Testament witnesses—cannot bypass careful attention to their literary and rhetorical shaping. To claim the support of Scripture without doing the hard work of exegesis is, from this perspective, presumptuous.

Because Scripture is perceived as a living and dynamic set of witnesses through which God's Holy Spirit not only spoke truly in and to the past but also speaks prophetically in and to the present, the theologian's relation to Scripture is also fundamentally reconceived. The writings of the Old and New Testaments are not regarded as a repository of oracles that provide support for doctrinal propositions, but as an arena for discovery, for new insight, for fresh challenge. The more a theologian is also an exegete, the more the theologian can learn from Scripture beyond the narrow range of doctrine that was not Scripture's main concern in the first place. To put it sharply: for the sort of theology practiced by the CDF, the truth is already adequately stated in dogmatic propositions, and Scripture's role is the secondary one of providing support; for the sort of theology practiced by many others today, even systematic theologians, the reading of Scripture comes first. In the ideal, this fresh reading of Scripture leads to an honest and positive engagement with traditional teaching; in some cases, unfortunately, it can lead to a simplistic dismissal of tradition. The decisive question is whether the reading of the New Testament today can lead present-day believers into a deeper and perhaps even richer understanding of the mystery of Christ than is possible to the formulaic expressions of tradition.

SPEAKING OF FAITH

My observations concerning the development of diverse discourses (or even epistemologies) and of an exegetically based theological inquiry have immediate pertinence to the matter at issue between Father Sobrino and the CDF, the faith of Jesus Christ.

The emergence of different ways of speaking about human beings has revealed ever more sharply the inevitable limitations of any single mode of discourse, including the ontological. That's the negative. The positive is that diverse discourses can add positive knowledge: what ontology cannot do, for example, psychology may be able to do; what psychology cannot get at, anthropology may be able to reach, and so on. There are ways of measuring the adequacy of each epistemology within its own range or competency: mathematical truths can be tested mathematically, but not literarily; moral truths can be tested by the rules of ethics but not by those of economics. By the same logic, epistemologies cannot make truth claims (or deny them) that lie within the realm of another discourse. I cannot appeal to the law of noncontradiction to deny the existence of literary metaphor; you cannot legitimately claim that a libretto is beautiful based on the morality of its theme.

The CDF appears to recognize these simple principles when it states, "Certainly, it is necessary to recognize the limited character of dogmatic formulations, which do not express nor are able to express everything contained in the mystery of faith, and must be interpreted in light of Sacred Scripture and Tradition." This healthy recognition, however, notably lacks any recognition of the contribution that can be made to theological understanding by diverse contemporary discourses. And it does not prevent the CDF from rejecting Sobrino's statements concerning Jesus's faith—based on his reading of Hebrews—precisely on the basis of such dogmatic formulations: "the filial and messianic consciousness of Jesus is the direct consequence of his ontology as Son of God made man." The CDF continues, "Jesus, the Incarnate Son of god, enjoys an intimate and immediate knowledge of his Father, a 'vision' that certainly goes beyond the vision of faith. The hypostatic union and Jesus' mission of revelation and redemption require the vision of the Father and the knowledge of his plan of salvation."

The CDF's statement has three further problems in terms of respecting the rules of discourse. The first is that the CDF states as obvious inferences that are by no means even necessary. According to the CDF there is a necessary link between Jesus being "true God and true Man" and that he enjoys the beatific vision from the start. Fair enough. But since it is not given to us humans to know what that vision is, deductions ought to be cautious rather than confident. The CDF moves from the beatific vision to "filial consciousness" to the "knowledge of the plan of salvation." It has shifted from ontology to psychology without a pause, moving directly from the "hypostatic union" to what it "requires" in terms of the content of Jesus's consciousness. But it is a large leap from a sense of filial relationship, or even the vision of the Father, and the human Jesus "knowing the plan of salvation." The second problem is that it refers only to those passages in the Gospels that might support this inference (although they do not do so in an unambiguous way) and fails to deal with the passages that do not support the proposition that Jesus's filial relationship with the Father led directly to his full and conscious awareness of the "plan of salvation." The third problem is the implicit monophysitism in the CDF's position. They deprive Jesus of any real human psychology, against the clear teaching of the church that his full humanity includes a soul. In answer to the question, "What was in Jesus's mind?" they allow only "what was in God's mind." But this is a category error of the first order, in which the technical ontological category of "person" (*prosopon*) is made to function as a psychological/moral category of "person."

On the other side, the CDF is certainly justified in objecting to Father Sobrino's language concerning the ontological categories used by the great councils. He is quoted to this effect: "While these texts are useful theologically, besides being normative, they are also limited and even dangerous, as is widely recognized today." The CDF, as I have noted, recognized the limited character of such language, but then (properly) took exception to the characterization of "dangerous." Father Sobrino would have done far better to give full and enthusiastic support to what ontological language can and does say about the mystery of Christ, and then rather than dismiss it as "dangerous," suggest the ways in which other epistemologies and discourses can enrich our appreciation for that element (the full humanity of Jesus) that the ontological language had the most difficulty expressing.

The dispute concerning the faith of Jesus also reveals, on both sides, the consequences of insufficient exegetical engagement with Scripture. The CDF rejects Father Sobrino's understanding of Jesus as the model of faith (based on his reading of Hebrews), we have seen, by appeal to the "consciousness of Jesus" that was necessary because of the hypostatic union. Jesus could not be a "believer like us," because whereas we do not have direct knowledge of God, he did. It is obvious that the CDF regards faith as a cognitive state, identifying it totally with "belief." But even if its argument on the point of belief was correct—that the Son of God could not "believe in God" in the way other humans do—their response is completely beside the point in the matter of the "faith of Jesus Christ."

The reason is disclosed by a close reading of the New Testament. In Greek, the single word *pistis/pisteuein* ("faith"/"having faith") lies behind the English translations "belief" and "faith." In English, furthermore, "belief" has a definite cognitive denotation, as in, "I believe there is a God." The New Testament certainly can use the *pistis* cognates in this fashion (see, e.g., Jas 2:19 and Heb 11:6, "Anyone who approaches God must believe that he exists and that he rewards those who seek him"). This is how the CDF understands the claim that the human Jesus had faith. The New Testament's predominant usage concerning *pistis/pisteuein*, however, is less cognitive than dispositional, less an intellectual assent than the commitment of the heart, less a matter of the mind than of the will. Faith is the complete response of human freedom to God, involving trust, obedience, and endurance.

There is no question that several New Testament writings ascribe *pistis* in this sense to Jesus. As Sobrino—and the entire history of Christian spirituality—recognized, the Letter to the Hebrews speaks of Jesus's human faith in terms of his obedience to God (3:1–6; 5:8–9; 12:1–3), although it requires a close analysis of the letter as a whole to bring out the full force of this ascription. The best recent work on Galatians and Romans, furthermore, has made the case that the "faith of Jesus Christ"—understood precisely as obedience—is an essential element of Paul's argument in these letters (see Rom 1:5; 3:21–26; 5:12–21; 16:26; Gal 2:16–21). And although the term *pistis* is not used, interpreters have long recognized that Jesus's prayer to his Father in the garden is the perfect expression of such faithful obedience (Mark 14:36).

Such scriptural evidence accords perfectly with Chalcedon's insistence that in the one person (*prosopon/persona*) of Jesus Christ there are two natures (*physis/natura*), and with the Council of Constantinople's condemnation of monotheletism, for if Jesus had no human volition, no genuine human freedom, then he could not have responded to the Father in the obedience we call faith. Paul declares in 2 Corinthians 1:19–20, "The Son of God, Jesus Christ, who was proclaimed to you by us, Silvanus and Timothy and me, was not 'yes' and 'no,' but 'yes' has been in him. For however many are the promises of God, their Yes is in him" (NAB). Paul's compressed language suggests that Jesus Christ is at one and the same time God's yes to humans and the human response of yes to God.

Here is where the CDF can find a legitimate (if minor) complaint at Father Sobrino's characterization of Jesus as "a believer like ourselves," for Paul makes clear that it is through Jesus's yes that we are empowered to say yes in obedient faith to God: "therefore, the Amen from us goes through him to God for glory" (2 Cor 1:20). For Paul and for Hebrews, it is not that Jesus "has faith just like ours," but rather that, through the power of his spirit, we can have faith like that of Jesus (Rom 3:26). Jesus is the model of faith, but more than that, he is the "pioneer and perfecter of faith" (Heb 12:2), the unique Son who accomplished what we could not on our own, because he was fully defined by the words with which he came into the world, "I have come to do your will, O God" (Heb 10:7).

SIMPLE LESSONS

If criticism and debate are inevitable and even positive elements of christological discussion within the church, and they are, whether among theologians as teachers or between theologians and the magisterium, perhaps the character of exchanges would be improved if all parties observed some straightforward rules. (1) Begin with the premise of good faith and reasonable intelligence among the participants; (2) recognize the legitimate diversity of discourses for thinking and speaking about Christ and learn something about the internal logic of those discourses; (3) stay within the boundaries of the mode of discourse one has chosen, and announce when another discourse is engaged; (4) don't commit the fallacy of epistemological imperialism by seeking to nullify another discourse from within one's own; (5) recognize and respect the several discourses of Scripture and of tradition as distinct and requiring equally energetic engagement and exegesis; (6) rather than automatically adopting the role of judge and seeking to silence a conclusion reached within a different discourse ("You can't talk that way about Jesus"), adopt at least for a time the role of learner and ask instead what that conclusion might mean for the discourse within which I am working ("What would it mean if I were to take that way of talking about Jesus seriously?").

Observing such rules will require of all participants in christological debates generosity of spirit, conceptual clarity, and a disposition sufficiently docile to learn from those who speak in a mode different from our own. If practiced, though, they may help school us all in the modesty appropriate to those who dare to speak of the mystery that defies all our definitions and surpasses all we can imagine.

7

DRY BONES

Why Religion Cannot Live without Mysticism

Published in a slightly different form in Commonweal *137, no. 4 (2010): 11–14.*

The greatest religious battle today is not that between believers and unbelievers, although that is an important and noisy conflict. Never before have the voices of religion's cultured despisers been more numerous, louder, or more confident than among contemporary proselytizing atheists. More significant even than that struggle, though, is the clash within religious traditions.

I have in mind the three monotheistic religions of the West, above all Christianity and Islam. The battle within each of them—already so far advanced as virtually to be decided—is between the exoteric and esoteric versions of all three religions. The exoteric has just about won, but the victory may only be prelude to the defeat of the tradition as a whole by secularism.

EXOTERIC AND ESOTERIC RELIGION

As the name suggests, the exoteric focuses on the external expressions of religion. Its concern is for the observance of the divine commandments, the performance of public ritual, the celebration of great festivals. It desires a common creed and identical practice. Its tropism is toward religious law, and it seeks to shape a visible and moral society molded by law. Exoteric religion is explicitly political: to form a visible community publicly obedient to the divine command requires an explicit social vision. The goal, after all, is the realization of the kingdom of God as an empirical reality. Such exoteric expressions are not by any means lacking in sincerity or passion; rather, the point of religion is its public dimension.

The esoteric, in contrast, finds the point of religion less in external performance than in the inner experience and devotion of the heart, less the public liturgy than the individual's search for God. The esoteric dimension of religion privileges the transforming effect of asceticism and prayer. It seeks an experience of the divine that is more intense, more personal, and more immediate than any made available by law or formal ritual. The esoteric element in religion finds expression above all in mysticism. Mystics pursue the inner reality of the relationship between humans and God: they long for true knowledge of what alone is ultimately real, and they desire absolute love for what is alone infinitely desirable.

Judaism, Christianity, and Islam are all best known as exoteric traditions. Each has the full array of formal worship, religious law, sacred books, and codes of morality. Yet each has also contained, from the beginning, a strong element of mysticism. The Judaism that formed in the second century on the basis of a strict interpretation of Torah, demanding of adherents observance of all the commandments, including dietary and purity regulations, also expressed itself mystically through the heavenly ascents accomplished by the adepts of Merkabah mysticism, the riders of the heavenly throne-chariot. The earliest Christian collection of books contains a powerful visionary composition (Revelation) and Christian mystical impulses found early expression both in Gnostic literature and among the desert fathers and mothers. In Islam, the Sufi movement, dedicated to the quest of God through renunciation and the prayer of recollection, grew together with the exoteric framework of the shari'ah—the system of Muslim law and observance.

INTERNAL TENSIONS

The great monotheistic religions have not found it easy to reconcile their exoteric and esoteric sides. The mystic's tendency to derogate the visible has sometimes led to the neglect of external forms in the name of purity of heart. Conversely, the lawyer's concern for common standards has led to the suspicion and even suppression of private devotion. Over the centuries, Judaism has proven most successful at harmonizing exoteric and esoteric expression. The masters of the heavenly throne-chariot were among the greatest scholars of the early rabbinic tradition and demanded of the mystic the punctilious outward observance of Torah. Similarly, practitioners of Kabbalah from the twelfth to the twentieth century assumed as the ground for their speculation a total immersion in the practices common to the community of faith. The early Hasidic movement worried some because of its apparently antinomian tendencies, but it also quickly became integrated in the exoteric tradition and is found today among the strictest of observant Jews.

To second-century champions of Christian orthodoxy, the sort of esoteric religion found among those termed Gnostics posed a direct challenge to the institutional church, and Irenaeus responded to the challenge by identifying what he considered the "heresies" of such esoteric groups, and constructed a defense of public Christianity based on creed, canon, and the apostolic succession of bishops. This extreme form of Christian (or near-Christian) mysticism eventually self-exiled from the larger community, finding a more congenial home in the new religion of Manichaeism. The mysticism of the desert fathers and mothers, in contrast, was thoroughly orthodox in its tendencies, and the mysticism that so invigorated medieval Catholicism gladly embraced the exoteric forms of the Christian faith.

Like Christianity, Islam early on faced the challenge of a radical esoteric movement that threatened the authority of the shari'ah. The earliest Sufis were adventurers of the spirit who sought immediate union with Allah through knowledge and prayer. Some of them issued statements that pushed the implications of ecstasy to the limits. The Sufi Mansur al-Hallaj (d. 922 CE), in fact, was executed because his claims of union with the divine seemed to outrage the fundamental conviction that Allah has no partners. The reconciliation of the esoteric and exoteric within Islam was accomplished by the monumental intellectual labors of Abu Hamid al-Ghazali (1058–1111), a man whose devotion to the Sufi way was absolute—he said it saved his soul—and matched only by his commitment to the shari'ah as the essential framework of true devotion. Al-Ghazali established the principle that the mystic's knowledge did not consist in new revelations but in an ever-deeper penetration of the truths disclosed by the Qu'ran. After al-Ghazali, Sufism flourished at the heart of Islam, becoming at times the dominant expression of the religion.

A HEALTHY BALANCE

The benefits of the exoteric to the esoteric forms of Judaism, Christianity, and Islam are clear: the framework of law and worship, creed, and Scripture, provided both a social meaning and shared social practices that enabled individual mystics to thrive. They shared with their nonmystical fellow believers the public practice of prayer, the study of sacred texts, and the deeds of charity. Their passionate quest for the experience of God through prayer was the more secure because it pursued the God proclaimed publicly in synagogue, church, and mosque. Their practice of asceticism was not an exception to but rather an intensification of the strict rules of behavior followed by the exoteric community. Mystics were able to swim freely, and dive deeply, in an ocean bounded by the public profession and practice.

Equally clear are the benefits to the outer tradition given by the mystics within. Most obvious is the way that mysticism provided a medium for the impulses of passionate devotion, producing in generation after generation the saints who represent the best within each religion. Perhaps less apparent, though no less important, is the way that mysticism—by recognizing all visible forms as less than ultimate—also challenges the claims of religious law to exercise total control over humans.

Mysticism stands as an anti-idolatrous witness within exoteric religion. It makes clear that religion is not simply another version of politics, but that at its heart, in its essence, it seeks to serve the Living God, that religion's efforts to stabilize the world are not solely about the assertion of human power but about the service of humanity. Because everything in religion must be measured by God, mysticism insists, and because God is not a controllable entity but remains hidden even when revealed, religion must always be measured by a reality beyond definition by the religion itself. By asserting an invisible presence as more real and more powerful than anything that appears, and by willingly sacrificing pleasure in this life for the sake of a future life with God, mysticism reminds the exoteric that it too is called to a service larger than itself.

By its positive affirmation of the heart's devotion, and by its negative critique of external forms, mysticism has been a powerful force of regeneration and reform within exoteric traditions.

For the greater part of the history of all three religions, a positive relationship was maintained between esoteric and exoteric tendencies. In Christianity, despite the excesses of exoteric control—inquisition, crusades, battles over the papacy—the great mystics served as the measure for what the religion was really about. Their personal lives bore witness to the reality of transforming grace, and their protests pushed prelates to reform. Above all, their writings gave vibrant testimony to a God whose transcendence was beyond comprehension and a Christ whose closeness never exhausted reflection. Think how impoverished the evidence for the spirit of the risen Christ would be without the writings of the Christian mystics. Indeed, consider how barren Christian literature would be without the writings of mystics from *The Cloud of Unknowing* through *The Interior Castle* to *The Sign of Jonas*.

In Islam equally, the Sufi fellowships dedicated to poverty, the renunciation of desires, and the practice of contemplation gave credibility to the Muslim claim to be more than a way to order society. Despite the violent split between the Sunni and Shi'a parties, the bloody wars between contending caliphs, and corruption within caliphates, the Sufi movement asserted that the heart of Islam was the human relationship with Allah. In the first centuries of Islam, saints like Rabi'a al-'Adawiyya (d. 801) provided a measure for what true *islama* (submission) to Allah meant. Sufis understood "*Jihad* in the way of Allah" not in terms of the conquest of infidel nations by the sword, but in terms of the submission of the entire self to the will of Allah, expressed above all by the constant effort to act in the name of "the compassionate, the merciful."

Sufi mystics likewise generated an astonishing amount of devotional literature that gave expression to such a life of sanctity and summoned others to it. Whether with an emphasis on the esoteric understanding of the Qu'ran and Hadith (as in the great Ibn al- 'Arabi [1165–1240]), or with an emphasis on extravagant love (as in the astonishing poetry of Julaladdin Rumi [1207–73]), the mystics of Islam stretched the limits of language and the symbols of the sacred text in their efforts to stretch the self toward the truly real, and in the process produced literature of surpassing depth and beauty.

In short, the classic realizations of Judaism, Christianity, and Islam all creatively fused exoteric practice and esoteric passion, thereby asserting that the deepest meaning of the public practice was the transformation of the individual soul and the quest for the Living God. The true purpose of both Christianity and Islam during most of their respective histories was to form saints. Living in imitation of Christ or in submission to Allah meant above all to see the present life as a journey of constant internal growth and transformation, a pilgrimage toward God that began in the present but only reached its goal in the eternal bliss of the divine presence. Because of this shared understanding, the classically formed Christian mystic Thomas Merton was able, even in the twentieth century, to recognize as a true brother the Algerian Sufi, Shaykh Ahmad al-Alawi (1869–1934).

Judaism, as I have suggested, has managed, not without difficulty, to hold the esoteric and exoteric together. Because for this diaspora religion the notion of a "Jewish state" was for so long oxymoronic, and even after the founding of the state of Israel remains problematic—to what extent is it or should it be "Jewish?"—Judaism has not experienced to the same degree the rupture between the exoteric and esoteric that has been experienced by Christianity and Islam.

EXPELLING THE ESOTERIC

In recent centuries, both Christianity and Islam have steadily diminished the importance of the esoteric. Christianity has slowly succumbed to the worldview of modernity, within which a life of renunciation as pilgrimage toward God makes little sense. With the collapse of a miracle-saturated world also comes the loss of a robust sense of the future life as the goal of enduring the present "vale of tears." In the eyes of modernity, the very concept of self-renunciation appears as a form of psychopathology. Simone Weil, by this measure, is simply a neurotic rather than a seeker of sanctity. The late "turn to the world" of Thomas Merton is celebrated precisely because it privileges the active over the contemplative, the politically engaged over the monastic retreat. Contemplative houses barely maintain their existence. Religious orders must have an "apostolate" that makes sense in social terms.

The marginalization of the mystical within Christianity becomes programmatic in movements like the social gospel or liberation theology, for which the esoteric life of the mystic is at best a form of self-indulgence and at worst counterrevolutionary—a resistance to the shaping of society according to the rule of God. Even for those explicitly opposed to liberation theology, Christianity seems to consist mainly in a social vision. Seldom do ecclesiastical exhortations focus on internal transformation of the self or becoming saints.

In Islam, the expulsion of Sufism has been even more explicit and severe. The "reform" movements initiated in Algeria by Muhammad ibn 'Ali as-Sanusi (d. 1859) and in Saudi Arabia by Muhammad ibn Abdul al-Wahhab (1703–92) began with questioning the centrality of Sufism. Especially al-Wahhab, a former Sufi, considered mysticism to be a distortion of authentic Islam. It was too otherworldly, too individualistic, too casual about external forms, too centered in spiritual leaders, too little concerned with the establishment of an Islamic state. The Sufi's spiritual understanding of *jihad* in the way of Allah must give way to a political understanding.

Islamic fundamentalism precisely matches that of Christian fundamentalism in this respect, namely that an absolute outer conformity to specific points or belief and practice is demanded, while little explicit attention is given to the intricate and difficult process of individual sanctification. Only by expelling the form of Islam that had dominated the religion for centuries—and had been such an important factor in the shaping of Islamic culture—could Islam recover its authentic roots. No longer the esoteric, mystical reading of the Qu'ran taught by the Shaykhs and studied by their disciples, should dominate Islam, but instead the "original" exoteric, political program of the prophet. Thus, the frequently stated axiom, that one can be truly Muslim only in an Islamic state, an axiom that would be meaningless to the Sufi.

CONSEQUENCES

Mysticism continues to attract people associated with Judaism, Christianity, and Islam, because it remains a fundamental and ineradicable way of being religious. But removed from the great exoteric traditions, mysticism suffers a perhaps inevitable trivialization. Kabbalism of the sort celebrated by Madonna and other celebrities is not recognizable as expression of the wisdom of Torah that it had been for centuries and is almost completely removed from the convictions and practices specific to Judaism. The Sufism popularized by Idries Shah (1924–96) and Inayat Khan (1882–1927) is a form of mind mastery divorced from the Qu'ran and Hadith and propagates itself as a form of universal wisdom. In Christianity, the "new Gnosticism" espoused by devotees of labyrinths and self-realization workshops eschews the dogmas of Christianity as underevolved and unenlightened.

Such deracinated forms of mysticism remain oddly superficial precisely because they draw no nourishment from the great exoteric traditions: Kabbalism apart from Torah observance is playacting; Sufism disconnected from shari'ah is vague theosophy; and mysticism that finds no center in the Eucharist or the passion of Christ drifts into a form of self-grooming. In a paradoxical fashion, it was the exoteric frame that enabled the esoteric to dig into deep soil rather than float off into vaporous fantasy.

Less visible but no less significant is the negative effect on the exoteric forms when contact has been lost with the esoteric life of individual transformation. A system of law unconnected to inner piety is simply an instrument of social control, a form of politics pure and simple. Whether it be an Islamic court issuing a fatwa to punish someone who has insulted the prophet, or the Vatican removing a theologian from a university faculty on suspicion of an inadequate Christology, the point is the same: control exercised through coercive force rather than through instruction, exhortation, and example. The more Catholicism resembles the Islamic state, and the more Islam resembles every other form of politics in the world, the less reason there is for anyone to grant these religions an exemption based on the supposition that they represent a transcendental value or supernatural vision.

Insofar as Christianity and Islam are defined by this-worldly goals and seek to accomplish them through the political instruments of coercion and repression, the more vulnerable both exoteric traditions are to the challenges of secular critics, who ask whether the vision of human society envisaged by these religions has anything special to recommend it. If religion is for this life only, then it must compete on an even plane with other this-worldly ideologies. And it is not unthinkable that such ideologies can offer a better and more humane society than that proposed by a religion that has been emptied of the transcendent and lacks any room for the spirit that soars toward God.

8

CARING FOR THE EARTH

Why Environmentalism Needs Theology

Originally published in Commonweal *132, no. 13 (2005): 16–20.*

There are good reasons why Christians, especially biblically formed Christians, are not often called friends of the earth, much less considered leaders in caring for the earth.

First, Christians have taken the command, "Be fruitful and multiply, and fill the earth and subdue it; and have dominion over the fish of the sea and over the birds of the air and over every living thing that moves upon the earth" (Gen 1:28), as license for a relationship to the earth—and all other living creatures—that dominates by subduing. Being created in God's image means not only eating first, but eating everything, considering all creatures as in service to human desires.

Second, Christians have widely been understood as interested only in the salvation of souls. The world's beauty is a seduction of the body and a peril to the immortal spark within humans that alone is worth saving. Fleeing the world is the secure path to eternal life. Christian Platonism hardly encourages a care of the material world.

Third, many Christians have an eschatology based on the Book of Revelation that gazes indifferently on the destruction of the late great planet Earth, since the saved will be removed by rapture to occupy a new heaven and earth. This earth is only a temporary package for the saints, which God will crumple and toss aside. Seeking to preserve the earth and its resources is a denial of the great cataclysm that awaits us.

Since many Christians hold some version of these views with greater or lesser intensity and clarity and act explicitly or implicitly on the basis of them, the terms *Christian* and *care of the earth* are not automatically equated. Still, ecological blindness isn't entirely the fault of the Bible or Christian theology. The links between cultural scripts and the way people actually live are often more complicated than we assume in the blaming and explaining game.

Three complications give us pause. First, Christians lived for centuries with these or similar views of the world, yet in remarkable harmony with other creatures. The outstanding example is monasticism. Although Benedictine monks subscribed to a form of *fuga mundi* and certainly sought to save their souls, their life within "the school of the Lord's service" was intimately attuned to the rhythm of God's time and the contours of God's earth. When Benedict instructed his monks to treat the tools of the monastery as they do the vessels of the altar, he inculcated a far-reaching and pervasive sense of piety toward the things of the body as well as those of the soul. Precisely such monkish attitudes, in fact, were once blamed for the failure of the world to develop technologically, and for humanity's failure to achieve its promethean ambition.

Second, material exploitation and despoliation are connected far more to attitudes that have developed in opposition to classical Christian tenets. It is the spirit of Enlightenment, after all, that seeks to demystify everything, reduce mystery to problem, magic to statistics. The infamous Cartesian dualism did more than Christian mysticism to cultivate the perception of the body as a machine and the world as the mind's laboratory. Above all, it has been the spirit of capitalism—fundamentally at odds with the classical Christian ideal of sharing possessions—that has fostered competitive acquisition as the measure of human success, and has succeeded in rendering all things material and spiritual as commodities.

Third, the effect of technological revolution and the human population explosion has fundamentally altered the relation between humans and the rest of creation in a manner no one could have imagined even two hundred years ago, much less when Christianity began or the Bible was composed. Only a short period of time has elapsed since the first serious warning calls by prophets like Rachel Carson, even shorter since awareness of the ecological disaster brewed by contemporary practices reached broad awareness, and still shorter since panic has gripped those aware of the impact our insatiable growth and consumption has on the survivability, not only of every other species of life, but—to speak in the most selfish manner possible—of the human species as well.

This wake-up call could not be heard even a hundred years ago. Even at that time, the consequences of the human drive for power, pleasure, and possession, abetted by astonishing technology, and multiplied by swarming populations, could not yet be imagined. Even a hundred years ago, nature seemed still to be infinitely vast, infinitely rich and varied in life and resource, even infinitely frightening compared to human cunning. We could not yet then leap to space and look down on our beloved planet as a stunningly beautiful yet suddenly fragile blue marble.

But if there is not a direct cause-and-effect linkage between Christian sensibility and ecological indifference, it is nevertheless true that Christians now bear distinctive responsibility for responding to the environmental crisis.

First, there are more Christians in the world than adherents of any other religious tradition. Two billion of the world's population claim to be Christian in some sense. What Christians think and do matters. If they continue on the path of destruction, the earth will be destroyed. If they turn about, there may be hope.

Second, of all the world's religions, Christianity has uniquely been corrupted by the spirit of modernity, that combination of Enlightenment reason, technology, individualism, commodification, and consumerism, so much so, that many American Christians have lost any awareness of the classic critique of precisely these idolatrous impulses in Scripture, and have blithely—I will not say innocently—merged Christianity into Americanism.

Third, and not incidentally, Christianity is the dominant religious influence in precisely the part of the world often designated the "first world," that is most responsible for the despoliation of the earth's resources in the quest for power, pleasure, and possession. If those calling themselves Christian live in a manner that reduces other humans to economic slavery and the earth's resources to the verge of depletion, and justify such heedless consumption in the name of Christian (-American) values like individualism, competition, or even the gospel of prosperity, and those same Christians have the ability, precisely because of their privileged position of power within the world, to change such patterns of consumption and change such perverse understandings of their religious heritage, then those Christians are deeply obligated so to change.

Such a change, or conversion, is not a matter of issuing apologies or engaging in symbolic protests. Nor does it suffice for each Christian to do his or her own little bit by recycling. The change required is massive. It involves a change of mind as well as a change of attitude.

Christians must engage in the difficult task of theological self-criticism, acknowledging those elements in its understanding that can have led to these consequences, engaging and challenging those elements in its sacred texts that have too long gone unexamined in light of changing circumstances. Conversion demands the painful work of hermeneutics, inquiring both into the moral implications of our texts, and the contemporary moral attitudes that allow us to read them responsibly or irresponsibly.

Conversion also demands a change of practices that is communal as well as individual. The church, as the Body of Christ, must become a laboratory of a life consonant with the care of the earth as God's creation. The church must learn, advocate, and cultivate practices that—at the very least—respect the precarious balance among the earth and all living creatures. The church as an embodied community must not weary the earth that provides it a home. But the church must also be a good citizen of the world community and engage the politics of that world as a good and honest advocate for the earth. The church cannot be content with avoiding environmental criminality, or even practicing environmental virtue. It must reach to learn leadership in being as a friend of the earth.

The church can hardly be a friend of the earth so long as its own self-understanding and way of life is based more on the individualism and consumerism of an increasingly savage capitalistic world order than it is on the gospel. When communities that call themselves church measure their success in terms that exactly mimic the market—growth in numbers, expansion in facilities, outreach through satellites, influence through money—rather than in terms that imitate the Messiah—fruitfulness rather than success, service rather than dominance, maturity of life rather than growth in numbers, suffering in solidarity rather than prosperity as the sign of blessing—then the church cannot be friend of the earth or advocate such friendship. It is corrupted by the very forces that pollute the earth. It has nothing to say.

A first step toward conversion is regaining a more properly theological sense of creation, one that is based on a better reading of Scripture, and, on the basis of that renewed sense of creation, rereading some biblical passages that reward careful reflection in light of the contemporary environmental crisis, which is also, I suggest, a crisis in Christian identity.

In the Nicene Creed, Christians profess belief in one God, the Maker of heaven and earth, of all things visible and invisible. Belief in God as Creator is fundamental to all other Christian profession, not least that in the resurrection of Jesus, for the two beliefs are intimately connected. Many Christians, however, have an impoverished view of creation. Influenced in part by deism—God is the cosmic watchmaker who wound up the mechanism and now just observes it ticking—and in part by the tradition of deriving the theology of creation only from the first chapters of Genesis ("in the beginning God created the heavens and the earth"), they think of creation as something that happened once as a chronological event, or perhaps better, as an event that began chronology.

Precisely this perspective gives rise to the bizarre phenomenon known as creation science, which tries to read the profound mythic account of beginnings in Genesis—which does testify to the most profound truth about creation, that everything that exists comes from God—in terms of natural science and ends up botching both religious and scientific truth. And because such a reading is driven by the fear of the theory of evolution, the temptation is even greater to make what is created simply a product, delivered perfect and complete by God within six days (however calculated). The seventh day on which God rested is, in this view, a signal that God's creative activity is finished. The world is now in the hands of humans to whom God has given dominion.

A more adequate theology of creation begins not with Genesis but with the Psalms, and with the biblical confession of God as the Living God. The Psalms also speak of God's creating the world, not in the distant past, but new every day. Psalm 104:27–35 says,

These all look to you
  to give them their food in due season;
when you give it to them, they gather it up;
  when you open your hand, they are filled with
    good things.
When you hide your face, they are dismayed;
  when you take away their breath, they die
  and return to their dust.
When you send forth your spirit, they are created;
  and you renew the face of the ground.
May the glory of the LORD endure forever,
  may the LORD rejoice in his works—
who looks on the earth and it trembles,
  who touches the mountains and they smoke....
Bless the LORD, O my soul.
Praise the LORD!

Creation is the world as coming-into-being by the power of God. Scripture, furthermore, speaks of God as the Living God and as the life-giver, not in the past, but in the present. The spirit that hovered over the abyss in Genesis is active throughout the story of Israel and in the story of Jesus and in our story today. This is the Holy Spirit that renews the hearts of humans and renews the earth.

It is this understanding of creation that enables Paul to compare the resurrection of Jesus to creation: "the God...who gives life to the dead and calls into existence that which is not" has raised Jesus from the dead (Rom 4:17, 24). It is more than a comparison: Paul speaks of the resurrection of Jesus as a "new creation"; by it Jesus becomes, not simply a living being like the first Adam, but becomes "life-giving Spirit."

If we think of creation not mechanically but existentially, then we acknowledge that all creatures come into being at every moment by the power of God, they are held out of nothingness at every second by an unseen power, their growth and change and development, and yes, their evolution, are all the exciting process of creation that has never ceased since God first announced, "Let there be light." We do not pretend to understand how God thus brings all that is becoming out of nothingness into being, but we confess that it is the case, and that it makes all the difference.

Four implications of this theology of creation touch our topic. First, if God creates the world at every moment, if creation is an ongoing process, then, as the Psalmist says, "The earth is the LORD's and the fullness of it" (Ps 24:1). The world that God brings into being belongs to him and none other. It is answerable to him and none other. It is constantly a gift from God and never becomes another's possession. The corollary of this truth is that however we understand humans being created in the image of God or being set over the works of God's hands, it does not mean that ownership of the earth has passed to humans, or that they can dispose of it without reference to the one whose power brings it—and them—out of nothingness into existence moment by moment. The earth is not a human possession but rather fellow creature. It is not an object to be manipulated for human gratification, but a gift that is given moment by moment and can never be arrogantly assumed to be a plaything or factory for humans alone.

Second, there is a wonderful equality among creatures, for at the level of existence, the smallest molecule is as real and valuable as the tallest mountain, at the level of coming-into-being out of nothingness, humans and dolphins truly are brothers and sisters, equally gifted by God with being, equally fragile in that existence; no more than the dolphin can any human add an inch to his or her stature or a moment to his or her life. It is not so much that we are arranged in the world in a hierarchy of being as that we dance in this world within a vast and interconnected web of existence, all of it dependent and interdependent, all of it coming forth at once from the same source, the all-powerful Creator God.

Third, the world is the medium of God's self-expression. God as spirit chooses to make that which is not spirit, and through the medium of matter make Godself known as spirit! How can we then not see the created universe as God's self-expression, the body that God uses to accomplish God's purposes? The implication of this is that the earth itself can reveal God. The Psalmist sings, "The heavens are telling the glory of God"—that is, the presence and power of God—

> and the firmament proclaims his handiwork.
> Day to day pours forth speech
> and night to night declares knowledge.
> There is no speech nor are there words;
> their voice is not heard;
> yet their voice goes out through all the earth,
> and their words to the end of the world. (Ps 19:1–4)

The entire biblical conception of revelation, indeed, is based on the revelatory capacity of the earth, for in this first instance paradigmatically is spirit expressed through matter, showing that matter also can express spirit. What is true of covenant, of prophecy, and of incarnation, is true first of all in creation itself. Or better: covenant, prophecy, and incarnation are all expressions of creation itself as an ongoing process from God. If God creates by a word, then the earth itself is articulate. It speaks its Creator in its very coming-into-being.

Fourth is the attitude demanded of humans toward all other creatures. If the earth is not ours but the Lord's, and if the material world is God's chosen medium of self-expression, then we are called to respond with reverence and awe, with attentive listening. If God seeks to declare a word to us from within the coming-into-being of all things, then must we not gaze at all things with eyes that are receptive and grateful, rather than calculating and measuring? Should we not listen to the earth with ears that are alert to the whispers of God's presence and power, rather than fill our ears with the din of noise and the clatter of our own voices? Does not the scarring and gouging of God's earth for the sake simply of human luxury seem in this theology of creation as more even than crass ingratitude, even a form of blasphemy?

In light of a more robust theology of creation, in turn, other Scripture texts appear in new light. I touch on only a few.

Genesis has two creation accounts. In the first, which I quoted in the beginning of this essay, God creates humans, male and female, in his image, precisely so that they might have "dominion" over other creatures, and, after creating them by a word in God's own image, commands them to multiply, fill the earth, and subdue it (1:26–30). But in the second creation account, humans are in a much humbler position. Adam is shaped out of the clay of the earth, and Eve from his side. Adam is placed by God in a garden, "to till it and keep it" (2:15). Note both terms: to achieve what God desires of him, he must till and preserve the earth he has been given to tend.

In this account, moreover, Adam is not given leave to eat from any seed-bearing plant on the earth, as in the first story (1:29), but is told, "You may freely eat of every tree of the garden; but of the tree of the knowledge of good and evil you shall not eat, for in the day that you eat of it you shall die" (2:17). Adam's use of the earth is circumscribed by God's commandments, for the earth is God's, not Adam's. Adam is simply the tender of the garden. Not all knowledge, furthermore, is life-giving. Eating some fruit leads to death. In this account, finally, Adam appears as closely enmeshed with God's other creatures. He names the animals, to be sure, but from among them, he is also seeking one like himself, a mate, and a partner, before God provides from his own rib a partner equal to him (2:18–25).

The second creation account in Genesis is in tension with the first. Humans are not simply created in the image of God and placed over other creatures. They are drawn from the same stuff as other creatures, and their sovereignty, if such it is, is the humble labor of gardening, which is never possible unless one understands how the earth gives life, unless one not only tills but also preserves. A lifetime would not be enough to exhaust the significance of the human vocation as one of tending the earth as gardener.

Such reflection might begin with consideration of the rebellion that follows this second creation account. Humans sought to become like God by eating what God's command had forbidden, by going beyond the limits of the human place within creation and seeking instead to assert a place like God's over all creation: we can eat anything! We will live forever! And let me remind you as well that, as Genesis has it, the enmity between humans and other creatures is a consequence of this rebellion against the limits that God had set to human ambition: Adam and Eve turn in accusation against each other; the serpent seeks to strike Eve's heel and she seeks to crush the serpent; she has pain in childbirth, and Adam must get his food from the sweat of his face and fight thorns and thistles to get any fruit at all, because "cursed is the ground because of you; in toil you shall eat of it all the days of your life" (Gen 3:1–19).

Such reflection might turn next to consideration of the Prophet Isaiah. We are familiar with his attacks on economic oppression in eighth-century Israel. But one of his most famous passages yields perhaps unexpected insight into our topic. I speak of Yahweh's love song for his beloved, "concerning his vineyard" in Isaiah 5:1–17. The passage begins with the image of a man who has planted a vineyard, expended labor on it, and expected to receive fruit, but got only wild grapes from it. His reaction? Ravage the vineyard:

> I will remove its hedge,
>   and it shall be devoured;
> I will break down its wall,
>   and it shall be trampled down.

I will make it a waste;
  it shall not be pruned or hoed,
  and it shall be overgrown with briers and thorns.

The garden will become wilderness.

The prophet then turns his poem on the people of Israel. They were meant to be God's vineyard but did not act according to righteousness:

He expected justice,
  but saw bloodshed;
righteousness,
  but heard a cry!

Isaiah recasts the garden story of Genesis in terms of the behavior of the people of his own day. But what form of injustice does he attack?

Ah, you who join house to house,
  who add field to field,
until there is no room for anyone but you,
  and you are left to live alone
  in the midst of the land! (5:8)

Can we not today read the prophet as saying, "Ah you who add house to house, who add factory to factory, until there is no room for anyone but you, and you are left to live alone on the earth?"

Isaiah declares that such practices will yield their own punishment:

The LORD of Hosts has sworn in my hearing:
surely many houses shall be desolate,
  large and beautiful houses, without inhabitant.

Those who lived only to satisfy their own luxuries, "who do not regard the deeds of the LORD, or see the work of his hands" shall not endure on the land: "therefore my people go into exile without knowledge." Nevertheless, says the prophet, the earth remains the Lord's, and when his righteousness is revealed, then "the lambs shall graze as in their pasture, fatlings and kids shall feed among the [human] ruins."

That Isaiah deliberately linked human injustice to the disruption of the created order, and the hope of God's righteousness to the restoration of harmony among creatures, can be shown by an equally famous passage in which the prophet speaks of a coming ruler in terms that Christians have always seen as prefiguring their Messiah Jesus, but can also be taken as sketching God's desire for the human mission with respect to the earth:

> A shoot shall come out of the stump of Jesse,
>   and a branch shall grow out of his roots.
> The spirit of the LORD shall rest on him,
>   the spirit of wisdom and understanding,
>   the spirit of counsel and might,
>   the spirit of knowledge and fear of the LORD.
> His delight shall be in the fear of the LORD.
>
> He shall not judge by what his eyes see,
>   or decide by what his ears hear;
> but with righteousness he shall judge the poor,
>   and decide with equity for the meek of the earth....
> Righteousness shall be the belt around his waist,
>   and faithfulness the belt around his loins. (Isa 11:1–5)

And what shall be the result of such an outlook and practice?

> The wolf shall live with the lamb,
>   the leopard shall lie down with the kid;

the calf and the lion and the fatling together,
  and a little child shall lead them.
The cow and the bear shall graze,
  their young shall lie down together,
  and the lion shall eat straw like the ox.
The nursing child shall play over the hole of the asp,
  and the weaned child shall put his hand on the
    adder's den.
They will not hurt or destroy
  on all my holy mountain. (Isa 11:6–9)

Why?

For the earth shall be full of the knowledge of the
    LORD
  as the waters cover the sea. (Isa 11:9)

This astonishing passage from the prophet challenges us as directly and forcefully as his hearers almost three thousand years ago. Except how much closer to desolating the earth has our lack of true knowledge and true fear of the Lord brought us! Except how much more do we need the spirit of wisdom, if we are not only to dream of the lion resting with the lamb, but even to dream of there being lions as well as lambs on the earth!

9

THE POLITICS OF THE CHRISTIAN CREED

From a conference lecture on faith and politics at Candler School of Theology, 2006.

I intend to make a twofold argument concerning the Christian Creed. By "the Creed" I mean the profession of faith used most widely in the liturgy by churches throughout the world, the Nicene-Constantinopolitan Creed, defined by the ecumenical councils of Nicea (325) and Constantinople (381), although my argument applies just as well to the Apostle's Creed. And when I speak of "churches," I mean not only the local iterations of the Roman Catholic communion—of which I remain a loyal if sometimes uncomfortable member—but all those everywhere, who, in Paul's words, "call on the name of the Lord" (1 Cor 1:2), and gather by two and three or by a thousand and two thousand in the name of Jesus (Matt 18:20).

The first part of my argument is that the Creed is a critical instrument for Christian self-definition in the contemporary world because (together with Scripture but with greater focus) it helps shape what might be called a politics of the church. The second part is that the Creed also helps shape the church as a participant in the politics of the larger world.

I call my presentation an argument because neither of these propositions is widely held even among Christians, whereas I want to assert that both ought to be at the heart of the church's reflection on its identity and action in the world.

OBJECTIONS TO THE CREED

My claims for the Creed's importance run against opposing cultural and ecclesiastical tendencies. Creeds in general have been regarded by Christianity's cultured despisers, at least since Friedrich Nietzsche, as the refuge of the inauthentic person who is frightened of critical thinking; today, affirming a creed is sometimes considered a form of religious fascism, a sign of low intelligence and bigotry. If there is a "politics" of the Creed, our culture says, it can't be one that is helpful or humane.

In fact, creeds are also explicitly or implicitly rejected by many Christians for similar reasons. Christians in the free church tradition in particular reject creeds because they are regarded as too little scriptural, too much the product of Hellenistic philosophy, and much too much the demonstration of ecclesiastical power.

Both outsider and insider objections to the Creed are connected to the same set of premises, namely that authenticity has to do with individuals rather than communities, that personal integrity can only be expressed by resistance to human authority and never by obedience to authority, and that the church is more of an obstacle than enabler of authentic discipleship.

My argument is based on the exact opposite premise, namely that the church as a community has as real a call to holiness as do its discrete members, and that the public profession of the community can be a "rule of faith" that is not only consonant with but also formative of personal integrity.

In short, I start with the assumption that Christianity is not a club one belongs to on one's own terms, but is a distinct historical community with specific marks of identity and with an essential witness to perform, and that it is precisely the erosion of this sense of communal identity and witness that has weakened to the point of collapse the credibility of Christian presence in the contemporary world.

THE CREED AS POLITICAL

The recovery of the Creed as an instrument of Christian self-identity, then, is not the only but is an essential step toward the reinvigoration of a more robust—and more scriptural—sense of the church as a public community with its own *politeia*, as well as a corporate body whose presence in and toward the larger world should have genuine political implications. Indeed, the very act of reciting the Creed publicly in worship ought to reveal—at least to the worshipers themselves—how odd and even countercultural a group they are. If you would allow me to quote from my 2003 book on the subject:

> In a world that celebrates individuality, [Christians] are actually doing something together. In an age that avoids commitment, they pledge themselves to a set of convictions and thereby to each other. In a culture that rewards novelty and creativity, they use words written by others long ago. In a society where accepted wisdom changes by the minute, they claim that some truths are so critical that they must be repeated over and over again. In a throwaway, consumerist world, they accept, preserve, and continue tradition. Reciting

> the creed is thus a countercultural act. (*The Creed: What Christians Believe and Why It Matters* [New York: Doubleday, 2003], 40–41)

Simply by reciting the Creed, I suggest, Christians act politically. This public profession of faith signals that the church is a distinct body within the world with definite convictions about the world.

Precisely the character of these convictions marks the church as countercultural, for its profession of faith flies in the face of, and challenges, the conventional wisdom of modernity, a wisdom, alas, that has steadily become dominant within the ranks of believers as well as of the cultured despisers of belief. And it is this side of creedal Christianity that I most want to discuss in this presentation. That Christians profess a common faith reveals them to be a political body. The common faith that they profess reveals the character of their politics.

The Creed's political potential is only realized, to be sure, when Christians act based on the principles they espouse in their liturgical recitation. Unless the Creed is a "rule of faith" for the practices of the faith as well as doctrine, the Creed remains politically neutral, and the church remains politically harmless—precisely the posture most secularists and even many Christians prefer.

If Christians are content to recite words that oppose the entire basis of the dominant culture's assumptions, but then act in their lives as though such words were "only worship," then they are correctly regarded as dreamers of fond but ineffectual dreams. They are like people who enjoy reciting the pledge of allegiance and dislike flag burning, but never connect the pledge to the conviction that the United States is a republic dedicated to "liberty and justice for all."

But if Christians actually acted on the principles enunciated by the Creed, then they would be perceived quite rightly as countercultural reformers, with the result that Christianity would become at once more interesting and more dangerous.

In reality, the church and most Christians do not for the most part act as though the Creed provided a guide for practice—this is what makes the Mother Teresas and Dorothy Days among us appear as both radical and strange. For most of us, the Creed is relegated to the category of doctrine, as though being Christian were mainly a matter of thinking certain things rather than a matter of acting in certain ways. My book on this subject had the subtitle, *What Christians Believe and Why It Matters*, but I had originally, in a spirit of candor, wanted it to be, "What Christians (say they) believe and why it (ought to) matter."

I recognize, therefore, the utopian nature of my argument. Not only have many Christians lost the sense of community cohesiveness that arises from and is expressed by the Creed, they have given little attention to thinking through the logic of the church's profession. In the remainder of this presentation, I propose for your consideration two statements in the church's profession of faith that have distinct implications for the church's political posture in the wider world.

THE PROFESSION OF GOD AS CREATOR

We declare at the start of the Creed, "We believe in one God, the Father all mighty, maker of heaven and earth, of all things visible and invisible." Scripture speaks of God's creation not simply as an activity of the distant past but as a constant bringing into being that which is not. God is the world's "beginning," not once long ago, but at every moment. The Christian confession of God as Creator is not a theory about how things came to be but a perception of how everything is still and is always coming into being. God is revealed in the world not through the "whatness" of things but through the "isness" of things. That anything exists at all is the primordial mystery that points us to God. Viewed this way, everything that exists is equally capable of revealing God simply by the fact of its existence.

This vision of creation, I suggest, has four practical corollaries that ought to position Christians in today's political discourse. The first concerns science and the teaching of science. The scriptural perception of creation enunciated by the Creed is entirely compatible with theories of evolution, including the evolution of species. The theories of the natural and biological sciences address, and can only address, the interconnecting causes of beings that have been or are now already in existence. They cannot account for existence itself. But concerning the sequence of becoming, scientific theories concerning the expansion of the universe and the evolving of species are full of important insight that Christians neglect or deny at the cost of intellectual integrity.

The peculiar exercise called "creation science" or "creationism" exemplifies such a loss of intellectual integrity. Reading the account of origins in the Book of Genesis as a source for scientific knowledge is both bad science and a disastrous misunderstanding of Genesis as a literary and religious text. Genesis is not a scientific tract, not even by ancient standards. Only those desperate to save inerrancy of the biblical texts and who lack any sense of how stories can be true without being accurate engage in such a dubious misuse of the mind. Genesis speaks the truth about the origins of the world, but not according to the standards of the natural and biological sciences. It speaks truth through literary metaphor and religious myth. It tells us plainly that everything existing comes from a God who is not part of the world but who brings the world at every moment into being by God's powerful word. It tells us, furthermore, that everything that exists, insofar as it exists, is good, and that humans in particular bear a responsibility toward the Creator because they bear God's image and likeness.

Because the Creed states clearly the "that" of God's creation and does not enter into the question of the "how" of the world's coming into being, it enables Christians to embrace simultaneously an openness to the religious truth of their own existence—they, like all creatures, come from and are directed to God the Creator—and an openness to the scientific truths concerning the wondrous ways in which the evolution of the world, and of humans, displays the wit and wisdom of God.

A second corollary of the Christian conviction concerning creation has to do with the care of the earth. Here, the logic of the Creed is just the opposite of the world-dominating and earth-exploiting attitude so often ascribed to Christians—and all too often practiced by them. Belief in God as Creator of heaven and earth ought to lead to an ecological consciousness and practice that is theologically grounded. If God is Maker of heaven and earth, then, as the Psalmist says, "the earth's is the Lord's and the fullness thereof." God retains ownership—indeed the Hebrew for "create" also means "possess"—and while the earth is given to humans, it never becomes their possession.

It follows also that there is, at the level of existence, a wonderful equality among creatures. However they may otherwise differ in size and significance, the tiniest cell exists just as truly as the largest constellation and can reveal God just as profoundly. Considered existentially, a mussel and a mountain are equally fragile and dependent on God for their existence. And if this is the case, then the world itself must be seen as God's chosen medium of self-expression. Spirit needs a body to communicate, and God's Spirit communicates through all the earthly bodies that the Spirit of God creates, in a continuum reaching from the expressive character of every leaf to the body language of covenant, the voice of prophecy, the incarnation, and the church as sacrament of the world. In light of all this, the Christian attitude and disposition toward the world is properly one of reverence and attentiveness, rather than one of manipulation and exploitation.

A third corollary touches on economics and social justice. The conviction that the earth's is the Lord's alone and that every good and perfect gift comes from God challenges the logic of idolatry that equates being with having and regards life as a zero-sum game in which those who die with the most toys win. Both the totalitarianism that deprives others of possessions so that the state might be strong and the savage capitalism that reduces all value to having and all worth to commodity must be countered by the good news that true worth and value are rooted in our creation by God and no amount of having can add to our being, and because the world is not a closed system but one God showers with more gifts of existence at every moment, we are called to a life of reciprocal gift giving rather than mutual theft, a life of cooperation rather than of competition, a community of reciprocal gift giving in which none are impoverished but all are made stronger.

A fourth corollary arises out of the Creed's own trope on God's creative activity. God is Maker of heaven and earth, the Creed says, "of all things, visible and invisible." If God creates all things, then all things that exist are good; evil, therefore, is to be found not in some aspect of created reality but in the willful distortion of God's creation by a disordered human freedom.

But the terms "visible" and "invisible" are more than a rhetorical rounding of "all things." They were probably added by the framers of the Creed to oppose the teachings of Marcion and the Gnostics that ascribed evil to material reality, and could celebrate a good god of the spirit only by postulating an evil god responsible for materiality. The logic of that radical dualism led to a rejection of any politics but that of rejection and withdrawal: since politics always involves the messy mingling of bodies, Christianity can only be pure by removing itself (if possible even within the church itself) from any contact with the material. By asserting that all material reality comes from the same "One God" who is also "Father of our Lord Jesus Christ," the Creed affirms the goodness of material things, and of the human body, and thereby implicitly valorizes both history and social engagement.

It is the addition of the word *invisible*, however, that seems particularly pertinent to the church's politics today. In contrast to antiquity, when spiritual realities seemed more certain than the treacherous transitoriness of bodies, today the material world is taken to be all that is certainly real. The success of technology in controlling the forces of nature makes this assumption appear self-evident. Based on scientific methods, we conquer disease and advance on death itself: what did the mind of antiquity yield of comparable worth?

Modernity has, in fact, progressively banished things invisible. First to go were spiritual realities other than human—these were considered the remnants of a superstitious supernatural view of the world discredited by empirical research. Then the soul was banished, replaced by mind, and now mind itself is quickly disappearing, since science is interested mainly in brain chemistry. Among intellectuals, talk about the spirit, much less spirituality, is a sign of soft and fuzzy emotionalism. In the realm of psychology, the immortal soul reduced to a tangle of electronic circuitry. Even among believers shaped by modernity, scriptural statements on spirit appear quite literally incredible, to the point that the New Testament's language about the resurrection state as *soma pneumatikon* ("spiritual body") is unintelligible and therefore ignored. It is not at all clear how some sense of spirit is to be recovered, and with it some sense of the mystery of being that lies within and beyond the merely material.

Part of the countercultural politics of creedal Christians lies in their willingness to affirm, first to themselves and each other, and then to an incredulous world, that faith itself is a legitimate way to know reality. Faith establishes contact with what is real in a manner distinct from but no less authentically the very limited ways of knowing the world by which the wheels of the world's empirical engine are kept spinning. This affirmation becomes a form of politics, to be sure, when Christians cultivate practices that reveal and reinforce a perception of the world that includes "things invisible" as much as "things visible." In particular, Christians need to claim the countercultural force of prayer, and consciously and joyously to embrace the politics of resistance to the status quo that is implicit in worship. Every time Christians pray to God through the risen Lord Jesus, say yes to God and mean it, they also thereby say no to a world defined on the basis of matter alone, a world run solely on the basis of measurement and manipulation. In the practice of prayer, Christians confirm the truth stated by the Creed that God creates heaven and earth, all things visible and invisible.

I have noted four possible political corollaries to the Creed's confession of God as Creator, which position Christians with respect to science and faith, to ecological awareness, to economic justice, and to the countercultural effect of prayer and worship. I do not suggest that these corollaries are obvious or even inarguable; some would reach different political implications from the same confession. What is most important to affirm, though, is that such public profession, when translated into community practice, does, and should have political effects.

THE PROFESSION OF JESUS AS LORD

The Creed's profession of "One Lord Jesus Christ" challenges the church itself with the scandal of divinity that lies at the heart of its paradoxical identity. The Nicene bishops put such emphasis on the Son of God because of the Arian heresy that reduced him to the status of creature; so we say, "God from God, light from light, true God from true God, begotten not made, one in being with the Father." The Creed asserts in the most straightforward fashion that

Jesus is more than an admirable teacher or prophet of change, that in his human existence, "God was in Christ reconciling the world to Godself," and that with his resurrection and exaltation, Jesus now shares fully in God's rule over all creation. This affirmation challenges the church today because Arianism thrives among those many Christians who for three hundred years have sought in some version or other of a "historical Jesus" that could save them from this embarrassing scandal of divinity.

The quest for the historical Jesus has never been motivated by history. It has from the start been a theological search for a Jesus stripped of the lordship of the classic Christian confession. True to its Enlightenment roots, the quest sought a Jesus within the bounds of reason, that is, within the bounds of Enlightenment historiography. But although the Creed grounds Jesus in human history with its stark reference to his being born of Mary and suffering under Pontius Pilate, it gladly embraces the language of myth as the narrative language appropriate to expressing the truth concerning Jesus, that he "came down from heaven," and "ascended into heaven." The Creed does not speak a truth about the past alone but above all about the present. When Christians declare that Jesus is Lord, they recognize him as ruler of all things and his authority over their own lives. We owe him the same obedience we owe to God. By calling Jesus Lord, indeed, we imply that the service we give to Jesus is the worship and obedience we pay to God.

This truth of the gospel has a real political corollary if it is taken seriously. To give absolute obedience to Jesus as Lord is to deny the same to any creature. We are pledged to serve no human authority, whether that of the church or the state, in preference to him. Thus, when ancient Roman prefects demanded a choice between Christ and Caesar, Christians understood that this was a choice between the power of God as revealed in the world through the crucified and raised Messiah Jesus, and the powers of the world as embodied by the Roman *imperium*. If they chose Caesar, the power of Rome assured that they would continue their mortal lives and, for the moment, escape death.

They knew also, however, that if they chose Jesus as Lord, they might as a result die in their mortal bodies, but they would live forever with Christ in the presence of God. To be sure, the choice for Christ in such a situation of danger would be nonsensical if Christians conceived of Jesus merely as a historical figure, even one who provided an example of speaking truth to power, for the real issue is the political: whose power is ultimate, who can ultimately save? The same choice has been demanded of Christians in every age, even when the setting and terms have not been so plain, and continues to be demanded of Christians today. The public profession of Jesus as Lord ought to mark Christians as not utterly reliable participants in the ordinary power politics of the world.

In light of this powerful—and prophetic—understanding, present-day objections to the use of *Lord* (as also *kingdom* and *king*) seem particularly unfortunate and misdirected. Some object to Lord and King being used of Jesus Christ not only because lords and kings are male, but because they represent patriarchal social arrangements that make some more powerful and privileged than others. Some translations of the New Testament seek to avoid this offense by using soft near equivalents, like *sovereign* (who could be either male or female) and *dominion* (which does not demand a monarch). These ploys may—clumsily—accomplish gender neutrality, but they do not mask the problem of power: a sovereign still rules, and a dominion is run by someone. Worse, they remove from the New Testament the terms by which Christians have understood themselves and their experience, not vis-à-vis each other, but in relation to God. And it must be agreed, I think, that it is theologically distorting to reduce the King of the Universe to the status of Citizen God.

More important, precisely such terms themselves offer an alternative to male dominance and unjust social structures. If

Jesus truly is our Lord, then none of us is lord over another. If Jesus is our lord, then we can all be slaves of Christ and none need be slave to another human. Being slaves of the Lord of creation ought to mean that we are free from any enslaving creature and free to inhabit all of God's own freedom. Terms like *Lord* and *King* have been used to support male power in unequal social structures, but it is important vigorously to resist the automatic equation of theological terms with social arrangements. To do this, Christians must be the most passionate reformers of social structures and reshapers of ideas concerning power; they ought of all people to struggle for the full equality in dignity among humans and for authority structures that enhance rather than detract from such dignity. The best way to do this, however, is through a serious and sustained criticism of the human tendency toward idolatry, of applying to our worldly arrangements what should only be applied to God. It is by recognizing and celebrating the truth of our existence in Christ—that he alone is our Lord—that we have the freedom to engage and change the structures and systems that obscure his Lordship over creation.

Perhaps even more difficult for many Christians today, though, is the Creed's later statement "his kingdom shall have no end." The conviction that Jesus's rule is eternal follows logically from the fact that the kingdom is God's own rule over creation that Jesus assumes because of his enthronement. Jesus, Christians claim, shares God's lordship over creation, and that kingdom by definition is never ending if God is to be God.

Many contemporary Christians stumble over these words, not because they object to the language, but because they cannot see that they are true in any real sense. The claim brings to a head all the difficulties that Christians have spent centuries trying to resolve about the delay in Jesus's coming again, the continuing reign of sin and injustice in the world, and the apparent absence, indifference, or impotence of God in face of all this. What sense does it make to profess a rule that has no end, if within our actual experience, it never seems to have had a beginning?

The problem is naturally most acute for those Christians who have identified God's rule with a visible social and political perfection (or at least improvement) in the world, and who interpret Jesus's proclamation of God's rule as the start of such a social reformation. Those whose hope in Jesus is directed only to his historical ministry, however, have no real kingdom to celebrate, for Jesus's prophetic ministry did not noticeably change society according to the measure of justice. Traditional Christians who have placed their hope for God's rule in the transformation of human freedom into a glad obedience to the Creator—a hope to be realized visibly in the community of the church—do not have much more evidence for a "kingdom without end." How few signs there are of lives made better. How often the church itself seems to have betrayed its own identity as the place in the world where the rule of God is to be so obvious that it can witness to the world's own possibility of redemption as a sacrament of what the world might eventually be.

Creedal Christians must acknowledge here above all how paradoxical if not absurd their confession seems, even to themselves, for here certainly is a belief in "things invisible." If Jesus is not even fully "my Lord," or in any obvious way "our Lord," how can we proclaim him as "Lord of lords and King of kings?" Is our profession, then, as our cultured despisers suggest, simply a stubborn refusal to acknowledge the truth about our lives? Is the Creed an exercise in willful self-delusion when we proclaim a kingdom to have no end when by the evidence it has no real existence at all?

Or should we look at the words of the Creed another way, not as a statement of what is, but as a profession of what we are committed to enact? Is the Creed in this instance, as in others, a witness that Christians bring against themselves and against their failure to live coherently according to God's kingdom? Is it a statement, not unlike the one that declares God the Creator of all things visible and invisible, whose truth is so difficult actually to imagine and embody that they must repeat it often among themselves and to themselves, even with gritted teeth in the face of evidence arguing the opposite, in the hope that they might glimpse and obey a truth that has grasped them even if they have failed to grasp it?

The cognitive dissonance between the Creed's profession in a rule of Jesus that is without end and an experience of the world in which there is little evidence of such rule can lead Christians in one of three directions.

They can cling to the Creed's statement as though it were fact rather than prophetic challenge and ignore the ways in which the world does not conform to God's will.

They can regard the Creed's statement as delusional and conform themselves to an understanding of the world in which the mystery of God's presence and power must conform to the standards of a reason that begins by eliminating mystery.

Or, they can take the Creed as a rule of faith that shapes Christian practice and commit themselves to living within the church as though the reign of Jesus were both actual and eternal, because it consists not in the conquest of visible enemies and not even in the victory over resistant social structures, but in the triumph of love and life, however halting and partial, over sin and death.

Making this real is the work of the Holy Spirit, and the place where that work can be made visible is in the practices of the church, and enacting such practices is precisely the shape of ecclesial politics demanded by the Creed.

What difference would it make if Christians took the four classic marks of the church, "one, holy, catholic, and apostolic," not as unassailable ontological status or as vague ideal, but as the prescription for specific practices?

The first thing that would happen is that Christians would need to engage in the internal politics of discernment and decision, as they moved from their deeply held and divergent understandings of these marks toward a common sense of how the church might actually act.

What if *unity* was translated not in terms of uniformity but in terms of a rich diversity? What if *holiness* were to mean "different" not only in terms of ritual or belief but in terms of the very structuring of the common life? What if *catholic* meant more than merely worldwide, and included a generous and world-embracing inclusiveness? And what if *apostolic* were not simply a matter of tracing a consistent tradition from the time of Jesus, but meant witnessing to the contemporary world in as radical a fashion concerning the resurrection of Jesus as the apostolic church did?

The unwillingness of contemporary Christians to struggle with such issues, in the name of tolerance and mutual acceptance, indeed the fact that few contemporary Christians even consider such questions important, is an indicator at once of the lack of a coherent politics within the church, and of the usefulness, or even necessity, of the reading and studying of the Creed as a step toward becoming a community that actually matters.

Part 3
THE CHURCH

10

SEX, GENDER, AND THE IMAGE OF GOD

Published as "The Church and Transgender Identity: Some Cautions, Some Possibilities," Commonweal *144, no. 5 (2017): 19–23.*

Our seemingly never-ending conflict over sexual identity, social cohesion, and political policy has settled in recent days on persons who are transgendered (in fact or in intention). Do they have the right to use public restrooms according to their gender of choice rather than their gender of birth? Must public institutions such as schools provide such designated restrooms, even for adolescents? Should public funds derived from taxes be used to enable gender-changing surgeries? To what extent is society obliged to formally recognize, approve, or provide appropriate (as defined by those being served) service to those claiming to have gender dysphoria? Should people who resist the rush to social engineering called for by the "transgender community," and advanced by executive orders, to be considered biblicist bigots? Or has liberalism at long last run amok, revealing itself to be plain silliness?

Veterans of the classic civil rights struggle for racial equality, who also gladly worked to realize the feminist dream of full gender equality, then with almost equal enthusiasm urged the acceptance of gays and lesbians and the rejection of language and practices that marginalized them, can be forgiven if they suffer a bit of battle fatigue, when they are now asked to consider the implications of the condition called intersex, and to approve—and work for society's acceptance—of bisexuality, polyamory, and the rights of the transgendered. Make no mistake, however, the pressure is on: Caitlyn Jenner not only appears on the cover of *Vanity Fair* but is the subject of a laudatory essay in ESPN (which has given her the Arthur Ashe Courage Award), connecting the triumph of her present transmogrification to the former Bruce Jenner's triumph in the 1976 Olympic Decathlon. In this, as in so many recent instances, it appears that sides must be taken. Immediately.

SOME RANDOM SOCIAL OBSERVATIONS

This latest stage in a heterogeneous society's effort to retain some coherent shape while tending to the special needs and desires of each segment of its population provides almost as many insights into the cultural condition of the United States as did the 2016 presidential campaign. It is obvious, for example, that the pace of social change, or the agitation for such change, is accelerated by the utilization of social media and the 24/7 cycle of news media. Actual on-the-ground experience finds itself magnified exponentially by an electronic universe of response and reaction. Equally clear is the great divide in social attitudes between those who dwell within that universe (of discourse?) and those who do not. For those defined by Facebook and Twitter, immediacy is all, and readiness is at best an afterthought.

It is clear as well that the understanding of civil rights continues its downward slide. A considerable distance separates the classic understanding of rights as correlative to obligations and an understanding of rights as a form of entitlement. The right to vote derives from the obligations of citizenship, the right of access to assemblies is correlative to the obligation to participate in assemblies; but what is the basis for the "right" to be recognized by others according to one's chosen gender?

Closely connected to the role of the media and the proliferation of language about "rights" is the polarization of political rhetoric, not least on some of our nation's most prestigious universities. Mudslinging, to be sure, is an honored American tradition. But it is startling to hear, especially among those otherwise so ostensibly committed to inclusion, language so divisive: liberals are not simply wrong, they are demonic; conservatives are not merely in error, they are evil. In a peculiar and paradoxical twist, agitators for the recognition of sexual difference in the name of diversity demonize any appeal to norm or nature as oppressive, a form of microaggression; they seem little aware that "diversity" easily becomes an equally hegemonic norm. The current craziness—there is really no better term for it—of discourse about gender on many college campuses is illustrative: when everything masculine is identified as "toxic" and in need of ideological correction (and behavioral control), it is not difficult to understand why gender dysphoria should be a feature of a young man's life.

The instantly political shape of the present social moment—its translation into federal, state, and local litigation—reminds us as well how confused our notions of public and private have become, a confusion only made worse by the omnipresence of streaming videos, Instagram posts, tweets, and all the other mechanisms of "social" media, and the direct discharge of such effluent into the (increasingly difficult to distinguish) "news" media.

Traditionally, one's sexual profile, given the standard plumage thought societally appropriate respectively to male and female, was considered largely a *private* matter, of interest only to oneself, one's partner, and God. In contrast to the baths of ancient Rome, in fact, modern public restrooms have been constructed to maintain as much as possible that tradition of privacy, as has been the elaborate protocol of custody of the eyes practiced by all decent people in such unavoidably public spaces. Unless they themselves draw attention to their gender difference, anyone dressed as a male is likely to go unnoticed at a Cracker Barrel men's room, and anyone dressed as a woman is likely to be unchallenged in the women's restroom at Target. Clearly, millions of visits to such facilities have taken place over the years without great physical or significant emotional damage done either to the transgendered or to the cisgendered in these traditional sites. Private modesty in public places is not an insignificant social value.

Perhaps most significant to note is a set of assumptions about the body that emerges among those in a distinctively privileged and luxury-laden society: that the social and physical world alike are answerable to each individual's "feelings" or "thoughts" concerning himself or herself and that such imperatives are as urgent as those having to do with violent crime or the economy; that sexuality is not primarily about human relationships, but about "identity"—always a slippery notion, especially in matters of sex, and above all among chronically confused adolescents; that the body is an instrument of human volition that is infinitely malleable, a problem to be solved rather than a mystery to be celebrated and suffered (to borrow Gabriel Marcel's language). Such assumptions encourage the notion that sexual or gender dysphoria, some degree of which is arguably "normal" and even a necessary component in psychosexual development, is a problem that can and should be fixed, and now.

Finally, there is the oversimplification of topics that inevitably happens when the primary mode of discourse is polemical. In the case of transgender, Rogers Brubaker's recent analysis (*Trans: Gender and Race in an Age of Unsettled Identities* [Princeton, NJ: Princeton University Press, 2016]) helpfully suggests three distinct meanings: the "trans of migration," in which the goal is to move from one gender to another, the "trans of between," in which one seeks to live idiosyncratically within both genders, and the "trans of beyond," through which a form of human existence that is in some sense "genderless" is the ideal. I take up here only the first and most frequently attested sense, that of persons seeking either to change to or identify with a gender other than the one "assigned" at birth.

Kierkegaard called ground-clearing observations such as these "preliminary expectorations" (or, more elegantly, "throat-clearings") that are sometimes necessary as preparation for the main topic. In this case, the question I want most to pursue is not the solution to our societal deformities, but whether Christian theology has anything to offer in response to the present situation. While all the points I have noted above deserve attention, my own small effort at thinking about these things from the perspective of wisdom rather than of knowledge focuses especially on the premises concerning the body that I have identified. And I begin by addressing a theological tendency that I regard as profoundly unhelpful precisely to the degree that it pays no attention to actual human experience, and therefore fails to "respond" at all.

GENDER IN RECENT THEOLOGY

The topic of gender has not been absent from recent theology. In fact, following Karl Barth's insistence that humans are constituted as male and female, and that it is impossible to think of a humanity apart from these categories (*Church Dogmatics* III, 4 [1978]), gender has played an important role among Catholic theologians such as Von Balthasar (*Theo-Drama: Theological Dramatic Theory*, vols. 2–3 [1978]), John Paul II (*Theology of the Body* [1997]), and Angelo Scola (*The Nuptial Mystery* [2005]). As recently demonstrated by Megan DeFranza (*Sex Difference in Christian Theology* [2015]), gender also appears as a fundamental category for thought about both humans and God in the influential Protestant theologian Stanley Grenz (as in "Theological Foundations for Male-Female Relationships," *Journal of the Evangelical Theological Society* 41 [1998]: 615–30).

Although these authors do not agree in every respect, they share a basic perspective, and the elements they hold in common make their approach to gender problematic, not only for addressing questions like transsexuality, but for thinking theologically about sex generally.

First, they take both the starting and end point for thinking about gender to be Scripture, not all of Scripture, to be sure, which has many and various ways of talking about real men and women, but the passages in Genesis 1—2 and the letters of Paul (especially 1 Cor 11 and Eph 5) that connect "male and female" to language about the image of God. Second, they read the ancient narratives and correspondence as though they yielded, without more ado, revealed truth concerning human ontology; thus, the shift from "he made them male and female" to "they are in the image of God precisely as male and female." Their approach to human sexuality, in short, is based neither on observation of human behavior, nor on genuine philosophical reflection on the behavior of real people, in conversation with all the texts of Scripture, but on selected texts of Scripture as having a distinct and absolute revelatory character.

Third, it is no surprise to find that conclusions concerning "male" and "female" among humans tend toward essentialism, with certain characteristics and dispositions taken as standard for the respective genders, a stabilization that seems to be demanded by making gender a constitutive element in being created in the image of God; the pure binary distinction begs to be filled out anthropologically (males are A, females are B; active/passive; giving/receiving). Fourth, quite shockingly, we find among such theologians the temptation to argue from analogy to something like gender roles in the interrelationship of persons in the Trinity, corresponding roughly to the complementary roles ascribed to human males and females. At times, such an argument from analogy seems to be something more like pure projection, from the happily gendered human family to a blessedly gendered trinitarian god. But it appears as necessary once one grants the conviction that gender is an essential and constitutive element of human personhood, and human persons must reflect "the image of God."

Such convictions tend naturally (even if not necessarily) to the ascription of traditional, "complementary" roles for men and women in the social realm. Thus, the almost frantic need among some Christians to assert that marriage is between a "male and female," with any other possibility being regarded as both unnatural and irreligious. These same understandings of gender support hostility toward feminism, and often in the same breath (see Angelo Scola), homosexuality. It scarcely needs stating that from this perspective, recognition of a "transgendered community" would prove to be deeply disturbing, a rejection of creation, and indeed of the image of God.

AN EXPANDED FRAMEWORK

A better theological consideration of human sexuality requires a more capacious hermeneutical framework. In less pretentious language, it needs to take more into account than the close reading of selected biblical texts. Interpretation of Scripture, as I have suggested, ought to at least encompass all the passages in which male and female figure and in which human sexual behavior (and misbehavior) is reported. But however important Scripture is as a witness to God's activity in the world, and however truly Scripture participates in divine revelation, it is wrong to proceed as though revelation is adequately contained in Scripture alone.

If theology has to do with the Living God, then it must pay attention equally—not more—to the ways in which God continuously manifests his power and presence in the world. Catholics have always regarded tradition as a second source of witness to God's work, in liturgy and creed, to be sure, but above all also in the living testimony of the saints. For the church must always pay attention to holiness, and where holiness speaks, the church must pay attention.

Theologians need to read Scripture within a complex conversation that includes the voices of tradition, but even more importantly, the witness offered in the contemporary world by human experience and human reason. For subjects like sex and gender, theologians run the danger of showing themselves deaf to the voice of the Living God if they do not listen carefully to what God might be up to in the sexual experience of actual humans, and in the best study of sexuality and gender offered by philosophy (especially phenomenology), anthropology, psychology, and—for goodness sake—biology. Such attention to what the disciplined application of the human mind can offer to the conversation with Scripture has usually been termed "reason." It is a necessary component of theology whose neglect leads to disaster.

Theologians are required, then, to give as much attention to the specifics of human experience in living human bodies as they do to the exegesis of ancient texts in dead languages, because they are convinced that God's self-disclosure continues in the process of God's constant bringing into being of the world, and that the special arena of God's self-disclosure is the human body, through which God's Spirit seeks expression. Such close and disciplined attention to the body is even more necessary because bodily expression is always ambiguous, always difficult to decipher. It is seldom obvious what word God is speaking through the complex diction of actual bodies. If we believe, however, that God lives and continues to touch us, then we must learn something of the grammar and syntax of real bodies.

By no means are the symbols of Scripture to be ignored or dismissed. On the contrary, we should have no clue about what to listen for in bodies were it not for the shaping influence of Scripture's language; we would not search for spirit in and through the body, we would not treasure each human body as in some fashion the image of God, were we not instructed by Scripture. My point is rather that attention to human reason and experience allows us to understand Scripture in new ways, just as Scripture helps us perceive reason and experience in fundamentally important ways. Sometimes, we are led to see that Scripture's language is true but not adequate; in such cases, attention to experience, and reason applied to experience, can help us appreciate the transcendent value, but also the very real limitation, of Scripture for theology.

The terms *male* and *female* in Genesis 1:26, the passage that figures so prominently in conservative interpretations of gender, offer a classic example. Just like the terms *night* and *day* in the same account, they identify in rough fashion what anyone can observe: as night differs from day so does female differ from male, a useful, and so far as it goes, true statement of reality. Males have penises, females have vaginas; night is dark, and day is light.

But closer observation exposes the descriptive inadequacy of *day* and *night*: the binary opposition must be supplemented by *dusk* and *dawn* as names for liminal stages between night and day; more analysis can identify still further gradations in light and darkness that challenge the adequacy without denying the truth of the terms *night* and *day*. So also in the case of the binary opposition between male and female: the observation of real humans reveals a variety of ways in which *male* and *female* can be individually embodied and expressed. The category is heuristically valuable, and its application covers most cases. But even where it applies, it camouflages as much as reveals the intricate and complex sexual differences even among those who fit roughly within the category.

AN AWKWARD EXAMPLE

An example of how rigid gender differentiation needs reconsideration is presented by the phenomenon called *intersex*. Here is not a case of sexual activity or "orientation," but of a condition at birth that demands attention. The numbers are debated by those who study the subject, but perhaps as many as 1 or even 3 percent of humans—a significant number whatever the percentage accepted—are born with unclear or inconsistent organic or hormonal gender markers. In one of several degrees, the most obvious being true hermaphroditism, they fall between the category of *male* and *female* as these terms are assigned to most babies. Such special births have always occurred and continue to occur: the infants are otherwise healthy, but their gender lacks clear definition. They are "inter-sex."

Even though Jesus is said to have recognized the distinctive character of "eunuchs who have been so from birth"—and by speaking of becoming eunuchs for the kingdom of heaven relativized the absolute status of marriage (see Matt 10:10–12)—and also stated that in the resurrection there would be no more marriage (Luke 20:34–38), the moral and theological implications of intersex are only slowly being addressed (see Margaret Farley, *Just Love: A Framework for Christian Sexual Ethics*, 2008; DeFranza, *Sex Difference in Christian Theology*, 2015).

Although in some societies such sexually ambiguous individuals have been recognized as such, and even given special roles, our society has medicalized the condition and "fixed" it—sometimes with unfortunate consequences—through surgery, hormone treatment, and socialization into one acceptable gender or another. In the same way that those who are single don't fit neatly within the theological concept of the image of God for those who conceive of that image in terms of male and female in covenant, so those who are intersexed would seem not to bear

God's image, if the words of Scripture, "male and female he created them" are taken as prescriptive for all human existence.

The "fact on the ground" of intersex, therefore, calls into question a theology that depends on Scripture alone, and on that basis, attaches the image of God to the hard distinction between male and female and their complementary (covenantal) roles. For a theological approach that begins in another place, namely with the question of what God is up to in the world of real bodies, of actual men and women, the phenomenon of intersex becomes above all an occasion for celebrating the playful inventiveness of the Creator and for asking what God might be up to in bringing humans into the world in such fashion.

A DIFFERENT ANGLE ON SCRIPTURE

From the standpoint of what experience and reason concerning gender teach us, we can approach, in addition to the texts of Genesis 1—2 (so beloved of John Paul II and the nuptial mystery crowd), and the passages in which Paul reinscribes traditional gender roles (Rom 7:2–3; Col 3:18; Eph 5:21–33; 1 Tim 5:14; Titus 2:4–5), those places in Paul where he states, in light of baptism, a more radical understanding of gender, ethnicity, and social status. His declaration in Galatians 3:28, that "there is no longer Jew or Greek, there is no longer slave or free, there is no longer male and female; for all of you are one in Christ Jesus" serves as the premise for his argument that the problem for relations in the church is not being either Jew or Gentile, but making being a Jew an absolute good: "In Christ Jesus neither circumcision nor uncircumcision counts for anything; the only thing that counts is faith working through love" (Gal 5:6). Ethnicity is made only a relative good in light of the "new creation" that is Christ (Gal 6:15).

A PAULINE PERSPECTIVE

The employment of experience and reason in addition to Scripture leads to the realization that gender is not properly either a moral or religious category. It is a biological and social category, rooted partly in physical facts and partly in social construction. Gender is therefore a relative rather than an absolute good. It is not constitutive of humans but is rather an accidental (if extremely important) dimension of being human.

Sexual behavior, in contrast, is both morally and religiously significant. As I have argued elsewhere, the church's concern for holiness requires that expressions of *eros* (both heterosexual and homosexual) be characterized by fidelity, fruitfulness, and chastity. Thus, irrespective of what organs are brought into play, the church cannot say yes to sexual behavior that is promiscuous, coercive, abusive, nonreciprocal, and violent, but must listen receptively to sexual lives (irrespective of what organs involved) that are faithfully covenanted, that nurture life, and that are chaste in manner. By this moral measure, note, polyamory is a nonstarter.

But if gender is a relative rather than an absolute good, how should we think about the effort to cross from one gender to another? I think it fair to state that the desire to change one's gender is not itself a moral issue. It is not in itself a disordered drive, or a form of rebellion against the Creator. It could be, to be sure, but it need not be; like the discovery of one's sexual attraction to persons of the same gender, it may in fact be a recognition of oneself that is deeply respectful of the Creator. In some cases, indeed, the dysphoria arising from one's present gender location may arise from deeply rooted circumstances of birth such as those we recognize in intersex.

Nor is the quest to change genders a religious issue—such as it must seem to those who connect "image of God" to a specific gender assignment. Gender is among the *adiaphora* (nonessential things) with respect to being rightly related to God; to borrow from Paul's statement on eating foods offered to idols, "'Food will not bring us close to God'; we are no worse off if we do not eat, and no better off if we do" (1 Cor 8:8). He states in another place, "The kingdom of God is not food and drink but righteousness and peace and joy in the Holy Spirit" (Rom 14:17); the principle Paul applies to food applies also to gender.

On the other side, if I make gender change an absolute (I cannot be myself in this body) rather than relative (what counts is serving God and others in any body), I may in fact reveal a disordered desire, a form of idolatrous impulse like all attempts to make that which is of only relative value to be of absolute value. Our gender is not the moral or religious issue, but what we make of it.

Christian theologians must take seriously both the order of creation and the order of the new creation. For Paul, the resurrection and exaltation of Jesus, who has now become "life-giving Spirit" (1 Cor 15:45) establishes us in a "new creation," whose full implications not even Paul was able to grasp: "If anyone is in Christ, there is a new creation: everything old has passed away; see, everything has become new!" (2 Cor 5:17; see Gal 6:15). What remains certain for Paul is that all those markers that were formerly taken to be absolute are now rendered relative. In his discussion of marriage and virginity (1 Cor 7:1–40), for example, he argues in the same way he did concerning the eating of foods: neither marriage nor singleness by itself matters, neither being male or female; what counts is service of the Lord.

In the middle of that argument, Paul shifts from the "male-female" binary to that of "Jew-Gentile" and "slave-free," making the same point concerning such "natural" markers within a world whose "present form...is passing away" (1 Cor 7:31). Circumcision, he says, means nothing, nor does uncircumcision: but "obeying the commandments of God is everything" (1 Cor 7:19). So also with slavery: the one in the condition of slavery is (in Christ) "a freed person belonging to the Lord," just as someone in the social condition of freedom is "a slave of Christ" (1 Cor 7:22). Now it is certainly the case that in his own circumstances, Paul's specific advice is that people "remain in the condition in which you were called" (1 Cor 7:20). But it is important to recognize that once gender, ethnicity, and social status are defined as *adiaphora*, the way is also open for persons to change, not because becoming a Jew or a male or a free person would put one in an advantageous position with God, but because it is possible to "keep the commandments of God" in any of those conditions.

CONDITIONS FOR DISCERNMENT

I have suggested here that attention to a different selection of texts from Scripture, stimulated by contemporary experience and disciplined by scientific inquiry, can lead to a more benign view of transgendering. But a degree of openness to what God is telling us through present day experience must also be accompanied by a firm commitment to the moral principles that attach to all expressions of human sexuality (openness to gender change does not equal openness to sexual vice).

More than that, Christians need always to remind themselves that, in light of the resurrection of Christ, their bodies are not first of all for their own disposal, but as Paul states, are first of all "for the Lord" (1 Cor 6:13). The point of embodiedness, for Christians, is not to find one's own special identity, and not to find one's own erotic fulfillment; our bodies are given to us for service to others and the world in that distinctive Christian expression of love (*agape*) that seeks not the good of the self but what is good for the other (1 Cor 13:4–7; Phil 2:1–4; Gal 6:2).

The hope for Christians to find wisdom concerning the body is clearly not to be found in the contentious and distortive context of contemporary academic, political, and media divisiveness and hostility. Because at its best the church is committed to such moral principles and to such an understanding of *agape* that must always transcend *eros*, it should be the ideal "safe space" for discernment by individuals and groups concerned about gender. Such discernment, it need hardly be stated, cannot proceed in the manner of the public disputes I characterized at the beginning of this essay. Rather than casual and careless use of the media, discernment requires face-to-face conversation; rather than the glare of publicity, discernment desires intimate and honest exchange; rather than forcing others to change through legal injunctions, discernment seeks to move together toward deeper insight and understanding of each other; rather than petitioning for one's own "rights," discernment seeks how to serve the needs of others; rather than regard the body as a machine that is infinitely malleable, such discernment appreciates the mystery of all embodiedness, and seeks carefully to see what the Spirit desires to be heard in our own and the bodies of others.

In sum, the church ought to be the place where openness to change is a corollary of belief in the new creation, but also the place where the goal of change is greater than the discovery of the self: "Now the Lord is the Spirit, and where the Spirit of the Lord is, there is freedom. And all of us, with unveiled faces, seeing the glory of the Lord as though reflected in a mirror, are being transformed into the same image from one degree of glory to another; for this comes from the Lord, the Spirit" (2 Cor 3:17–18).

11

A DISEMBODIED "THEOLOGY OF THE BODY"

John Paul II on Love, Sex, and Pleasure

Originally published in Commonweal *128, no. 2 (2001): 11–17.*

Papal teaching on human sexuality has received some positive reviews recently. A number of these have appeared in the journal *First Things*. In "Contraception: A Symposium" (December 1998), Archbishop Charles J. Chaput, OFMCap, declares that Pope Paul VI has a lock on the title of prophet because, in *Humanae Vitae*, he was right. In the same issue, Janet E. Smith thinks that people who regard the papacy's condemnation of contraception to be based on the "artificial" methods employed simply have not acquainted themselves with the richness of papal teaching. In particular, she says, "those who appreciate precise and profound philosophical reasoning should read Karol Wojtyla's *Love and Responsibility*," while offering a strong recommendation also for "the extensive deliberations of Pope

John Paul II." Even more recently, Jennifer J. Popiel states that "unlike many women, I find the church's doctrinal statements on contraception and reproduction to be clear and compelling," and argues that Natural Family Planning is fully compatible with feminism, since "only when we control our bodies will we truly control our lives" ("Necessary Connections? Catholicism, Feminism, and Contraception," *America*, November 27, 1999.)

George Weigel joins this chorus of praise in his biography of John Paul II, *Witness to Hope* (New York: Cliff Street Books, 1999). Under the heading, "A New Galileo Crisis," Weigel traces the pope's systematic response to the "pastoral and catechetical failure" of *Humanae Vitae* in a series of 130 fifteen-minute conferences at papal audiences beginning on September 5, 1979, and concluding on November 28, 1984. The conferences were grouped into four clusters: "The Original Unity of Man and Woman," "Blessed Are the Pure of Heart," "The Theology of Marriage and Celibacy," and "Reflections on *Humanae Vitae*." These talks were brought together under the title *Theology of the Body: Human Love in the Divine Plan* (Boston: Pauline Books and Media, 1997).

Weigel himself considers John Paul II's work to be a "theological time bomb" that may take almost a century to appreciate fully, or even assimilate. It "may prove to be the decisive moment in exorcising the Manichaean demon and its deprecation of human sexuality from Catholic moral theology," because the pope takes "embodiedness" so seriously. Weigel considers these conferences to have "ramifications for all of theology," and wonders why so few contemporary theologians have taken up the challenge posed by the pope. He is surprised as well that so few priests preach these themes and only a "microscopic" portion of Catholics seem even aware of this great accomplishment, which he considers to be "a critical moment not only in Catholic theology, but in the history of modern thought." Weigel provides three possible reasons for this neglect: the density of the pope's material, the media's preoccupation with controversy rather than substance, and the fact that John Paul II is himself a figure of controversy. It will take time to appreciate him and his magnificent contribution.

Is Weigel right? Have the rest of us missed out on a theological advance of singular importance? Can the claims made for the pope's theology of the body be sustained under examination? Recently, I devoted considerable time (and as much consciousness as I could muster) to reading through the 423 pages of the collected conferences, and I have reached a conclusion far different from Weigel's. For all its length, earnestness, and good intentions, John Paul II's work, far from being a breakthrough for modern thought, represents a mode of theology that has little to say to ordinary people because it shows so little awareness of ordinary life.

I want to make clear that I am here responding to the theological adequacy of papal teaching. I do not dispute the fact that in some respects papal positions can legitimately be called prophetic. Certainly, John Paul II's call for a "culture of life" in the name of the gospel, against the complex "conspiracy of death" so pervasive in the contemporary world, deserves respect. Likewise, the pope's attention to the "person" and to "continence" stand as prophetic in a time of sexualized identity and rationalized permissiveness. It is small wonder that those worried about moral confusion in matters sexual would want to accept all the papal teachings, since some of them are incontestably correct.

But I want to ask whether we ought to make some distinctions even where the pope does not, whether while approving some of his positions we can also challenge others. Weigel is correct in noting that these conferences are dense and difficult to read—what must they have been like to hear? But Weigel fails to note how mind-numbingly repetitious they are. He does not seem to notice that the pope only asserts and never demonstrates, and that he minimizes the flat internal contradictions among the conferences. For example, on October 1, 1980, the pope declares that a husband cannot be guilty of "lust in his heart" for his wife, but a week later, in the conference of October 8, he states confidently that even husbands can sin in this fashion. But beyond such relatively minor deficiencies (how many theological writings are not dense, repetitious, and inconsistent?), the pope's theology of the body is fundamentally inadequate to the question it takes up. It is inadequate not in the obvious way that all theology is necessarily inadequate to its subject, and therefore should exhibit intellectual modesty, but in the sense that it simply does not engage what most ought to be engaged in a theology of the body. Because of its theological insufficiency, the pope's teaching does not adequately respond to the anxieties of those who seek a Christian understanding of the body and of human sexuality and practical guidance for life as sexually active adults.

If the pope had only made casual or passing comments on the subject in a homily, then a critical response would be unfair. But everything suggests that John Paul II intended these conferences to be read as a "theology of the body" in the fullest sense of the term *theology*. The pope uses academic terms like *phenomenology* and *hermeneutics*, refers to contemporary thinkers, provides copious notes, and in the very commitment to the subject over a period of five years in 130 conferences, indicates that he wants his comments to be given serious attention. It is perhaps appropriate to offer a number of observations concerning things that someone far removed from the corridors of doctrinal declaration, but not unschooled theologically, and certainly not disembodied, might want to see yet does not find in John Paul II's discourses.

PRELIMINARY OBSERVATIONS

A starting place is the title itself, which, while perhaps not chosen by the author, legitimately derives from his frequent reference to a "theology of the body" and his constant focus on "human love in the divine plan." Surely, though, an adequate theology of the body must encompass far more than human love, even if that were comprehensively treated! The pope cites 1 Corinthians 6:18 approvingly: "Flee fornication. Every sin a person commits is apart from the body. But the one who fornicates sins in his own body." But Paul's rhetorical emphasis cannot be taken as sober description. Do not the sins of gluttony and drunkenness and sloth have as much to do with the body as fornication, and are not all the forms of avarice also dispositions of the body?

Reducing a theology of the body to a consideration of sexuality falsifies the topic from the beginning. Of course, an adequate theological phenomenology of the body as the primordial mystery/symbol of human freedom and bondage must include every aspect of sexuality. But it must also embrace all the other ways in which human embodiedness both enables and limits human freedom through disposition of material possessions, through relationships to the environment, through artistic creativity, and through suffering—both sinful and sanctifying. The pope's title provides the first example of the way in which a grander—or to use his word, *vast*—conceptual framework serves to camouflage a distressingly narrow view of things.

The pope's subtitle is *Human Love in the Divine Plan*, but no real sense of human love as actually experienced emerges in these reflections. The topic of human love in all its dimensions has been wonderfully explored in the world's literature, but none of its grandeur or giddiness appears in these talks, which remain at a level of abstraction far removed from novels and newspapers with their stories of people like us (though not so attractive). John Paul II thinks of himself as doing "phenomenology," but seems never to look at actual human experience. Instead, he dwells on the nuances of words in biblical narratives and declarations, while fantasizing an ethereal and all-encompassing mode of mutual self-donation between man and woman that lacks any of the messy, clumsy, awkward, charming, casual, and, yes, silly aspects of love in the flesh. Carnality, it is good to remember, is at least as much a matter of humor as of solemnity. In the pope's formulations, human sexuality is observed by telescope from a distant planet. Solemn pronouncements are made based on textual exegesis rather than living experience. The effect is something like that of a sunset painted by the unsighted.

The objection may be made: isn't it proper to base theology in Scripture, and isn't John Paul II correct to have devoted himself so sedulously to the analysis of biblical texts, rather than the slippery and shoddy stuff of experience? Well, that depends on how seriously one takes the Catholic tradition concerning the work of God's Holy Spirit in the world. If we believe—and I think we have this right—that revelation is not exclusively biblical but occurs in the continuing experience of God in the structures of human freedom (see *Dei Verbum* 2.8), then an occasional glance toward human experience as actually lived may be appropriate, even for the magisterium.

As for the pope's way of reading Scripture, the grade is mixed. Certainly he is careful with the texts. Nor does he misrepresent those aspects of the text he discusses in any major way—although he leaves the impression that Matthew's "blessed are the pure of heart" (5:8) refers to chastity, when in fact he knows very well that the Beatitude does not have that restricted sense. Even more questionable are the ways John Paul II selects and extrapolates from specific texts without sufficient grounding or explanation. First, he scarcely treats all the biblical evidence pertinent to the subject. His discourses center on a handful of admittedly important passages, with obligatory nods at other texts that might have rewarded far closer analysis, such as the Song of Songs (three conferences) and the Book of Tobit (one). Other important texts are given scant or no attention. A far richer understanding of Paul would have resulted, for example, from a more sustained and robust reading of 1 Corinthians 7, which truly does reveal the mutuality and reciprocity—and complexity—of married love.

Second, John Paul II does not deal with some of the difficulties presented by the texts he does select. For instance, he manages to use Matthew 19:3–9, on the question of marriage's indissolubility, without ever adverting to the clause allowing divorce on the grounds of *porneia* (sexual morality) in both Matthew 5:32 and 19:9. What does that exceptive clause suggest about the distance between the ideal "in the beginning" evoked by Jesus, and the hard realities of actual marriages faced by the Matthean (and every subsequent) church?

Third, for all his philosophical sophistication, John Paul II seems unaware of the dangers of deriving ontological conclusions from selected ancient narrative texts. He inveighs against the "hermeneutics of suspicion," but the remedy is not an uncritical reading that moves directly from the ancient story to an essential human condition. He focuses on the Yahwist Creation account in Genesis 2, because that is the account cited by Jesus in his dispute with the Pharisees concerning divorce (Matt 19:5), and, I suspect, because its narrative texture—not to mention its human feel—allows for the sort of phenomenological reflection he enjoys. But as the pope certainly understands, this creation account must also be joined to that in Genesis 1 if an adequate appreciation of what Jesus meant by "from the beginning" (Matt 19:8) is to be gained. If Genesis 1—which has God creating humans in God's image as male and female—had been employed more vigorously, certain emphases would be better balanced. John Paul II wants, for example, to have the term *man* mean both male and female. But the Genesis 2 account pushes him virtually to equate *man* with "male," with the unhappy result that males experience both the original solitude the pope wants to make distinctively human as well as the dominion over creation expressed by the naming of animals. Females inevitably appear as "helpers" and as complementary to the already rather complete humanity found in the male. Small wonder that in virtually none of his further reflections on sexuality do women appear as moral agents: men can have lust in the hearts but not women; men can struggle with concupiscence but apparently women do not; men can exploit their wives sexually but women can't exploit their husbands sexually.

Such tight focus on male and female in the biblical account also leaves out all the interesting ways in which human sexuality refuses to be contained within those standard gender designations, not only biologically but also psychologically and spiritually. What appears in the guise of description serves prescription: human love and sexuality can appear in only one approved form, with every other way of being either sexual or loving left out altogether. Is it not important at least to acknowledge that a significant portion of humans—even if we take a ludicrously low percentage, at least tens of millions—are homosexual? Are they left outside God's plan if they are not part of the biblical story? Would not an adequate phenomenology of human sexuality, so concerned with "persons," after all, rather than statistics, take with great seriousness this part of the human family, who are also called to be loving, and in many fashions to create and foster the work and joy of creation?

Even within this normative framework, out of all the things that might be taken up and discussed within married love and the vocation of parenting, John Paul II's conferences finally come down to a concentration on "the transmission of life." By the time he reaches his explicit discussion of *Humanae Vitae*, it is difficult to avoid the conclusion that every earlier textual choice and phenomenological reflection has been geared to a defense of Paul VI's encyclical. However, there is virtually nothing in this defense that is strengthened by the conferences preceding it.

WHAT THE POPE LEAVES OUT

John Paul II is certainly to be appreciated for trying to place the knotty and disputed questions concerning procreation into a more comprehensive theology of the body. But there are several things lacking in these conferences and in the various declarations of the pope's apologists. I will simply list some obvious ones without development.

Most important, I would like to see a greater intellectual modesty, not only concerning the "facts" of revelation but also with the "facts" of human embodiedness. In everything having to do with the body, we are in the realm of what Gabriel Marcel called *mystery*. The body does not present a series of problems that we can solve by detached analysis. The body rather is mystery in two significant ways. First, we don't understand everything about the body, particularly our own body. The means by which we reveal ourselves to others and unite lovingly with others are not unambiguous. The body reveals itself to thought but also conceals itself from our minds. Second, we cannot detach ourselves from our bodies as though they were simply what we "have" rather than also what we "are." We are deeply implicated and cannot distance ourselves from the body without self-distortion. Our bodies are not only to be schooled by our minds and wills; they also instruct and discipline us in often humbling ways. Should not a genuine "theology of the body" begin with a posture of receptive attention to and learning from our bodies? Human bodies are part of God's image and the means through which absolutely everything we can learn about God must come to us.

In this regard, I find much of contemporary talk about "controlling our bodies" exactly contrary to such humility, whether such language derives from technocrats seeking to engineer reproductive processes or from naturalists who seek the same control through continence. I am not suggesting that a lack of continence or temperance is a desirable goal. But self-control is not the entire point of sexual love; celibacy is not the goal of marriage! And it may help to remember, in all this talk of controlling the body, that Dante assigned a deeper place in hell to the cold and the cruel than to the lustful. It can be argued, especially from the evidence of this century, that more evil has been visited upon us by various Stalins of sexless self-control than by the (quickly exhausted) epicures of the erotic. Recognition of the ways in which we suffer, rather than steer, our bodies is a beginning of wisdom.

Along these lines, I would welcome from the pope some appreciation for the goodness of sexual pleasure—any bodily pleasure, come to think of it! Pleasure is, after all, God's gift also. A sadly neglected text is 1 Timothy 6:17, where God supplies us all things richly for our enjoyment. Sexual passion, in papal teaching, appears mainly as an obstacle to authentic love. Many of us have experienced sexual passion as both humbling and liberating, a way in which our bodies know quicker and better than our minds, choose better and faster than our reluctant wills, even get us to where God apparently wants us in a way our minds never could. Along the same lines, papal teaching might find a good word to say about the sweetness of sexual love—also, I think, God's gift. Amid all the talk of self-donation and mutuality, we should also remember, "plus, it feels good." Come to think of it, why not devote some meditation to the astonishing triumph of sexual fidelity in marriage? Faithfulness, when it is genuine, is the result of a delicate and attentive creativity between partners, and not simply the automatic product of "self-control." In short, a more adequate theology of the body would at least acknowledge the positive ways in which the body gifts us by "controlling" us.

As with pleasure so with pain. A theology of the body ought to recognize the ways in which human sexual existence is difficult: how arduous and ambiguous a process it is for any of us to become mature sexually; how unstable and shifting are our patterns of sexual identity; how unpredictable and vagrant are our desire and craving as well as our revulsion and resistance; how little support there is for covenanted love in our world; how much the stresses of life together—and apart—bear upon our sexual expression. John Paul II and his apologists seem to think that concupiscence is our biggest challenge. How many of us would welcome a dose of concupiscence, when the grinding realities of sickness and need have drained the body of all its sap and sweetness, just as a reminder of being sentient! I would welcome the honest acknowledgement that for many who are married, the pleasure and comfort of sexual love are most needed precisely when least available, not because of fertility rhythms, but because of sickness and anxiety and separation and loss. For that matter, a theology of the body ought to speak not only of an "original solitude" that is supposedly cured by marriage, but also of the "continuing solitude" of those both married and single, whose vocation is not celibacy yet whose erotic desires find, for these and many other reasons, no legitimate or sanctified expression, and, in these papal conferences, neither recognition nor concern.

The pope does not examine these and many other aspects of the body and of "human love in the divine plan." Instead, the theology of the body is reduced to sexuality, and sexuality to "the transmission of life." The descent to biologism is unavoidable. What is needed is a more generous appreciation of the way sexual energy pervades our interpersonal relations and creativity—including the life of prayer!—and a fuller understanding of covenanted love as life-giving and sustaining in multiple modes of parenting, community building, and world enhancement.

REVISITING *HUMANAE VITAE*

John Paul II's conferences and the recent articles I have quoted have meant to defend the correctness of *Humanae Vitae*, but paradoxically they remind readers with any historical memory how flawed that instrument was, and how badly it is in need of a fundamental revisiting. George Weigel calls it a "pastoral and catechetical failure," as though the encyclical's deficiencies were merely those of tone or effective communication. John Paul II's biblical reflections, in fact, appear as nothing less than a major effort to ground *Humanae Vitae* in something more than natural law, an implicit recognition of the argumentative inadequacy of Paul VI's encyclical. As my earlier comments indicate, I would judge his success as slight. It would be a weary business to take up the entire encyclical again, but it is important at least to note five major deficiencies that require a genuinely theological response rather than enthusiastic or reluctant apology.

In these comments, I will speak of "artificial birth control" only in terms of using a condom, diaphragm, or other mechanical device, mainly because I have considerable unease concerning chemical interventions and their implications for women's long-term health.

First, the encyclical represents a reversion to an act-centered morality, ignoring the important maturation of moral theology in the period leading up to and following Vatican II, which emphasized a person's fundamental dispositions as more defining of moral character than isolated acts. I am far from suggesting that specific acts are not morally significant. But specific acts must also be placed within the context of a person's character as revealed in consistent patterns of response. The difference is critical when the encyclical and John Paul II insist that it is not enough for married couples to be open to new life; rather, every act of intercourse must also be open, so that the use of a contraceptive in any single act in effect cancels the entire disposition of openness. But this is simply nonsense. I do not cancel my commitment to breathing when I hold my breath for a moment or when I go under anesthesia. Likewise, there is an important distinction to be maintained between basic moral dispositions and single actions. The woman who kills in self-defense (or in defense of her children) does not become a murderer. The focus on each act of intercourse rather than on the overall dispositions of married couples is morally distorting.

Second, the arguments of Paul VI and John Paul II sacrifice logic to moral brinkmanship. When Paul VI equated artificial birth control and abortion, he not only defied science but also provoked the opposite result of the one he intended. He wanted to elevate the moral seriousness of birth control but ended by trivializing the moral horror of abortion. Similarly, from one side of the mouth, John Paul II recognizes two ends of sexual love, unitive intimacy and procreation. But from the other side of his mouth he declares that if procreation is blocked, not only that end has been canceled but also the unitive end as well. He has thereby, despite his protestations to the contrary, simply reduced the two ends to one. This can be shown clearly by applying the logic in reverse, by insisting that sexual intercourse that is not a manifestation of intimacy or unity also cancels the procreative end of the act.

Third, the position of the popes and their apologists continues to reveal the pervasive sexism that becomes ever more obvious within official Catholicism. I have touched above on the way John Paul II's reading of Scripture tends to reduce the moral agency of women within the marriage covenant and sexual relationships. This becomes glaringly obvious in the argument that artificial birth control is wrong because it tends to "instrumentalize" women for men's pleasure by making the woman a passive object of passion rather than a partner in mutuality. Yet the argument makes more experiential sense in reverse. Few things sound more objectifying than the arguments of the natural family planners, whose focus remains tightly fixed on biological processes rather than on emotional and spiritual communication through the body. The view that "openness to life" is served with moral integrity by avoiding intercourse during fertile periods (arguably times of greatest female pleasure in making love) and is not served (and becomes morally reprehensible) by the mutual agreement to use a condom or diaphragm, would be laughable if it did not have such tragic consequences. And what could be more objectifying of women than speaking as though birth control were something that only served male concupiscence? How about women's moral agency in the realm of sexual relations? Don't all of us living in the real world of bodies know that women have plenty of reasons of their own to be relieved of worries about pregnancy for a time and to be freed for sexual enjoyment purely for the sake of intimacy and even celebration?

Fourth, the absolute prohibition of artificial birth control becomes increasingly scandalous in the face of massive medical realities. One might want to make an argument that distributing condoms to teenagers as a part of sex education is mistaken, but that argument, I think, has to do with misgivings concerning sex education—and a general culture of permissiveness—as a whole. But what about couples who can no longer have sexual relations because one of them has innocently been infected by HIV, and not to use a condom means also to infect the other with a potentially lethal virus? When does "openness to life" in every act become a cover for "death dealing"? Given the fact that in Africa AIDS affects tens of millions of men, women, and children (very many of them Christian), is the refusal to allow the use of condoms (leaving aside other medical interventions and the changing of sexual mores) coming dangerously close to assisting in genocide? These are matters demanding the most careful consideration by the church and the deepest compassion. It is difficult to avoid the sense that the failed logic supposedly marshaled in the defense of life is having just the opposite result. If the political enslavement of millions of Asians and Europeans led the papacy to combat the Soviet system in the name of compassion, and if the enslavement and murder of millions of Jews led the papacy to renounce the anti-Semitism of the Christian tradition in the name of compassion, should not compassion also lead at the very least to an examination of logic when millions of Africans are enslaved and killed by a sexual pandemic?

Fifth, and finally, shouldn't *Humanae Vitae* be revisited rather than simply defended for the same reasons that it was a "pastoral and catechetical" failure the first time around? It failed to convince most of its readers not least because its readers knew that Paul VI spoke in the face of the recommendations of his own birth-control commission. The encyclical was, as Weigel calls it, a "new Galileo crisis," not simply because it pitted papal authority against science, but also because the papacy was wrong both substantively and formally. It generated an unprecedented crisis for papal authority precisely because it was authority exercised not only apart from but also in opposition to the process of discernment. Sad to say, John Paul's theology of the body, for all its attention to Scripture, reveals the same deep disinterest in the ways the experience of married people, and especially women (guided by the Holy Spirit, as we devoutly pray) might inform theology and the decision-making process of the church. If papal teaching showed signs of attentiveness to such experience, and a willingness to learn from God's work in the world as well as God's word in the tradition, its pronouncements would be received with greater enthusiasm. A theology of the body ought at least to have feet that touch the ground.

Since God is the Living One who continuously presses upon us at every moment of creation, calling us to obedience and inviting us to a painful yet joyous quest of wisdom, theology must be inductive rather than deductive. Our reading of Scripture not only shapes our perceptions of the world but is in turn shaped by our experiences of God in the fabric of our human freedom and in the cosmic play of God's freedom. Theology that takes the self-disclosure of God in human experience with the same seriousness as it does God's revelation in Scripture does not turn its back on tradition but recognizes that tradition must constantly be renewed by the powerful leading of the Spirit if it is not to become a form of falsehood. Theology so understood is a demanding and delicate conversation that, like sexual love itself, requires patience as well as passion. If we are to reach a better theology of human love and sexuality, then we must, in all humility, be willing to learn from the bodies and the stories of those whose response to God and to God's world involves sexual love. That, at least, is a starting point.

12

SEXUALITY AND THE HOLINESS OF THE CHURCH

Presented as keynote address at the Covenant Network of Presbyterians, November 6, 2004.

Thank you very much for asking me to be here with you. I am honored to be with you this morning, although as I stand before you to talk on the subject of sexuality and holiness in the church, I don't know whether this is an act of stupidity or valor. These are three of the most important and difficult subjects imaginable.

The issue of sexuality doesn't need to be advertised for us to regard it as important. That is one of the reasons we have come together. It is in the headlines. It is in the elections. It is in our church controversies. And it is just interesting!

But sexuality is of importance for us right now, I think, because it intersects these other two realities, namely holiness and the church. And whether or not sex was on our minds, the church and its holiness remain the most important, disputed questions facing Christians today, as they have faced earlier generations of Christians; and we are obliged to grapple with them as were previous generations of Christians.

I want to begin with the difficulties of each of these subjects, taking them in turn—not that you are unaware of them, but so that we can have a kind of shared framework as we move forward in our conversation, which I hope it will eventually turn out to be, and to keep our expectations realistically low.

To begin then with sexuality, it seems to me that we have five kinds of issues here. The first is (and I think we always need to begin here) that our emotions are involved. And I'm not simply talking about our sexual feelings and our sexual passions and the unexpected leanings and longings of our hearts and our bodies, but I'm talking about powerful emotions of fear and of anger, of guilt and shame, whether imposed on us or interjected by us, and a widely pervasive distrust. I think that we need to begin and acknowledge the fact that none of us are free from emotion as we approach the subject of sexuality today.

The second issue is that each of us is subjective. Each of us brings a story to this topic. No one comes to the subject of sexuality in the church either neutral or innocent. We are all implicated. Some of us have abused. Some of us have been abused. Some of us have used. Some of us have been used. Some of us should be ashamed, and some of us have had shame put upon us. We all bring these tangled stories. Each of us has a tangled story to tell regarding sexuality, which is, by the way, not entirely perspicuous even to the person whose story it is. None of us, I think, knows ourselves that well. If we were as honest with each other as we would like to be, I think that many of us would want to say that sexual identity is not a fixed point but rather a sliding scale of sexual expression, feeling, and desire that never stands still until we die.

The third problem with sexuality is that it is not a problem. It is a mystery. Here I mean that human sexuality is a matter of embodiedness. It is not, therefore, as Gabriel Marcel has reminded us about all things in which body and spirit touch, a problem to be fixed like a broken carburetor. It is, rather, a mystery that is to be at once celebrated and suffered. We cannot detach ourselves from our own sexual embodiedness without distorting the subject. We are implicated in our sexual bodies. In this respect, sexuality is very much like our relationship to our bodies regarding being and having possessions, only more so. We are at that delicate place in human reality where bodies express spirit, and spirit needs a body in order to express itself, and the spirit is implicated in the dispositions of the body.

The fourth reason why sexuality is complicated today is that all of us have a sense of disordered forms of sexuality in our culture. We would be fools to deny this: pervasive voyeurism, pornography, prostitution, the sexualization of the media, of advertising. The victims are above all among our children and among the youth of this country, and we are quite rightly deeply anxious about the way in which the distinction between "selling sex" and "sex sells" is almost indistinguishable.

And finally, fifth, all of us certainly in this place recognize and are angry at the phenomenon of scapegoating—the focusing in the church and in the culture on homosexuality, that wonderfully abstract term, as a form of disorder that can be *othered*, and therefore can be considered outside the pale and allow the church and society *not* to look at the pervasive disorderedness of sexuality across the board. It is a massive form of deflection from what needs paying attention to. I find it fascinating, for example, that we have all of this stuff about homosexuality, and churches meeting in conferences and convocations and gatherings and so forth, while the church seems utterly silent in its inability to speak about the reality of a multibillion-dollar pornographic industry. Yet by the simple process of deduction, the promoters of that industry are male Christians, presumably mostly heterosexual.

Our thinking about the church is equally complex and conflicted. Here also we have individual stories and attendant emotions. Some of us have a sense of grief at the loss of a church that we once had, or fear of a threat of change in the church, or anger at the church's refusal to change. Some of us come as immigrants from other traditions seeking a saner place here in this communion, and others of us have been made to feel as strangers within their own place—I think the technical word is *alienation*.

But beyond those emotional reactions and those multiple stories is the plain fact that we don't share an understanding of church. That is the real difficulty. We are not on the same page in our understanding of what church is.

Here are some of the elements that are up for grabs. Where is the church? Is the church in the local assembly, primarily, where two or three are gathered, and the Spirit moves in acts of worship and of healing; or is the church more powerfully present in the denomination and its organizational mechanisms; or is it, perhaps more importantly, found ecumenically? That is a matter of place.

But what about our sense of the church? Here, I think, we have widely differing views. Do we regard the church, as so many Christians in America today do, as a voluntary association, a place of services that are offered, a place that we join because of its market niche, or because it agrees with us, or because it offers us services that we can't find somewhere else? With that understanding of the church as a voluntary association, we can expect the church to ask very little of us. We can just go down the street to the other club that will accept us on our own terms. Or is our church more properly Reformed in character? Do we understand the church in strongly covenantal terms, that we have been called by God into covenant, and that covenant places upon us real and deep obligations to God and to our neighbors, and that therefore we can, both in private and public, expect our neighbors to support us and to challenge us when we fail to keep covenant as we also are obliged to challenge and question our neighbors when they do not meet the covenant? Or do we have a sense of the church that is ontological: the mystical body of Christ, the place where the resurrected Jesus is powerfully present among us?

Those are three very different visions of what we are about in the church. We don't agree, I expect, in this room, on the marks of the church and how important they are: one, catholic, apostolic, and holy. Above all, I don't think we agree on what the politics of those four marks of the church should be. Is the church one, holy, catholic, and apostolic in terms of an eschatological hope only; or is there a way holiness, oneness, catholicity, and apostolicity can be expressed politically and visibly within the communion?

This brings us, finally, to the subject of holiness, which is, perhaps, the hardest of all. Again, here are individual stories, and our emotions are frequently running in opposite directions. People of my age tend to be running in fear and some relief from a heritage of holiness that can roughly be identified with the Puritan or Jansenistic past, in which holiness was set against witchcraft and godlessness of all sorts. But as we are running (my folks) in one direction, we are meeting our children running in the opposite direction from the moral relativism of the sixties and all that represents—namely us. I am not sure, especially within the Reformed tradition, how much it's allowed to talk about holiness. There are some very substantial kinds of issues, it seems to me. One is a connection between the religious reality in which we find ourselves and moral behavior. How do faith and virtue connect? Second, once more, is it personal and individual, or is it public and political?

Now, on the personal side, it seems to me that one of the reasons why "practice" is now such a buzzword in Protestant theology—that is, the practicing of our faith, the practice of prayer, the practice of hospitality, the practice of fasting, the practice of almsgiving, the practices of chastity and modesty, even of the custody of the senses—the reason why Protestant theologians far and wide are beginning to try to think about practices and shared practices is that we don't do them. That's why Protestant theologians have been looking to us Catholics and saying, "Teach us about these things." That would have been great if we had not given them up just a couple of decades ago, too. I think it is safe to say that most of us do not have a highly structured notion of what personal holiness looks like in terms of the practices of faith.

We also have a difficulty regarding the public dimension. I think all of us will sort of acknowledge that the Eisenhower era was one of very clear private virtue that was comfortable with various forms of public vice, and the Clinton era, in opposition, was one that was very deeply committed to public virtue (this was the generation of the sixties), but was also equally comfortable with private vice; and in each case, you see, sex was a player. For the Eisenhower era, only private, domestic sexual morality counted. Issues of gender didn't matter. Issues of segregation, issues of repression didn't matter. Certainly those of us who came from the sixties were all about nondiscrimination, were all about gender issues, power issues, and egalitarianism. But it is not quite clear how we connect that with things that are going on with our bodies, that is to say in private (if anything is private). And none of us have a very clear sense of what should be regulated and observed and open and is anybody else's business! So we exist in a society in which it is possible for abortion not to be a criminal action, but a mother who brings a child to term but has taken cocaine or is drunk and bears a damaged child can be subject to criminal charges. None of us want to be regulated, but all of us want to regulate—at least on the issue of carcinogens and so forth. This is a very confused time.

So, what do we make of the fact that holiness is a mark of the church? What do you and I understand by that? That's our challenge, and once we understand something about it, what are we going to do about it?

Another difficult issue is how to bring Scripture to bear on these questions as a resource for trying to think together as church—about church, about holiness, and about sexuality. Once more we find ourselves in disputed and troubled waters. Let me say immediately that I simply reject the usefulness of two forms of modernity regarding Scripture, named fundamentalism and historical criticism. Fundamentalism distorts the witness of Scripture by paying no attention to the context of language, either in the past or in the present, and assuming that the past can speak directly to the present, and the traffic moves only in one direction. Fundamentalism is, in effect, a denial of the Living God. But so is historical criticism. Historical criticism distorts the witness of Scripture because it keeps the text simply in the past and deprives Scripture of its prophetic force, and so equally denies the Living God.

We need a more complex form of conversation with Scripture. Let me recommend two things for our consideration. The first is that we need to work hard to cultivate theological imagination. One of the worst things that happened in the Enlightenment was the banishment of the imagination to the epistemological attic. The only thing that counted was the empirically verifiable. We all became positivists. We all became, in Brooks Holifield's wonderful phrase, "Baconian evidentialists."

We need to recover and embrace a scriptural imagination, to imagine the world as Scripture imagines it, not looking for proof texts, not trying to do an archeological dig, but trying to recover the sense of Scripture as a living city in which we are citizens, whose language we know and whose byways we know, because we live there.

The second thing we need to cultivate is a loyal and critical engagement with the imaginative world of Scripture. I emphasize both things because they go together. You can only be critical if you are loyal; and the deepest form of loyalty is criticism: the criticism that doesn't simply question the ancient text but questions those who approach this text. That means listening to Scripture together with the other formative sources of our life—tradition, reason, and the experience of God and the world, above all the experience of God as discerned in real human lives today. Theology is an inductive art. Its business is trying to catch up with what the Living God is doing in the world. We begin there; and then we try to figure out how Scripture can speak prophetically to it.

What I want to do is recommend that we engage Paul in a conversation about church, holiness, and sexuality, briefly, to be sure. This is a conversation opener, not a closer.

Paul is a good place to begin to prompt our thinking on these subjects, for three reasons. First, Paul has the most powerful understanding of this new thing that has happened in Jesus. For Paul, the resurrection is not a historical event of the past that is adequately understood as the resuscitation of Jesus. For Paul, the resurrection affects all of us. Jesus, the last Adam, has become life-giving Spirit. The resurrection reality is the outpouring of the Spirit upon all flesh, and therefore the reality of Jesus as Lord, not in the past but in the present, in whose name we have gathered today, affects and determines all other relationships through time and space, and all other bodies through time and space. For Paul, the resurrection is not simply a new covenant, it is a new creation. "If anybody is in Christ, [*kaine ktisis*] it is a new creation. [*Ta archaia parelthen*] The old things have gone away. [*Idou gegonen kaina*] Behold, all things are new" (2 Cor 5:17).

Second, Paul is also important because he understands that these new and eschatological and creation-renewing experiences of the Living God find embodiment, have to be worked out, in bodies of the first creation, and that we are not in the end-time totally yet. Therefore, there is always going to be stress and tension between the first creation and the new creation, between the new human and the old human, between flesh and spirit. To make matters more complicated for Paul, he knew that these forms of embodiment had to be worked out among urban Christians of the first century who were multicultural and came from very different understandings of what bodies should mean in the world, whether coming from the side of Judaism or coming from the side of Greco-Roman culture. Different cultures, different traditions, different perceptions.

Paul had to try to figure out what these new realities meant in terms of an *ecclesia*, a church, which met in a household, and so we always find a stress and a tension in Paul between the utopian ideals—in Christ there is neither male nor female, slave nor free, Jew nor Greek—and the social realities of the household, in which gender and social status meant a great deal indeed. The reason why Paul is so valuable to us is that he shows us both poles of that tension without reducing them. That is his great gift to us, because the same tensions exist today. No matter how profoundly egalitarian our ideals, we must always come up against the hard, intractable elements of bodies and cultures and different perceptions of how societies should work.

Third, Paul is important for us to engage because his characteristic demand of his communities is that they think. Let's face it: this is why we don't like Paul. It's not his personality. It's the fact that he's a thinker, and he asks us to think. We don't want to think. It doesn't matter what side of the debates you are on. Most of us (let's be honest) would rather put it on a bumper sticker and drive off. Thinking is hard. Thinking demands stuff of us. So Paul asks them to discern, to think about the connections between the power of the resurrected Lord poured out on this community, and specific ways of being embodied, specific ways of acting in the world. And he provides for them a measure for that thinking that he calls "the mind of Christ" (1 Cor 2:16) or the pattern of the Messiah (Gal 6:2). That ought to be, as well, the measure of our thinking.

Paul, then, is most important, not because he solves or creates our problems, but because he gives us exactly what we need to struggle with. And so the point is not learning Paul, and the point is not dictating to Paul. The point is thinking with Paul.

Let me touch on the three topics here that we have selected for today: Paul's view of the church, Paul's view of holiness, and finally, Paul's understanding of sexuality. On one side, Paul's view of the church, as you know, is extraordinarily strong and high. He falls into that Body-of-Christ ontological understanding of the church. We have all drunk the one Spirit, he says, and therefore we are the one Body of Christ. If you were to ask Paul, "Where is the resurrected body of Jesus?" he would say, "Look around." The church is the Body of the resurrected One. We are "in the Lord." We are "in Christ," that characteristic Pauline language of the deepest kind of intimacy between the risen Lord who, because he shares the life of God, can be more intimately present to our body than we can be to each other's body so that all relationships are defined by this relationship to the Lord.

At the same time, Paul recognizes how astonishingly fragile his communities are, so we have an ideal of the church as the Body of Christ. Yet he recognizes that sociologically his communities are fragile, intentional communities that are parasites on Jewish and Greco-Roman cultures but belong to neither. They are sort of free-floating household churches that have absolutely no basis for continuation in the world except their shared collusion in understanding that they have been called out from the world to be together in the power of the Lord. For Paul, one of the most important elements in the life of the church is what he calls *oikodome*, edification, building the community. Repeatedly when Paul asks what should be done in the community, his answer is, "Does it build the community in its own distinctive identity?" This is going to be characteristic of Paul. "It's not about me, it's about the community." It is interesting that for Paul, even gifts of the Holy Spirit might not build the community. This is the case of *glossolalia*, or tongues. Speaking in tongues is perfectly fine. You can pray it, you can sing it, you can do all this stuff, but unless it is translated and can build the community, it must be kept under control. The test is not spirituality but church. What builds the church in its distinctive identity? The point is not what makes me feel good. The point is what supports and strengthens God's presence in the world.

Again, on the subject of holiness, Paul's view is, first, amazingly strong. They have been sanctified. They are the saints. They have been given the Holy Spirit. They are the Body of Christ and the temple of the Holy Spirit. The church is holy in its very identity. Holiness is a gift to the church because the church lives and breathes by the Holy Spirit of God.

But, Paul says, holiness is also a mandate. You have been called to holiness. This is God's will, he says to the Thessalonians, your sanctification or your holiness, so the gift bears within it a mandate. I think Paul shared the Jewish understanding of holiness as being *other* in the world, of being different in the world. The Holy Spirit is holy because we can't generate it. It's God's, and God is utterly other than us. When God said to the Israelites, "Be ye holy as I am holy," what this meant is that they were to be different *in* the world as God is utterly different *from* the world. So, the way they signaled the holiness of God was through the various ritual and moral commandments they kept. Paul retains this sense that to be in the church, to be the holy ones, to be saints, means to be *other than* world. There is a very real question as to whether the church can authentically be church if it is not countercultural, if it is not in some way other than the world.

For Paul, such holiness is a matter of behavior. In this he agrees with the Pharisees. Paul does not think that the church can maintain its holiness by having a completely separate existence as monks. You cannot go out of the world. So holiness doesn't consist of having a Christian education system, Christian poetry, Christian literature, Christian rock music, Christian cocaine, whatever! It is a matter of being in the world as a community and yet somehow being markedly different within that community. That's very much Paul the Pharisee.

But unlike the Pharisees, Paul does not regard this as a matter of ritual, but a matter of moral behavior. Here is where it becomes complicated for Paul. At one level Paul can quite blithely identify the difference between the world and the saints in terms of virtues and vices. So, in 1 Corinthians 6:9–11, he says, You used to do evil in the past, and now you are different, and he gives a list of virtues and vices as understood by ancient Greco-Roman and Jewish culture. So to be holy appears to mean simply being good.

And yet there are two complications of this in Paul. First, Paul can call a pagan vice a Christian virtue. In pagan thought, *tapeinophrosynen* was regarded as a vice. It was the mark, not of a good and virtuous person, but of somebody who was craven. In fact, it was identified with slaves (there's your class issue), because it was lowly mindedness. So, the only way Paul could get from a pagan vice to a Christian virtue called humility or lowly mindedness was through the crucified Messiah. Holiness in the church is not simply a matter of being good by the world's measure of being good or philosophy's measure of being good. It also means something about being marked with Christ.

And when Paul says that in Christ is neither male nor female, slave nor freed, Jew nor Greek (Gal 3:28), everybody recognizes that Paul has here relativized the three great status markers of antiquity—namely ethnicity, social location, and gender—and has said that in this Christian community, these distinctions are not to separate and divide and put one over the other, but they are to become opportunities for gift giving. That also is part of the holiness of the church, the otherness of the church for Paul, because the world doesn't operate that way. In the world, status is what matters. So this business of egalitarianism in the community is not a matter of political correctness. It is a matter of theological correctness. It is a matter of gospel.

But then you've got the problems of sex. Here we come, finally, to Paul's understanding of sexuality. Paul's understanding of sexuality, we must understand, is both strong and subtle, extraordinarily subtle, and extraordinarily strong. Paul does not view sex the way Greco-Roman philosophers viewed it, as a matter either of self-care, as Foucault has pointed out, or as a matter of self-control and anxiety. Nor does he view sex simply in terms of marrying the right girl and maintaining ethnicity, as in Judaism. Paul regards sexuality as personal engagement. This is quite distinctive in antiquity—it's unparalleled. It's not that Paul diminishes the significance of sex. Paul heightens the significance of sex. Why? Because he heightens the significance of bodies, as communicators of spirit. So, sexuality is personal and relational, and if we want to treasure those aspects of sexuality, we have Paul to thank, because that is where it comes from.

Now, in terms of how to act sexually, Paul doesn't tell us a great deal in detail. He has a very definite boundary. Sex cannot be involved in *porneia*, which is broadly and correctly translated as sexual immorality. Now what Paul understood by sexual immorality, I think, is clear. He did not think that men should sleep with men or women should sleep with women. He did not think that people should engage in prostitution. He certainly did not think that people should commit incest. He did not think that people should be violent in their sexual acts or that they should be adulterers or fornicators. All of these things for Paul fall under the sort of boundary line of sexual expression called *porneia*, and for him all of these modes of sexuality, in one way or another, did not adequately reflect the body and our bodies' relationship to the Lord.

Two things must be said about the positive expressions of sexuality, for Paul. First, they are multiple, so that one can marry, one can be a virgin, one can be a widow. And, more importantly, one's sexual status does not determine one's standing before the Lord. How one is sexually at one level is among the *adiaphora*.

But everywhere in Paul, *agape* trumps *eros*. Generally, the New Testament is the world's least erotic literature. By that I don't mean that it simply doesn't have many good stories. It's simply that *eros* does not register. We must go somewhere else besides the New Testament to find *eros*. But *agape* trumps *eros*. Alterity trumps egoism. Adulthood trumps childhood.

Once we have imagined the world that Paul imagines, we must also engage it with loyal criticism, taking into account the continuing work of God in our world. Here is my basic premise: the Living God continues to disclose Godself in the world, and Scripture does not contain everything that we need to learn about God, the world, our bodies, our sexuality. So our loyal criticism must hear our discernment of what God is up to as an equally important voice. We must read Paul through the lens of the new creation as it has continued to unfold and disclose itself in human life, in the world that God brings into being at every moment.

I think we need to ask, not whether we fit into Paul's understanding of church, but how we understand church. I am putting down these challenges to you as conversation points. How do we understand church?—because holiness will mean something very different if we are a voluntary association to meet my spiritual needs, or if we are the Body of the resurrected Christ in which the relationship to the risen Lord deeply affects every other relationship. How do we understand edification? Which means that we must come to grips with what we consider private and public.

Before we can talk coherently about holiness or sexuality, we need to talk about church. I want to propose that whatever we decide about church must include holiness, and not simply the holiness of the individual but the holiness of the church corporately. We must not reduce holiness to sexual morality, as though that were all of it. Holiness involves every dimension of life, and as many folks have pointed out, another form of deflection represented by the scapegoating of homosexuality has been our willingness to ignore the way Christianity has colluded with a view of the economic world in which no scrap of the gospel is detectable.

What are the implications of the resurrection of Jesus, of the lordship of Jesus, of the new creation, of our bodies being Christ's Body? Here is a fundamental difference for us. I don't think we can be Enlightenment people regarding the body and still be Christians. I don't see how we can do it. I don't see how we can think of the body simply as an assembly of eyeless monads who happen to be colliding together here or gathered here or agreed to meet this morning. If we don't understand church and holiness, which somehow involves the presence of the resurrected Lord, then why should we bother? Why should we bother with what we do individually and privately with our bodies? We could fool everybody, including ourselves, if we are not answerable to the Lord. It is a big issue. I want to add, how are we corporately other than the world? And is personal holiness to be defined totally by conventional virtue, or can it mean a witness to a life outside the bounds of social acceptability? If it does, how do we discern that witness?

Finally, our understanding of holiness cannot be reduced to sexuality, but must include sexuality. I will conclude with three points here, which I offer to you as my best offering at this point:

1. We must level the playing field. I don't see how the church can make any distinction between these two terms, *heterosexual* and *homosexual*, regarding sexual morality. To start, I don't believe in the terms. Obviously we hook up with different kinds of bodies, but in sexuality, there really is a very sliding scale, and I think using terms like *homosexual*, even if we multiply gay/lesbian/transgender, break it up into eighty kinds of different things, then we have to do the same thing on the hetero side as well, because it is not just A and B. Therefore, if we want to think about chastity, we must think about chastity on the heterosexual side, and we must think about chastity on the homosexual side. If we are going to think about *porneia*, we can't put it all over on the homosexual side. We must really come to grips with *porneia* on the heterosexual side, and I would

argue, statistically, there is a lot more of it, and it goes a lot more unattended. So, we cannot obsess that "gay people aren't faithful like us heterosexuals." Look at the statistics! How much fidelity is there on the heterosexual side? Leveling the playing field, I think, must be our task in terms of thinking about this. In other words, in my rendering of Galatians 3:28, "In Christ there is neither homosexual nor heterosexual."

2. We are obliged, mightily obliged, to rediscover the dimensions of *porneia*. What does it mean? We can no longer afford simply to work with the biblical understandings of *porneia*. We need to think through the ways in which our sexuality is disordered—again, on the level playing field, on both sides: the ways in which manipulation, violence, abuse, coercion, promiscuity are on both sides of the plain, and I would argue represent *porneia* on both sides. I don't think the church can ever say yes to *porneia*. If the church is asked to accept, let us say, a gay bathhouse style of promiscuity—the church can't; but neither can it say yes to a *Playboy* or *Penthouse* style of promiscuity.
3. We need to try to begin to think creatively, again with a level playing field, about the expressions of sexuality that are holy. I would like to offer four dimensions of holiness as I see it in sexual life.
   a) Holy sexual activity is relational. Here I think Paul is right. Sex can't simply be recreational. It simply can't be like eating peanuts—food for the belly, the belly for food. It can't simply be reduced to bodily fluids, relief of tension. Of course, we all know it is. We are not entirely in the new creation. I am very serious about that! I don't think that we should pretend to theologize our existence—sex is always going to be out of our control to a large extent. But in its highest expression, what the church wants to affirm as holy is not going to be recreational sex but

rather relational sex, because it is in relational sex that body expresses spirit.

b) I think the church wants to affirm, on both sides—fidelity, covenantal sexual life. Now, does fidelity fail on the heterosexual side? Yes. Should the church stop affirming it because of that? No! We are not holy. The church is holy. The Spirit is holy. We are drawn into a holy community to be lifted up, not to reduce the community to our lowest common denominator. So, I think the notion of covenantal sexual love is extremely important, bearing in mind the level playing field.

c) I would like to offer as a test of sexual relations the generation of new life. But I want to do it on a level playing field. Don't jump to children. That is obviously one way in which sexual love can be generative; but I think if we read Paul in terms of egoism giving way to alterity, of *eros* being trumped by *agape*, by childhood giving way to adulthood, I think we are called in the church to have our sexual love embrace others and give life to them. It can involve begetting children or adopting children or caring for others or fostering others or reaching out to our neighbors—there are all kinds of ways that we can do this. But I think it is a test of holiness whether our sexual love is just about me, and just about me and you, or whether it is a good thing for others as well that we embrace each other and bring others into our embrace.

d) How do we find a way of restoring those ancient Christian values without which we are all going to end up in a ditch somewhere?—chastity, modesty, custody of the senses, these practices that help us move away from a pansexualization of identity that surely is ruinous. The notion of being disciplined in our sexuality, it seems to me, is an important place to go.

I really do think this is not a problem that we will or can solve. It is a mystery in which we both suffer and celebrate. And I would simply ask of us that we be gentle with each other and with those who cannot see or speak or hear as we do or, rather, as we would like to think that we do.

13

A NEW GNOSTICISM

An Old Threat Made New

An edited version of this appeared in Commonweal *131, no. 19 (2004): 28–31.*

Historical analogies are both tempting and tricky. They are tempting because we always like to learn about the present from past examples. They are tricky because the search for instructive examples can distort both past and present. Try hard enough, and any age can begin to look like the fall of the Roman Empire.

Despite the danger, I want to suggest just such a historical analogy in the life of the church. My interest is partly historical but mainly moral. I think there is a genuine analogy between the situation of the church in the mid-second century and in the early twenty-first century. I will argue that in both cases there is a crisis of identity and even of survival, and that both the shape and the resolution of the crisis in the second century has lessons—and a challenge—for the church at the start of the twenty-first century.

I am scarcely the first to invoke ancient Gnosticism as a category for analyzing contemporary movements. In fact, the January

26, 1927, issue of *The Commonweal* has an editorial entitled "The Newer Gnostics." But in contrast to my predecessor in these pages, who was genially content to skewer aspects of popular religion in contrast to the serene stability offered by the simple truths of faith espoused by the church, I am concerned about the future of the church as a witness to those truths.

THE CRISIS IN THE SECOND CENTURY

The powerful controversies that swept the scattered Christian communities between 130 and 190 and created a crisis of identity happened long before Constantine made Christianity the imperial religion. Christians had no great buildings or wealth. Martyrdom was a real possibility for those whose convictions about Jesus were sufficiently powerful or public to irritate ruling authorities.

In the first part of the century, Ignatius, Polycarp, and Justin were leaders in a movement that had no state support, no cultural approval, and little by the way of central organization. How faith in Jesus Christ made a difference with respect to Judaism or Hellenism was still not clear. Although the letters of Paul, the Gospels, and some other early compositions had been exchanged for some time, and local communities gathered collections of apostolic writings, there was yet no need for a firm canon. And even though creedal statements were frequent, they were not yet much elaborated or standardized.

By the end of the century, though, teachers like Irenaeus of Lyons and Tertullian wrote extensive treatises against heretics on the basis of what they called the "rule of faith," argued for a set canon of Scripture, and located the teaching authority of the larger church in the bishops, regarded as the successors of the apostles.

I have two reasons for narrating this remarkable transition. The first is to raise the question concerning the shape of the tendencies within the church that generated such a decisive response. The second is because the same tendencies are powerful today but generate little effective response.

Irenaeus's tripod of creed, canon, and apostolic succession not only shaped Christian orthodoxy, but provided the strategy for Christian self-definition from the second to the twentieth century: whenever there was controversy over doctrine or morals, bishops met in council, debated and discerned the Scripture, and elaborated or defended the creed. The "new Gnosticism," as I call it, not only questions the shape of Christian faith, but does so by questioning this traditional strategy of response.

The first Gnosticism was a complex phenomenon, so complex that some scholars have suggested the term has outlived its usefulness. But some things are clear enough. Toward the middle of the second century, new revelations from Jesus were circulated in literature associated with well-placed Christian leaders and their followers. The literature claimed an understanding of reality superior to that found in the traditional writings, and an authority based in divine revelation. The Gospel of Thomas is today the best known of those compositions, but there were many others, including the Gospel of Truth and the Gospel of Philip.

Producing new literature was not itself an issue; the Christian movement had been vigorously literate from the first. But producing literature that claimed to arise from new revelations of Jesus (often to apostles after the resurrection) served to undermine the authority of the apostolic writings widely used in the churches. And the content of the new revelations also subverted the good news as found in those earliest writings.

Although it is impossible to systematize these revelations—indeed, much of Gnostic literature remains unintelligible to us—

they have certain common traits that, when combined, form an alternative version of Christianity. These common traits all arise from a fundamental dualism that privileges the spirit and deprecates the body. What is precious and salvageable in humans is the divine spark of spirit within them, the piece of the divine that somehow got lost and trapped in bodies. Through ignorance or malice, a lesser god created this material world.

Saving knowledge is the awareness—available only to the few—that they belong to a higher order of being. Christian Gnostics regard Jesus as the emissary from the light, the teacher-revealer who saves by sharing this knowledge of self-realization. The resurrection is not a matter of a body being exalted, but of a divine existence realized. Authentic Christian existence, then, is a form of individual mysticism, in which each individual cultivates the spirit and (as literally as possible) eliminates the flesh. Celibacy and fasting are the obvious mechanisms of liberation.

Gnostic literature placed Christianity within a more encompassing understanding of existence. The Nag Hammadi library makes no discrimination among writings that speak of Jesus and those that do not. Christianity is part of a universal scheme of revelation and salvation. What is true within it is universally available, for it is spirit. What is particular in it is false, for the particular is always material. In a very real sense, Gnosticism was an argument for spirituality over religion.

Gnostic teachers like Valentinus and Ptolemy were successful in purveying this vision through a variety of literary productions, and, perhaps even more significant, they were also adept at interpreting even the writings of the New Testament according to this dualistic code. In their reading of Paul, for example, "flesh" and "spirit" at war were read as the tension between an individual's body and soul, not as the conflict between attitudes driven by selfishness and those guided by God's Holy Spirit. "Opening the canon" to new writings, then, was more than a form of openness to new revelation; it was a strategy for reinterpreting earlier tradition in accord with the ideology found in the new writings.

The brilliance of the Gnostic position lay in its ability to claim a form of Christianity that was more inclusive (it was universal in scope) and at the same time a form of Christianity that was appropriately exclusive—it was obviously superior to that practiced by the ordinary folk (the *hylics*) who lacked the divine spark. Those who came to self-realization (*gnosis*) correspondingly participated in a larger world of spirituality while salvaging what was true in the partial revelation found in the traditional Scriptures. The Gnostics achieved "true" Christianity precisely by transcending it. Logically, then, Christians who insisted on the adequacy and ultimacy of the particular revelation of Christ found in the New Testament, by that very fact automatically showed themselves to be unenlightened. There is a polemic edge in Gnostic writings like the Gospel of Mary and the Gospel of Philip against the stupidities of the "apostolic men."

The second-century struggle over books was really a struggle over the identity of Christianity. For the orthodox party, the issue was which books should be read publicly in the assembly at worship; for the Gnostic party, the issue was whether something so public and physical as an assembly was even important.

The crisis over identity was not trivial, for the profound dualism of the Gnostics had several corollaries. If it's the spirit and not the body that counts, then it is the individual and not the assembly that matters. The messiness of life together is a distraction from the serious work of personal transformation.

Gnostics read their revelations in private or discuss them in small conventicles with those who are similarly enlightened. Participating in meaningless rituals with the great unwashed who mistake them with reality is hard on those who have passed (in their own minds) through the veil of appearances. Certainly there is no point to building the church as a public and political presence in the world, no point to the sharing of possessions—or having and raising children—not even any point to the witness of martyrdom. The spiritual refinement of the individual not the moral practice of the group is the point.

If only the spirit counts, then Jesus is important not because he revealed God in his body or died for our sins or showed us the pattern of radical obedience toward God and selfless love toward "the least of the brethren," but because his words contain timeless truths that assure me that all I need to do is look within to find the only important truth—that I am not like other people.

If this material creation is the work of a mischievous god, and if liberation means detachment from all materiality, then the visible and all too material church is clearly a perversion of the genuine good news, is indeed a continuation of that distorted revelation found in the Old Testament and continuing to be propagated by that most particular and physical and resistant of all peoples, the Jews.

And if the apostolic writings advance so particular a view of reality—that the Jews remain within God's plan, that Jesus became flesh, that resurrection means a future bodily existence, that the sacraments make God present in embodied fashion—then those writings need either to be abandoned or dramatically subverted by the higher revelation delivered by Gnostic literature.

The genius of Irenaeus was partly that he saw more clearly than anyone the need for a threefold strategy of response to this challenge: the claim of esoteric teachings he countered with the public rule of faith; the claim of secret gospels he countered with the writings read publicly in the assembly, the canon of Scripture (Old Testament as well as New); the claim of private teacher/revealers he countered with the public tradition of bishops extending from the apostles to his own day.

But his genius was also in constructing a coherent understanding of the creed, canon, and apostolic succession that was intellectually convincing and spiritually powerful. He elaborated a story of human existence from creation to resurrection as a continuous and progressive revelation of the one God who sought throughout to elevate humans to a share in his own life. Within that narrative, the church as a public body is not an inhibition to the spirit, but rather the essential vehicle for the spirit truly to work. Irenaeus's vision was sufficiently capacious to embrace the renewing movements of popular religious experience, the ardent quests of mystics and the adventurous speculations of theologians, within a visible, sacramental, institutional church.

THE CRISIS IN THE TWENTY-FIRST CENTURY

What I call the new Gnosticism does not resemble the old Gnosticism in every respect. There is little explicit rejection of the body, for example, and few claims to new and authoritative revelations from Jesus. But the new version does have real connections with the original, and, more important, it poses the same sort of challenge to the identity of the church in the twenty-first century that the original Gnosticism did in the second century.

The five features of the new Gnosticism that I describe—mostly based on my own observation and random reading—are generally well known and recognized, so I will be brief. What is most remarkable about this contemporary version, however, is that it is found among some members of virtually every Christian congregation in the United States, that it is found often among the most educated and committed members of these congregations, and that such members sense no incompatibility between these tendencies and classic Christian identity.

The saving knowledge that gives present-day Gnostics their sense of superiority to ordinary Christians does not derive from experiences of divine revelation but from initiation into the historical consciousness provided by higher education. By historical consciousness I don't mean the knowledge of historical events. I mean rather a set of perceptions about human life that are common to late-Enlightenment intellectuals. One of these perceptions is that there is no special revelation to one people that excludes others, or one special history; instead, every culture and people has its own special story.

Unenlightened people know only their own story and think it unique. The enlightened understand that all traditions are variations on a theme and rise above exclusive allegiance to a single version. To know and live by only one tradition is to be exposed as *hylic*. A vision that embraces the truth of all traditions is the mark of the Gnostic. It follows that traditional Christianity is false insofar as it is exclusive and is improved to the degree that it is elevated to a more universal view.

Another shared perception of the educated is that all transcendent claims can be reduced to the play of human politics. There is no arena of activity free from human self-interest, including religion. The hermeneutics of suspicion enables the detection of whose interest is at work in any historical development, and the recovery of other voices enables a more liberating politics for the present. "Liberating" often means precisely an expansion beyond the bonds of the material and the particular: women are "liberated" when they are not defined by biological or patriarchal imperatives but are free to develop as they choose.

These perceptions come together to form the contemporary Christian Gnosis. Not new divine revelations, but the historical recovery of the original Gnostic compositions, has provided the wedge to challenge the traditional canon, and with it, the traditional construction of Christian identity. Scholars calling themselves Christians write books that enjoy enormous popularity among the (educated) laity, not to defend or interpret the tradition, but to attack its foundations on the basis of the higher historical knowledge: the canon was the political work of patriarchal bishops; they excluded all the good writings that taught an inward spirituality (i.e., the larger view) in favor of those that focused on public behavior; they suppressed the female in favor of the male (read: suppressed the spiritual in favor of the institutional).

No one has been more successful at popularizing this view than Elaine Pagels, whose books are regularly reviewed by the *New York Times* and just as regularly—no surprise—appear on the *New York Times* best-seller list. How popular? A recent novel by Jim Harrison (*True North*) involves a guilt-ridden heir to an ill-gotten fortune whose theological education at Seabury-Western failed to provide relief or understanding. His only real spiritual help comes from his defrocked, randy, and alcoholic uncle who dabbles in world spiritualities. The uncle recommends Pagels's *Gnostic Gospels*, and in that book, the hero discovers a beautiful spirituality available in Christian clothing that the institutional church had kept from him. The only implausible element in this story is that the hero could have gotten through seminary without one of his professors recommending Pagels.

The specific historical-ideological argument embedded in scholarly and popular publications joins a widespread preference for the universal over the particular, for the spiritual over the religious among many present-day Christians who consider themselves well-educated, but whose specific knowledge of history and theology (or religion) is slight, making them the perfect target for the ersatz spirituality and scholarship hawked at Barnes & Noble. And these tendencies among the educated elite also connect to the even more widespread and intense individualism that has affected even the most traditional and conservative Christians, who increasingly think of religion in terms of personal salvation and individual satisfaction rather than in terms of communal commitment and shared practice, and who prefer retreat and workshop and small-group discussion with the like-minded to the messiness and confusion (and yes, small-mindedness) of the local parish.

The four characteristics I have enumerated—superior knowledge given by historical consciousness, individualism, preference for universal over particular, and preference for spirituality over religion—amount to a new form of dualism, corresponding roughly to the ancient Gnostic dislike of the body. The contemporary dualism dislikes the embodiedness that is institution. The effect of the hermeneutics of suspicion is most obvious here. The structures that make up tradition are not considered as a gift from the past, but a burden on the present and a shackle holding back the future.

The pervasive prejudice against ecclesiastical institutions is exacerbated when bishops and priests are regularly exposed as less well read than the laity and, alas, not markedly more moral. In recent years, the same anti-institutional bias has strengthened an antipathy toward canon and creed. For many Christians, it is now axiomatic that the New Testament canon is a political tool and inadequate to a fully mature spirituality. For some Christians, especially those for whom history has become the criterion of all truth and who have embraced the various versions of the historical Jesus, the Nicene Creed is increasingly unintelligible and alien, easily regarded as another instrument by which the ancient episcopate distorted Christianity.

THE UNCERTAIN FUTURE

Many of these tendencies have been around for some time, but they have come together in recent years in a particularly forceful way. But because of the convergence of two factors, the challenge they pose now to the future of the church as a visible and coherent witness to the good news of God in Jesus Christ is real and severe.

The first factor is the already reduced significance of the institutional church in the lives of most Christians. Already, the church is not the exclusive or the most trusted source of religious truth. Already, laity are better and more widely educated than the clergy—in Protestantism as well as Catholicism—and are open to the learning available from other sources. Already, many Christians regard the church, not as the essential community by which their lives are defined, but as one among other voluntary associations that provide certain services in a competitive market.

The second factor is the doubtful capacity of present church leadership to respond in the manner of Irenaeus and Tertullian, by making an argument for the sacramental church, with its Creed and canon and visible leadership that is intellectually coherent and morally convincing. The hierarchy appears to be so obsessed with its own power—especially with regard to women—that the feminist argument concerning the ancient bishops seems all too obvious, and the craven behavior of the hierarchy in response to the sexual scandals of the recent years has further eroded confidence in official leadership.

But even scarier for those who love the richness of the orthodox tradition is the obvious lack of intellectual breadth or depth among the church's official teachers—and for that matter, among contemporary theologians. Where are the successors of the creative and faithful theologians and scholars—many of them priests, some even bishops—of the Second Vatican Council? Perhaps there are a few. But do *they* have successors? The *Catechism of the Catholic Church* is useful. Papal encyclicals have their place. But they are isolated spasms of intellectual activity in a great and fearful desert of mediocrity.

Irenaeus became bishop of Lyons because his predecessor was martyred. Being Christian was still a dangerous occupation. When Irenaeus wrote *Against Heresies*, he thoroughly understood his opponents' views—indeed, he made more sense of them than they deserved—and responded with a deep sense of loyalty to the tradition he had received, an ability to support that tradition from an exhaustive grasp of Scripture, an outstanding dialectical ability, and even humor. Above all, he responded with a vision of the world as God's place of self-revelation, and of the church as witness to that revelation, which made the pretensions of the Gnostics back then appear as puny and unattractive alternatives to that tradition.

Is it possible, in the present situation, to hope for champions of the tradition with such courage and passion, with such intelligence and imagination? If not, then neither is there much human reason to hope for a future of the church that is continuous with the church of the apostles.

14

INTELLECTUAL FREEDOM AND CATHOLIC THEOLOGIANS

Originally published in Commonweal *133, no. 1 (2006): 10–14.*

Suppose we indulge our fondest hopes. Let us imagine that Pope Benedict XVI turns out to be quite unlike what many expected, and that he embraces a spirit of theological openness and generosity within the church. No longer would a respected and respectful editor of a Jesuit journal be removed for the sin of advocating fairness; no more would a leading theological ethicist be removed from a tenured position, or a systematic theologian be quelled by threat of the same.

In this new atmosphere, local pastors would no longer be called to account in Rome on the basis of parishioners' calls to the bishop (as priest friends of mine have been), scholars (like me) would not be disinvited to conferences on Aquinas because they criticized John Paul's *Theology of the Body*, or asked to sign a statement that they would not do anything to "embarrass the Church" when lecturing at a university, or on the basis of other anonymous calls, be warned by the vicar-general of an archbishop who is now a cardinal, against being "soft on the bodily resurrection" of Christ when teaching New Testament to adult Catholics. All this would disappear.

The "big chill" within contemporary Catholicism includes all those mechanisms, overt and covert, by which the Vatican has deliberately sought to suppress theological intelligence and imagination in the name of doctrinal and moral correctness. Now suppose all these measures stopped because Benedict XVI turned out, not to be John Paul II's attack dog, but rather someone who actually moderated the previous pope's repressive instincts, and now, in his own pontificate, seeks to encourage the gifts that formerly he was thought to suppress. Would the church then be in a state beatific? Would a healthy balance between magisterial authority and theological inquiry then be struck?

I am not sanguine. For one thing, the chill has become systemic. The episcopacy shaped by John Paul II will continue to perpetuate its fearful distrust of the life of the theological mind all on its own. Priests get out of line at their peril; priests teaching theology either self-censor or are removed from their position. Defenders of the DFC argue that this is a matter of "truth in advertising"—Catholic theologians in Catholic colleges should teach the way the church says they should teach. But this is convincing only if "theology" is reduced to "catechesis." Catholic theologians who are not priests, in turn, are being silenced in another but equally effective fashion, which is simply not paying them any attention.

And the chill has become pervasive, permeating to more distant and lower regions. A recent *Chronicle of Higher Education* reports that the Cardinal Newman Society is demanding the firing of eighteen faculty members in Catholic colleges who represent, in its view, the "culture of death" because they supported the removal of Terry Schiavo's feeding tube. In my own quite moderate parish of Sacred Heart in Atlanta, the effort to form faith-sharing groups during "Renewal 2000" was almost derailed by lay voices fearful of the doctrinal chaos that might result from lay Catholics talking together about Scripture without a clerical monitor, as though the point of faith sharing was doctrine in the first place, and as though the laity today—better educated than in any previous generation, and often enough better educated in theology than some of the clergy—are not able to exercise critical judgment on matters of faith away from clerical control.

Most of all, though, if we focus our hope for the church on the personality or policy proclivities of this or the last or the next pope, we simply perpetuate the Vatican's own tendency to equate the church with the magisterium and the magisterium with the pope, and strengthen the conviction that all theological wisdom must spring from a single source. This fixation is problematic even if—perhaps especially—we grant that John Paul II and Benedict XVI are genuine and even important theologians. What is saddest about this is the steady theological impoverishment of the church as a whole, precisely at a time when the task of articulating the church's faith in the world is urgent and daunting, demanding the best gifts of theological intelligence and imagination that any of us can contribute. The effort to control theological debate reflects little trust in the capacity of theologians to criticize each other—something they have never been reluctant to do—and even less trust in the best-educated laity in Catholic history that is hungry for an intellectual engagement with the faith that is not condensed and condescending.

THE CHURCH

CONDITIONS CHRONIC AND ACUTE

The crisis of intellectual freedom and institutional responsibility within the church has become acute, but it is rooted in chronic systemic conditions that require serious and sustained analysis. In this essay I am able only to suggest a framework for thinking about a way forward. We might be able to work together more fruitfully to enable a healthier theological ecology in the church if we recognize certain basic issues that require candid conversation among all those who love the church. I propose that Christianity bears within itself certain intractable tensions that cannot be resolved completely without diminishing the community's life in one way or another, and that the church is healthier when the disparate values that push against each other are allowed full play. I also suggest that the New Testament provides distinct metaphors for the church and its role in God's revelation, that one of these metaphors is inappropriately dominant today, and that a greater appreciation of the other metaphor would help us imagine a way to celebrate and negotiate a livelier theological life within the church.

Every version of Christianity in every age must struggle with deep intrinsic tensions that derive from its peculiar and paradoxical character. On one side, there is what we might call the resurrection principle: the powerful gift of the Holy Spirit that comes from the exalted Lord Jesus pushes believers toward transformation and growth, toward the exercise of spiritual gifts and of responsible freedom in response to the urgings of the spirit. "The Lord is the Spirit," declares Paul, "and where the spirit of the Lord is, there is freedom" (2 Cor 3:17). This resurrection principle asserts God's own sovereignty and freedom, as revealed in the death and resurrection of Jesus, which transcended all previous human understanding of the law and prophets. And because this spirit of freedom comes from the Lord and not from humans, its exercise must ultimately be responsible to the Lord rather than to humans. Peter faced the duly constituted religious leaders of his day, and when told to stop preaching in the name of Jesus, invoked the witness of the Holy Spirit in his response: "We must obey God rather than humans" (Acts 5:29–32).

On the other side is what might be called the incarnational principle. Christianity is embodied in the same way that the human Jesus was embodied, which means that, like Jesus himself, the church is always particular, historical, and conditioned by the social realities of each age in which it exists. The church is a "clay vessel" and the glory of God shines through the cracks of its fragility (2 Cor 4:7). The church does not exist in an ideal plane removed from the mess of embodied and social existence. In sociological terms, it has always been an intentional community that continues in existence because of the commitment of its members. It is, therefore, an inherently unstable community. Those who grasp this also appreciate that tradition is a delicate business. Tradition does not seek to live in the past, but to remember the past in order to secure a future, and therefore, tradition needs carefully and respectfully to be tended.

Of all Christian communities, Catholics have best understood this embodied dimension of the faith. Catholics celebrate Irenaeus's triad of self-definition: Creed, canon, and apostolic succession. For Catholics, *institution* and *authority* are not terms of opprobrium any more than are *sacrament* and *saint*, and for the same reasons. Catholics consider it is axiomatic that the diverse movements of the spirit must be discerned, and that freedom is not absolute but a matter of service to the truth, and that boundaries must both be set and maintained by ecclesial authority, if the church is to be faithful to its socially embodied as well as its spiritual character.

As the long history of heresy and schism within the church has shown, maintaining a healthy tension has never been easy.

Those who value tradition and good order have found it convenient to regard impulses toward liberty as a dangerous enthusiasm. And those who treasure freedom and creativity have dismissed the concern for tradition as legalism and authoritarianism. It is extraordinarily difficult to honor equally both impulses, both sets of values.

The difficulty has become acute since the Second Vatican Council. Here was a case in which the spirit of theological openness and imagination, which had survived in the shadows cast by the war against modernism, was invited into the highest deliberations of the church and honored, as bishops sat as students of theologians who had somehow survived that earlier ice age. More than that, the spirit of open inquiry seemed even to have been institutionalized by the council's statements on ecumenism, collegiality, the role of the laity, and religious liberty. The fifty years since the council, in contrast, have seen a steady retreat from the spirit of intellectual freedom. Censorship is justified by some as a necessary response to the excesses of enthusiasm and creativity unleashed by the council. But others see it as a betrayal of the spirit of the council, and indeed, of the Holy Spirit, less a necessary adjustment in the direction of tradition than a deliberate suppression of freedom for the sake of power.

The present situation is acute above all because values that should be mutual and held in balance are championed as though they were opposed to each other. As a result, we too often find ourselves in a state of polarization rather than collaboration. Those who emphasize the value of freedom and the spirit of theological inquiry can so exaggerate that value as to obscure the value of loyalty to tradition. And those who value loyalty to tradition sometimes speak and act in ways suggesting that intellectual freedom is a luxury too dangerous for the church to afford. It is, indeed, increasingly difficult to assert a middle position in which theological inquiry and intellectual freedom is understood as essential to a genuine loyalty, and loyalty is understood as requiring intellectual integrity—that is, freedom. More than that, it is increasingly difficult in this contentious environment, to be perceived by others as combining both loyalty and freedom in such reciprocal service.

Exacerbating the ideological polarization is a tendency on both sides to deny the need to make distinctions between what is of lesser and greater importance in the practice of the faith. On the left, making such distinctions smacks of intolerance, and in the name of freedom, all boundaries are ignored if not denied. And on the right, making such distinctions is regarded as tantamount to eroding the faith: everything is of equal importance, with no distinction possible without the loss of everything. But such polarization profoundly threatens the integrity of theology within the church, which thrives precisely on the making of distinctions, and on the delicate negotiation of fidelity to tradition and openness to new understandings of tradition.

Theology has always differed from catechesis precisely in this, that its role was not simply to transmit the faith but also to interrogate the faith in the name of and on behalf of truth. Without catechesis, theological imagination can run amok into an amorphous spirituality. I have written recently in these pages about "the new Gnosticism," and proponents such as Matthew Fox are easy to spot. But without theology, catechesis can become a sterile repetition of formulas that become less and less intelligible for not being interrogated. The experience of watching Trinity Broadcasting is literally stupefying, and the rigidity and fear found among Steubenville graduates does not give encouragement.

The greatest theologians in the church, from Origen through Aquinas to Rahner, have claimed this delicate and dangerous place as their specific service to the church. All of them were profoundly loyal to the tradition and could, in sermon and in lesson, express that faith with utter simplicity, and in their lives, expressed that faith in lives of genuine discipleship. But each of them was also willing, indeed, impelled, to bring the most stringent questioning to the tradition, questioning generated by the circumstances of Christians in their age.

Do those who now regard Thomism as fundamental for Christian theology not understand how radical and dangerous a thinker Saint Thomas Aquinas was? Do they not recognize that his willingness to address the wisdom of the nations (Greeks and Muslims) and allow the tradition to be challenged by Aristotle required a kind of loyalty to tradition and an intellectual integrity that could never be commanded or controlled from the outside but could find its resolution only by giving his great mind and heart the liberty to find a way to a new expression of the good news? Do they not see that the best way to imitate Thomas is to engage, with equal fidelity and creativity, the intellectual challenges posed by our own day? Can we really suppose that there is no wisdom God wants us to learn from the movements for women's liberation, for democracy, for freedom of conscience? Is not the challenge presented by evolution at least as great as that posed by Muslim philosophers of the Middle Ages?

THE CHURCH AND REVELATION

No less are theologians today obliged to ask hard questions in the language of this age concerning the truth of the gospel, not in order to erode or compromise that truth, but precisely in order to let its splendor be more powerfully manifest. Among the hard questions into which theologians of this age, as of every age, are obliged to inquire is the ways in which the structures and processes of the church itself best serve the truth of the gospel, or how they might need to be reformed, not in capitulation to the capricious desires of a single generation, but in obedience to the Living God who calls the church in every age to a deeper and more creative fidelity. Theologians best make such inquiry not as a way of asserting their own importance but as a way of serving the church and its Lord. And theologians best pose hard questions to the church not out of the ethos of their own age (though the pressing concerns of their age are not irrelevant), but out of the Spirit-inspired Scriptures by which the church claims to be guided.

Pertinent to the present situation, as I suggested above, are two distinct understandings of the church and its relation to God's revelation. Both understandings (or metaphors or models) are found in the New Testament—indeed, both are found in the letters of Paul. Both contain genuine, even indispensable values. But the relation of the church to revelation is distinct in each. In one, there seems to be little place for the theologian. In the other, the role of the theologian is critical. I want to argue that one model has today almost totally eclipsed the other, and that a renewed appreciation for both as held in a creative tension might show us a way to think about the role of the theologian in the church.

One metaphor for the church is the household. The image has roots in the metaphor of "house" for the people of Israel but is even more directly connected to the Hellenistic household (*oikos*) in which early Christians gathered as an assembly (*ekklesia*). The image leads naturally to thinking of the church in terms of authority—moving from top to bottom as in the patriarchal household of antiquity—and good order. The image is especially associated with the Pastoral Epistles. Paul tells his delegate Timothy to tend to "how one ought to behave in the household of God, which is the church of the living God" (1 Tim 3:15). By no means is the image disconnected from the power of the Holy Spirit. Paul elsewhere speaks of the Corinthian community as "God's building" (1 Cor 3:9) and as "God's temple" since "God dwells among you" (1 Cor 3:16). But the metaphor's entailments move in the direction of an administration of "God's mysteries" by those, like Paul and Apollos, who are "servants and household managers" (1 Cor 4:1). And in the Pastoral Letters, when Paul is faced with deviant teaching that threatens the truth of the gospel, the image serves to help secure a chain of authority that will preserve the deposit of the faith (2 Tim 1:13; 2:2). Already in these letters, we see Paul speaking of the "supervisor" (*episkopos* = bishop) of the community in terms analogous to the head of the household: the moral and intellectual qualities appropriate in one are appropriate in the other as well (1 Tim 3:1–7; Titus 1:7–9).

This model of the church is positive and powerful and does some things very well. It is good at preserving tradition and passing it on to new generations and protecting it from massive distortion through false teaching. What the model does not do well is provide for contributions from others than the head of the household or learn from those outside the household. Small wonder that this image proved so attractive to a Christianity that first sought to secure its place in the world. It maintained the boundaries of the "household of faith" over against the rival claims of Jew and Gentile, and, already in the second century, over against the confusions perpetrated by heretics.

In Catholicism, the image of the household has been merged with a strongly juridical reading of Matthew 16:18–19, which reports Jesus designating Peter as the rock on which "I will build [as a house = *oikodomeso*] my church [*ekklesia*]," and gives Peter the keys of the kingdom of heaven and the power to bind and loose. Ecclesial development in Catholicism has tended toward the establishment of the Bishop of Rome as the supreme "head of the household of the faith." Just as Caesar was the *paterfamilias* of a worldwide household, the *oikoumene*, so the pope is the *paterfamilias* of the ecumenical church. The line of authority—and of teaching—moves downward from pope to bishops to priests to laity.

Even in the best of circumstances (assuming the integrity and intelligence of the hierarchy), what this arrangement does best is catechesis: the handing on of the tradition as it has already been formed. If we understand God's revelation in static terms as doctrinal and moral and ascetic teaching, and as adequately contained in such teaching, then this arrangement may suffer from a certain inevitable stagnation and rigidity, but it cannot be accused of being negligent with respect to God's word. But even here, when the pope is not only final arbiter of fidelity to the deposit of faith but also its only source of theological reinterpretation, there is surely at least an impoverishment of the church's theological life.

But catechesis does not embrace all of theology. And the premise that revelation is closed is simply wrong. To think thus would be to adhere to a dead rather than a Living God. If Jesus truly shares the life of God as "life-giving spirit" (1 Cor 15:45), then we must consider that God, through Jesus Christ, can continue to reach us in new ways, and must conclude that revelation as open and continuing in the world, specifically in human experience. And if God acts in human stories both within and outside the structures of the church, then the church's relationship to revelation is not simply that of protector and purveyor. The church must also find a way to become an effective interpreter of God's self-disclosure in the world and seek to be faithfully obedient to the word of God that is spoken in and through human lives. This is not a plea for the privileging of every private human experience. Not every human story reveals God. But it is a plea to consider the implications of the millions of stories of believers (such as women and homosexuals) whom the church has persisted in regarding as "objects" to be "explained" rather than subjects, and persons through whose struggles the Holy Spirit speaks a word to the church.

Paul's letters offer another image of the church that is no less embodied than that of the household, but that is more directly responsive to the resurrection character of Christian existence. This is the metaphor of the "body of Christ," which Paul uses for the church in Romans 12:4–5, Colossians 1:18, and Ephesians 1:23; 2:16; 4:16; 5:23–28, but develops most fully in 1 Corinthians 12:4–31. It should be noted at once that Paul does not oppose this image to that of the household. We find the images side by side in 1 Corinthians 6:15–18, and even merged in Ephesians 2:16–22. He plainly regards the metaphors as compatible and complementary. But they are not identical; each image captures a distinct set of values. That of the household, I have suggested, communicates the values of authority and order and the passing on of tradition in a way that the image of the body cannot. So the question arises: What values does the image of the Body of Christ communicate that the metaphor of the household cannot?

Most obviously, it sees the church as a living organism immediately and intimately joined to the risen Lord Jesus as its source of life, and as intimately and immediately directed by the Holy Spirit in its activities (1 Cor 12:4–6). Paul emphasizes the diversity in unity that should characterize the body. No member can replace or do the work of another, and the work of each member should be for the well-being and growth of the body as a whole: "To each is given the manifestation of the Spirit for the common good" (12:7). Nor can any member of the body dismiss another as useless; all are needed: "If the whole body were an eye, where would be the sense of hearing? If the whole body were an ear, where would be the sense of smell? But as it is, God has arranged the organs in the body, each one of them, as he chose." Thus Paul provides a list that includes apostles, but also prophets and teachers. Their gifts are not identical, nor are their roles. He lists also gifts of healing and governance and speaking in tongues and interpretation; these also are not all seated in one member but are distributed according to the will of the Holy Spirit (12:28–30).

Paul sees some of these gifts, moreover, as having a specific role regarding the continuing revelation of God's word in the assembly. The Corinthians are attracted to the spectacular gift of speaking in tongues, but Paul insists on the greater importance of a "revelation or knowledge or prophecy or teaching" (14:6). The revelatory function is not restricted to the apostle, but is dispersed throughout the assembly: "When you come together, each one has a hymn, a lesson, a revelation, a tongue, or an interpretation" (14:26). Paul places particular emphasis on the gift of prophecy, a form of public discourse that, in contrast to tongues, makes use of the mind (14:14–19). Prophecy both builds the church within (14:4) and convinces outsiders that God is truly present in the faith community (14:20–25).

Paul does not think of the spiritual gifts exercised by the community as being without norm or good order. They must cohere with the confession that Jesus is Lord (12:3) and must build rather than tear down the community (3:16–17; 14:5), and all the gifts should be practiced "decently and in order" (14:40). All spiritual utterances must be discerned. Paul tells the Thessalonians, "Do not quench the Spirit. Do not despise prophecy. But test everything" (1 Thess 5:19–21). But this testing or discerning is carried out by the whole community rather than by governors or administrators only. The utterances of prophets, Paul says, "are subject to the prophets" (1 Cor 14:32). When a word is publicly declared in the assembly, he adds, "Let the others discern" (14:29). The process of discernment, like the gift of prophecy itself, is public and serves to build up the community. To do this, discernment must also be carried out by the entire community. This role of discernment is the one gift that Paul implies is universally distributed in the community, to be exercised by all.

If the metaphor of the household excels at catechesis but lacks a capacity to respond to God's ongoing revelation, the metaphor of the Body of Christ excels at responding to the prompting of the Holy Spirit among all the faithful, but lacks a capacity for consistent communication of the tradition. The two images are complementary rather than in competition. But it might be appropriate to ask which image is more capacious, that is, can include the other within itself. Here, I think it is clear that the image of the Body of Christ that can encompass the positive dimensions of the other image—remember that governance and administration and teaching are among the gifts—whereas the image of the household finds little or no place for the diversity of gifts among all the faithful. We can also ask which image is more adequate to the good news of the resurrected Christ, and again our answer would necessarily be the metaphor of Christ's body, which lives and is directed by the Holy Spirit that comes from the resurrected Lord. Above all, the image of the church as the Body of Christ allows for gifts and speech and discernment among all the faithful, rather than simply a few officials, and for an openness to God's continuing self-disclosure, rather than simply the transmission of truths already learned. The church is not simply a place where precedents are handed down, but a place where God's word for the world can find expression in new ways.

THE ROLE OF THE THEOLOGIAN

I am not suggesting that theologians in the church today should be regarded as prophets, although some may be. Rather, I suggest that the image of the church as the Body of Christ provides a framework for our thinking about the role of the theologian. If God's self-revelation continues in the world in and through the lives of humans both in and outside the church, and if the church is obliged to respond to God's self-disclosure with faithful obedience, then the church needs all the eyes and ears and hands and *minds* it can get, for the practice of discerning God's word is constant and demanding.

In some fashion, as I have argued extensively in my book *Scripture and Discernment: Decision Making in the Church* (Nashville: Abingdon, 1996), all in the church should practice theology, in the sense that all are called to discern and bear witness to the ways in which God is at work in their lives, and all are needed to help the community as a whole discern how God's

Holy Spirit is moving within and around them in the circumstances of their lives, so that they might respond faithfully as a community to the Living God. The term *church* is distorted when it is made to refer only to the universal organization and not first of all to the local assembly, where the Spirit can first be discerned, and discernment can then rise to various levels, reaching at least the universal level. The Catholic principle of subsidiarity ought to apply to the inner life of faith communities. The pope's authority, in short, ought not to preempt such a process of discernment at every level of the church, but ought rather to respond to it.

A special place in this process is held by those whose charism and training enables them both to take part in this process of discernment of real-life experience, and to engage in critical reflection on the ways in which this discernment is in continuity or discontinuity with the tradition of the church, not only in canon and Creed, but also in the teaching of the magisterium through the ages. The task of carrying on this delicate conversation requires spiritual gifts, to be sure, but also requires great learning. It is not enough to be a skilled listener of human stories; the theologian must also know the tradition in great depth and breadth if the conversation between the present and the past is to be healthy and productive, and "build the church."

The theologian must be more than a catechist if the church is to be a place where God's living word is to be articulated in and for the world. To demand of the theologian that he or she be nothing more than a catechist, one who hands down what is already known, is to "quench the spirit" and "despise prophecy" (1 Thess 5:19). To require of theologians that they strip themselves of all critical intelligence and imagination so that they present no danger and better serve the church is actually to place the church in a position of much greater danger, namely of not responding to the work of the Holy Spirit in the world.

Is the free employment of critical thinking and theological imagination dangerous? Of course, just as all true living is dangerous. There are, to be sure, dangers from ignorance and arrogance. Theologians are no more exempt from sin than are bishops. But there are even greater dangers in engaging the Living God with human speech at all. The Letter to the Hebrews reminds us that "falling into the hands of the living God is a fearful thing" (10:31). But within the church as the Body of Christ, the dangers of false prophecy are mitigated by the practice of discernment by all in the community, especially of other prophets. Theologians are capable of discernment and require of themselves to respond to faulty thinking and fatuous imagination. And if theologians are loyal as well as critical—as we should always assume until it is absolutely necessary to conclude otherwise—they also understand that their thought and imagination must also be in constructive conversation with the church's catechists, above all the hierarchy.

THE STARK REALITY

The image of the church as the Body of Christ, in which a diversity of gifts is celebrated and practiced in a harmonious reciprocity of revelation and discernment that builds the church, is no longer operative. It has totally been swallowed by the metaphor of the household. This model has no place for the role of the prophet or of the theologian, for all teaching comes from the top down. And today, this hierarchical model is more rigid than ever. For a vast number of Catholics, especially younger Catholics, it is axiomatic that the pope is not only chief pastor but also sole theologian, with the rest of the hierarchy serving as stages of transmission to a passive laity. On every matter, the pope is not only the last word (arguably a legitimate and even necessary role) but also the first word (arguably a dreadful displacement of ecclesial functions).

The timing could not be worse. The current efforts to suppress every theological voice except that emanating from Rome is both more effective and more appalling because of the loss of theological talent and commitment elsewhere. Bishops of the past may not have been universally gifted with great minds or bold spirits—their job, after all, was to administer, shepherd, and catechize—but there were always prophetic voices to be heard among them. Religious orders like the Jesuits and Dominicans specialized in producing fine theological minds in the service of the church. But not only have these orders been particularly targeted for control, their diminished and aging ranks do not have the talent they once did. As for diocesan priests, the talent pool for the future episcopacy, the kindest thing that can be said is that the tradition of the learned clergy is lost. Some of the best theological talent available to the church today is found outside the clergy. But if they teach in Catholic colleges or seminaries, they are placed under strict control. If they teach in Protestant or secular schools, they are largely ignored.

The theological impoverishment of the church today is real and, if something is not changed, will undoubtedly get worse. The best minds and most loyal hearts in the church will either wilt, or increasingly absent themselves from a system that seeks to chill all critical intelligence and imagination. It may be too much to hope that the present model of the church as household can open itself to a healthy conversation with the image of the church as the living Body of the resurrected Christ, particularly if the present heads of household think that theirs is the only model that is true to revelation and that to alter anything is to endanger everything. But they are wrong. The alternative (and, I insist, complementary) image of the church is if anything truer to the good news as found in Scripture than the dominant model. Those of us who long for a church in which it is possible to be both smart and holy, both loyal and critical, live in hope that something of this vision might gain recognition. But suppose the big chill continues, through the papacy of Benedict XVI (despite our fondest hopes) and the papacies to follow. What can theologians do? They can continue to speak prophecy and to practice discernment among God's people. What is at stake is the integrity of the church's witness to the Living God.

15

CHRISTIANS AND JEWS

Starting Over

Originally published in Commonweal *130, no. 2 (2003): 15–19.*

How should Christians think about Jews? Or better, how should Christians think about themselves with reference to Judaism? This will always be a necessary question for Christians to ask and will never be an easy question for them to answer.

It is a necessary question because Christians and Jews each lay claim to a body of sacred texts and the story found in them as their texts and their story, but they do so in such different terms that each claim appears to challenge the other. It is necessary as well because Jews and Christians share a history of internecine rivalry. The primal trauma experienced by the first Christians is expressed in the New Testament's polemic against nonbelieving Jews. Christian payback extends across the long centuries of anti-Semitism supported and even sponsored by the church. It is necessary also because the Holocaust of the twentieth century and the subsequent rise of the state of Israel have fundamentally altered the terms of the conversation.

Recent exchanges in this and other journals indicate that the question remains as difficult as ever to address from either side. Even as many Jewish scholars and religious leaders seek a more informed and less inflammatory context for constructive conversation (see *Christianity in Jewish Terms*, 2000), other Jewish scholars and religious leaders find additional reasons for rage, not only because of the uncovering of historical evidence concerning the church's role in the Holocaust, but because of the Vatican's obtuseness in pursuing the canonization of Pius IX, Pius XII, and Edith Stein (see "Continuing the Conversation: The Church and Daniel Goldhagen," *Commonweal* [March 8, 2002]: 7–8). Christian voices are equally divided and perhaps even more confused, as indicated by the recent exchange in *America* (October 21, 2002) between Avery Dulles ("Covenant and Mission," 8–11)—who thinks that, despite everything, Christians should still proselytize Jews—and members of the Christian Scholars Group of Jewish-Christian Relations (Mary Boys, Philip Cunningham, and John Pawlikowski)—who defend their statement that "revising Christian teaching about Judaism and the Jewish people is a central and indispensable obligation of theology in our time" ("Theology's Sacred Obligation," 12–16).

In this essay, I do not hope to answer the question of how Christians should think about Jews, because I think that is the wrong way to put the question. I hope instead to suggest a way that Christians might begin to think of themselves with reference to Jews. If Christianity is not supersessionist, is it anything? I think so. But discovering what Christianity is apart from supersessionism will require more work and clearer thinking than has usually been in evidence.

THE CHARM OF SUPERSESSIONISM

It is an odd word, *supersessionism*. The *Oxford Dictionary of the Christian Church*, a reference work that defines almost everything, has no entry for it. The term is used for the conviction that Christianity has replaced Israel as God's chosen people. Israel has lost its place and Christianity now occupies it. Supersessionism is shorthand for the dominant Christian theological position regarding the Jews.

The claim that supersessionism is already explicit in the writings of the New Testament is an exaggeration. The New Testament, it is true, provides plenty of ammunition for later supersessionist arguments. Avery Dulles's recent use of Hebrews shows how easy such appropriation is ("Covenant and Mission," 10). But the New Testament compositions were not written from a position of Christian superiority to Judaism. They were, rather, composed in the context of competition between sects within the framework of Judaism. For Dulles to speak of Hebrews as "the most formal statement on the status of the Sinai covenant under Christianity," is at the very least, anachronistic.

Supersessionism in the proper sense emerges in the middle and late second century, when Christianity had become almost entirely Gentile, and when history seemed to be running against the Jews. The failed Jewish war against Rome in 67–70 and the suppression of the Bar Kochba Revolt in 135 meant the destruction of Jerusalem and its temple, and the apparently permanent scattering of the people. Justin Martyr, Origen, and Tertullian make the explicit claim that the Jews have been displaced as God's people and replaced by Christians.

The claim seemed to be magnificently confirmed by historical events. As the Gospels show, Jesus fulfilled the messianic prophecies of Scripture in great detail. In Matthew, everything from Jesus's virgin birth to his betrayal for money fulfilled specific prophecies (Matt 1:22–23; 27:9–10). The embarrassing fact that Jesus did *not* fulfill other messianic prophecies—in particular, those predicting a triumphant rule over Israel's enemies—was managed by hermeneutical sleight of hand: those prophecies concerned Jesus's second coming, not his first. Jesus's own prophecies had even more impressively been confirmed by history: the temple had been destroyed just as he had predicted, and the people had been punished and scattered. The gospel, moreover, had been proclaimed to the Gentiles and received by them (see Mark 13:1–37; Matt 24:1–51; Luke 21:5–36). Real historical events confirmed Jesus's status as prophet. They also showed the emptiness of Jewish counterclaims. How could Jewish messianic expectations be accomplished when there was no longer a temple and no longer a people on the land, and when the failed Bar Kochba uprising had proven how futile was the hope for a Jewish king?

As the sole legitimate heirs of the biblical promises, Christians had the right and the obligation—so they supposed—to define those whom they had supplanted, especially since Jews themselves seemed to ignore the clear lessons of history and insisted on persisting. How can such odd obduracy be understood? What might God have in mind? Do they survive in order to bear the curse they brought on themselves for the death of Jesus? Is their continued presence an object lesson? Whatever conclusion Christian theologians reached, they assumed that their historical victory gave them the right to define Judaism in Christian terms.

HISTORY'S LITTLE TURNS

Things have changed. Christianity today is the world's largest religion, but it can no longer claim to be history's darling. Four developments in recent centuries suggest that history has abandoned Christians. First, world exploration revealed how tiny a territory—and how short a time span—Christians and Jews had been debating: history and geography no longer fit in the frame of the Bible. Most humans on the planet also needed to be considered. Second, while the Enlightenment toppled revelation generally from its throne and installed human reason in its place,

Christianity was secular reason's special target. Third, the age of revolution removed Christianity's political clout, making it no more than one more competitor for secondary allegiance within the secular state. Fourth, the Holocaust of the mid-twentieth century revealed the moral rot in Christian consciousness concerning Jews. The logic of isolation and exclusion that had been Christian policy for centuries found diabolical expression in the machinery of concentration camps and mass murder. In the face of these jolting historical realities, many Christians find it harder to maintain theological smugness.

Even worse—from the perspective of supersessionism—the same historical turns that toppled Christianity from its place gave Judaism a place of its own. The state of Israel is not only an unexpected, perhaps unprecedented, historical resurrection of an ancient nation, it enables Jews to read the Bible again as something more than the revelation of God's commandments. They can once more read Torah as the story of a people and a land pointing to a fulfillment in present-day Jews as the people on that land. A keystone of Christian supersessionism was the impossibility of reading Torah in terms of material fulfillment. With the appearance of the state of Israel, that argument disappears (see, e.g., E. Fackenheim, *The Jewish Bible after the Holocaust*).

WHO'S LAUGHING NOW?

After the necessary time of silence and witness following the Holocaust, the classical forms of Jewish observance and thought have reappeared with new vigor and confidence. The Talmudic tradition thrives in the open market and exercises political influence in Israel. Jewish scholars' engagement with the Torah is on their own terms rather than on the terms dictated by Christians. They celebrate the breadth and fecundity of Midrashic study in contrast to the narrowness and aridity of historicism. Although many Jewish scholars are deeply interested in Christianity as another way of reading Torah, they approach conversation not as the rejected but as the elder child, fully confident of the special place of this people before its God. They simply do not need to take Christians into account in order to account for themselves.

Christians, in contrast, find themselves deeply divided in their responses to the changed historical circumstances. On one side we find Christians acting as though nothing significant has changed. Many evangelicals seek the conversion of Jews to Christianity. Many millenarians find the state of Israel a welcome bit of fuel for the final conflagration: having a literal landscape for Armageddon helps enormously when charting the course of the final days.

Roman Catholics vacillate. The Second Vatican Council's *Nostra Aetate*, for example, disavows any basis in Scripture for regarding Jews as "repudiated or cursed by God," but precedes that line with the bald statement, "the Church is the new people of God." And while deploring "the hatred, persecutions, and displays of anti-Semitism directed against the Jews at any time and from any source," it fails to acknowledge the church as one of those sources and takes no account of the Holocaust or the papacy's less-than-stellar performance in the face of the Nazi regime (*Nostra Aetate* 4). Small wonder that one Jewish respondent (Rabbi David Polish) called the declaration "a unilateral pronouncement by one party which presumes to redress on its own terms a wrong that it does not admit" (cited by Claud Nelson in *The Documents of Vatican II* [1966] 669–70). The same combination of contrition and obtuseness has characterized subsequent Vatican statements and gestures down to the present.

Other Christians, especially though not exclusively from mainline Protestant denominations, see everything as changed. They experience such moral revulsion at Christianity's sponsorship of anti-Semitism and its complicit role in the Holocaust that they vigorously eschew every trace of supersessionism (see, e.g.,

C. Williamson and R. Eckhart). Certain Christian historians and theologians seem willing to eviscerate Christianity altogether. The major difficulty in many Christian-Jewish dialogues today is finding any real representation of a Christian position that is not so self-denying as to be in danger of disappearing. They see the New Testament as so drenched in anti-Judaism that they apply the logic of the medieval church's Talmud burning on their own Scripture: Christianity must find another basis than these fatally flawed—in Harold Bloom's phrase, "pragmatically murderous"—compositions. Rosemary Radford Ruether's provocative equation of Christology and anti-Semitism (see *Faith and Fratricide*, 1974) has for recent authors acquired the status of an unquestionable premise (see James Carroll, *Constantine's Sword*, 2001). To borrow James Carroll's image, Christianity must atone for its past by throwing itself on the same sword it wielded against Jews. Only the suicide of Christianity is sacrifice sufficient to answer the Holocaust.

Such showy self-immolation is scarcely a solution, not only because no moral high ground is available for Christianity regarding its past, but because public self-negation simply continues the pattern of Christian grandiosity. But this reflex among Christians shows how devastating the long history of supersessionism was. It led to the persecution and murder of Jews. But it also fundamentally distorted Christian identity as well. Nothing so reveals the powerful hold of supersessionism on the Christian consciousness than the evidence provided by the present situation. Some Christians simply can't shake themselves free of it, and those who do find that they have no Christianity left.

With respect to the first consequence, the persecution and murder of Jews, Christians need to do more than make symbolic gestures or eloquent apologies. They need to pray for the mercy of God and ask for the prayers of those Jews who have survived their savage stupidity. And, most of all, they need to repent. The word means change. And that brings us to the second consequence, the distortion of Christian consciousness. With respect to this, Christians need to change in fundamental ways. But they need to change *as* Christians. Self-annihilation serves no purpose.

SIMPLE REMINDERS

A healthier conversation might begin by Christians recognizing that what makes supersessionism wrong is not its political incorrectness but its lack of theological imagination. If, in fact, two parties should make contradictory truth claims on precisely the same point, then it would be necessary that one claim cancel the other. If you should say that you alone inherit this property but I say that I alone inherit it—and we are the only available heirs—then one of us being right means the other must be wrong. But putting the matter that way in the case of Jews and Christians is to put it wrongly, for two reasons.

The first reason is that, if we truly believe that there is but one God for all humans (see Rom 3:29–30), then Jews and Christians are not, either together or separate, the exclusive recipients of God's gifts. All humans are God's children. A sibling rivalry between two children in complete disregard of the larger family is both self-centered and silly. For either Jews or Christians to understand "election" in terms of an exclusive claim on God's revelation or care is to diminish God as well as the religious impulses of all the world's peoples. It is imperative that Christians and Jews move into modernity at least in this respect, that they recognize that the biblical story is not world history and the self-disclosure of God in Scripture does not exhaust God's capacity for self-disclosure to humans. The "Gentiles" of the present day also need to figure into Jewish and Christian thinking about God.

The second reason is that the internal claims of Jews and Christians are markedly different and do not cancel each other. In Jewish terms, for example, Jesus must be considered a failed

Messiah even if he is not regarded as a false Messiah. He did not, after all, make things better for Jews, and that is the minimum requirement for a Jewish Messiah. But Judaism is fundamentally misconstrued when it is reduced to messianism. Defining Judaism in terms of messianic expectation is defining it from a Christian rather than a Jewish perspective. Not even in the first two centuries of the common era, when messianism was rampant in Palestine, do we find a trace of it in the Diaspora, where most Jews lived. From Bar Kochba to Sabbatai Sevi, and from Sabbatai Sevi to Zionism, Judaism has flourished religiously apart from any significant messianic impulses but centered in community patterns of observance, study, and worship, based on the commandments of God.

On the other side, the Christian claim that Jesus is Messiah is connected not to any manner of empirical leadership over the Jews, but to his exaltation to God's right hand as the resurrected Lord. For Christians, Jesus is not a new Moses who displaces the old law with a new one, but the New Adam, whose "life-giving Spirit" (1 Cor 15:45) inaugurates a "new creation" (2 Cor 5:17; Gal 6:15). Christians understand the "promise to Abraham" not in terms of flourishing of the people on the land, but as the eschatological gift of the Holy Spirit poured out on all flesh and capable of transforming human freedom itself (Acts 2:17–39; 2 Cor 3:17–18). Christians understand righteousness as measured not by the observance of the commandments but as measured by the obedient faith of Jesus (Rom 3:21–26).

The texts shared by Jews and Christians, in short, are read in fundamentally different ways, not simply because Christians read TaNak in light of the New Testament, but because the New Testament itself is based on distinctive religious experiences and convictions not recognized as their own by Jews past and present.

Although these are simple and (at least ought to be) obvious points, they require repetition, because Christians have apparently forgotten them. Christians and Jews are not and should never have been in the present situation of Jews and Muslims in Israel today, wrangling over specific geography because of religious associations. The saddest theological aspect of the Crusades was not the violence they fostered toward Jews as well as Muslims but the way they distorted the point of Christian faith, for which "the Jerusalem above" ought to be the only Jerusalem that matters (see Gal 4:26; Heb 12:22).

Given the fact that Jesus is clearly not a Jewish Messiah in any manner that makes sense to Judaism, and given the fact that Judaism honors God by its profound and enduring witness to God's holiness through its own understanding of Torah and its demands, there is every reason for Jews to continue within and celebrate their own tradition with no particular concern for what Christians might think. Christians have not lost the right to define Judaism. They never had the right. That so many Christians over the centuries have assumed that they had that right simply shows how far they were confused about Christianity's distinctive experience and conviction.

TOWARD A TRUER CONVERSATION

Christians can begin to contribute toward a healthier and truer conversation by cultivating three unaccustomed attitudes and turning each attitude into a consistent practice.

The first is an appropriate theological modesty. Even after being stripped of their political, cultural, and intellectual pretensions, Christians still manage to display theological arrogance. The arrogance is found as much among those who propose reconstructing Christianity from the ground up as among those who think that no real change is necessary. From neither side does one hear any sense that Christians, like all other humans, are caught up in a mystery that goes beyond easy definition or calculation. From neither side does one learn how obscure and difficult are the texts of Scripture, which heal even as they wound. Spokespersons for Christianity seem to have forgotten that they do not represent the most logical and reasonable of religions—Judaism and Islam are both far more perspicuous—but the most paradoxical, based not in God's coherent revelation of law but in God's self-revelation in the crucified and raised Jesus. They seem, oddly, not to have learned that the God who so brings life out of death in Jesus challenges all human pretense of grasping or controlling God. They have not learned the most important lesson taught by their first and greatest theologian, the Apostle Paul, who spoke not of knowing God but of being known by God (1 Cor 8:3; Gal 4:9), and who concluded his own anguished search—as a Jew—into the mystery of God's ways among Jews and Gentiles with a confession of God's indecipherable and inscrutable ways (Rom 11:33–36).

And if such modesty is appropriate, even imperative, for any Christian at any time who proposes to speak about God, how much more should those claiming the name of Christian today abandon all arrogance in theological discourse. For, in plain truth, Christianity today is not in a good position even to represent itself, much less speak for God. The partial collapse of supersessionism has revealed the degree to which Christianity has defined itself negatively—in terms of contrast to Judaism—rather than positively—in terms of the experience of God in the resurrection of Jesus the Lord. Even the heroic Christian theologians who—like Ernst Kaesemann—disavowed Nazi anti-Semitism, continued in their own reading of the New Testament to perpetuate an implicit Marcionism in their reading of Paul and the Gospels. What was essential to Christianity had to be what was unique to Christianity, and what was unique to Christianity could only be measured by means of favorable contrast to a stereotypical Judaism. The same tendency persists, alas, even among questers for the historical Jesus.

Marcus Borg's Jesus, with his "politics of compassion" in contrast to the law's "politics of holiness," is only a contemporary variation of the same old anti-Semitic strand in Christian theology. The entire phenomenon of the historical quest for Jesus, in fact, is testimony to Christianity's own confusion about its own foundational experiences and convictions.

The attitude of modesty can manifest itself in practices of speech and behavior that counter Christianity's tendency toward arrogance. Christians might refrain for a season from declaration and pronouncement and definition. They might confess ignorance and confusion as well as moral inadequacy in the face of the mystery with which they have been entrusted—who knows why? They might relearn the delights of honest labor and inquiry, as they seek into their peculiarly complex Scriptures and traditions. They might, above all, acknowledge that they are required above all to learn who they are—what they actually believe and what they actually practice—before they can undertake to declare anything about others.

The second attitude for Christians to adopt—in truth a manifestation of theological humility or modesty—is a patient attentiveness to the truth of the gospel. Such is the fractured state of Christianity that Christians need first to engage in serious and sustained conversation about what they believe and what they do, in a humble quest for self-definition that is both internally coherent and consistent with the gift that God has given them through Jesus.

That there is a truth to the good news from and about God in the death and resurrection of Jesus is the continuing reason to be Christian. But patient attentiveness is required if Christians are to recover the heart of that truth through a difficult process of discernment and relearning. Christians need to rediscover and reclaim the experiences and convictions that truly define their own religious tradition. Even this simple statement will meet vigorous objections among some calling themselves Christian.

Some will say, "Who are you to define Christianity, why should Christianity need definition, why should definition be a matter of experiences and convictions?" The long and slow erosion of identity that has, at the beginning of the twenty-first century, made Christianity a club that one joins on one's own terms, gives rise to such objections. But the partial collapse of supersessionism ought to reveal how imperative it is for Christians to seek together for a positive coherence in their commitment. If Christianity is not simply "not Judaism," then what is it? If the church is not the replacement of Israel, then what is it? If Jesus is not the Jews' Messiah, then what kind of Messiah is he for Christians? These questions have not adequately been answered by the tradition. In the aftermath of the Holocaust, Christians must address them.

The two obvious starting points for such discernment among Christians are the New Testament and the Creed. A rigorous and sustained reading of the New Testament in its entirety and with critical loyalty should have the effect of disqualifying the careless and partial and uninformed readings that move either in the direction of anti-Semitism or in the direction of self-despising despair. A careful and communal reading of the New Testament ought also to lead Christian readers into a positive encounter with what is positive and life-giving in these texts. They do not need to define Christianity as a religion of grace over against a religion of law, because they discover in the actual words of Paul that no such contrast exists in his letters. And in the actual reading of the New Testament—as opposed to reading *about* the New Testament, they can be touched by the power of the transforming Spirit and recognize anew the meaning of declaring "Jesus is Lord."

Recommending the Creed for purposes of Christian self-discernment is more controversial, precisely because substantial numbers of people calling themselves Christian have grave doubts about creeds in general and the early church creeds in particular. Many ministerial students think that the point of studying theology is to develop "their theology" rather than be prepared to adequately proclaim the faith of the church. But for that very reason, the Creed—Apostles' or Nicene does not matter for this purpose—can serve as a valuable instrument for Christian self-examination. The Creed, after all, seeks precisely to define the faith of Christians, and it does so with a remarkable and possibly miraculous parsimoniousness. The Creed does not ask us to subscribe to specific theories of atonement or pronouncements on Mary. It does not define sin or righteousness. It says nothing about the church except that it should be one, holy, catholic, and apostolic. It says nothing at all about the Jews.

The Creed does state the basic Christian convictions concerning triune God as Creator, Savior, and Sanctifier, and the basic Christian story from creation through incarnation to the world to come. If Christians study the Creed together, it helps them sort out what in reality they are willing to confess and what they are not willing to confess, and bring to light the dramatically different ways in which they understand that which they confess. This process can encourage as well a serious intellectual engagement with the profession of the church, so that Christians can begin to ask not simply whether they believe in the incarnation and the resurrection and the ascension and the future judgment, but if they do, what that belief means for Christian practice and politics. They can begin to ask whether the heart of Christianity is not eschatological rather than historical, and whether it is necessary to recover the language of ontology to express what God has done in Christ.

The third attitude that Christians should cultivate is another manifestation of theological modesty, namely the willingness to learn from Judaism rather than presume to define Judaism in Christian terms. The ignorance of Christians with respect to their own tradition is exceeded only by their ignorance of Judaism, not only concerning the past but also the present. Although there has been a great deal of splendid historical work done on ancient Judaism in the time of the New Testament carried out by both Jewish and Christian scholars, too little of this learning has found its way to theological conversations, and very little of it has entered ordinary Christian consciousness. Knowledge about Christianity among Jewish scholars, to be sure, is not much more developed. Christians formerly thought they had the luxury of defining Jews based on their own literature. They no longer have that supposed luxury. Christians are obliged to learn now not about Jews but from Jews, not out of a fear of Jews, but out of the need to discover and appreciate the shape of their own heritage through a deeper knowledge and appreciation of the gift that God has given—and keeps giving—as well to the Jews.

These proposals are simple. But they are difficult. Keeping silence about things they do not know will be hard for garrulous Christian theologians. Paying attention to the heart of their tradition will be anguishing for communities who would rather do anything than define their belief and practice. Learning about Judaism from Jews as a way of gaining in wisdom means learning as well an unaccustomed humility. If Christians can manage such small steps, they will begin to learn what repentance truly means.

16

MENTORING IN THE ROMAN CATHOLIC TRADITION

Published in Mentoring: Biblical, Theological, and Practical Perspectives, *ed. Dean K. Thompson and D. Cameron Murchison (Grand Rapids: Eerdmans, 2018).*

In the centuries-long tradition of Catholicism, mentoring has played a prominent role, and has several distinctive features. It has had little or no connection with the sort of mentoring for worldly success in a career or profession that current use of the term suggests. Rather, its main goal has always been the transformation of personal character in the search for sanctity. This sort of mentoring has deep roots in Greco-Roman moral philosophy and Hellenistic Judaism, in which the "guidance of souls" (*psychagoge*) had a significant place. The expressions of such mentoring have been various across the centuries, but every form includes a teacher/disciple relationship, the transmission of wisdom through oral instruction, and (perhaps most critical) imitation of the teacher by the disciple. Over time, a considerable body of "devotional" literature was generated, which enabled even those excluded from such a personal mentoring relationship to follow the same path.

In this essay, I first sketch the historical antecedents and the successive expressions of mentoring within the Catholic tradition. And since being "Catholic" means embracing the entire tradition rather than the short period since the Counter Reformation when the modifier *Roman* became necessary, my survey goes back to the beginning. Along the way, I note significant literary expressions of this mentoring tradition. Then, I spend some time on the actual shape of such mentoring: how was the path to sanctity understood, why was it thought to be perilous, and why was careful guidance required for those who undertook it? I close with some comments about the effects within Catholicism of the loss, or at least the substantial weakening, of this mentoring tradition.

BACKGROUND AND FIRST STAGES

Christianity inherited an already well-developed tradition of mentoring in the philosophical life. In the time of the early empire, philosophy had become a matter more of therapy than of theory. Moral philosophy paid close attention to the formation of virtue (health) as opposed to vice (sickness). Although philosophical schools differed on many points of doctrine, they agreed on the need for the transformation of character, and that such transformation required a special form of *paideia* (education/discipline). Wisdom was a matter of practical living and was best learned through imitation of a living example.

Thus, in the patriarchal structure of the ancient household, a father was expected to provide both wise sayings (maxims) for the guidance of his son, and to serve as a living exemplar of proper behavior. For those seeking more than merely conventional morality, however, training in the philosophical life required the instruction, but even more, the example of the philosophical mentor. The Stoic Epictetus, for example, praised the way his own teacher, Musonius Rufus, had insight into even the secret vices of his students, and Epictetus offered himself to his own students not only through his lively sermons (discourses) but as well through the manner of his life. The condemnation of "false philosophers," in turn, tended to focus on the disparity between their words and their practice; it was important to learn authentic virtue from an authentic exemplification of virtue.

Attention to the formation of would-be philosophers was given more formal structural expression among the Pythagoreans, whose communal life featured the sharing of possessions and the ordered transmission of the *apophthegmata* (wise maxims) of Pythagoras. Entrants to the Pythagorean community had to undergo a period of probation before they were admitted among the mature members. Such structural elements are found as well among the Essenes at Qumran, who resemble the Pythagoreans not least in their exceptional practice of communal possessions. Philo of Alexandria's description of the *therapeutai* also suggests the goal of spiritual transformation among such Jewish practitioners of the philosophical life through the study of Scripture, teaching, and prayer.

The canonical Gospels contain elements that situate the activity of Jesus and the apostles within this mentoring tradition: Jesus is portrayed as a teacher who instructs his disciples, and his command to "follow me" points to his role as a model to be imitated. In his letters, Paul presents himself as a model to his readers, and instructs them in the moral life. But mentoring in any real sense is not found in the New Testament writings, which are directed primarily to the formation of communities, rather than the transformation of individuals. The same is true of the extant Christian literature of the pre-Constantinian period. With the very partial exception of such Gnostic writings as Ptolemy's *Letter to Flora*, there is little attention given to the spiritual progress of individuals. As the figures of Ignatius and Polycarp and Justin and

Origen remind us, the centuries when the church lived under the threat of persecution and martyrdom demanded a posture of public witness in the face of death more than the patient cultivation of the virtues under the guidance of a mentor.

A clearer expression of mentoring emerges after Constantine, when Christianity was established as the imperial religion. The relatively comfortable circumstances of Christian life in urban centers led some to become discontented with what they regarded as a compromised form of discipleship and to seek a more strenuous form of witness—a "white martyrdom"—in the wilderness of Egypt, Palestine, and Syria. The conflict these fathers and mothers of the desert engaged was not with the demonic forces of the empire threatening death through martyrdom, but the demons of their own passions (desire, lust, envy, avarice, sloth) that threatened to turn disciples from the way of Christ. The publicity gained by some of these early saints (see Athanasius's *Life of Antony*) led thousands to seek their presence and their guidance, so that virtual "cities in the desert" grew up around the men and women who could provide direction to others in the quest for holiness.

Many of their maxims on the spiritual combat, as well as anecdotes about their practice of prayer and fasting, were collected and published (see the *apophthegmata patrum*), enabling those who could not physically be in their presence to share in their wisdom. The fourth-century *Lausiac History* by Palladius describes the way in which wealthy men and women from cities would travel from one holy person to another seeking such guidance; the literary expression of their quest similarly enabled readers to participate in the same mentoring at a distance. And the early fifth-century monastic founder John Cassian, who had studied with monks in Palestine and Egypt, compiled the wisdom of the desert monks concerning the path to God in his *Conferences*, which enabled readers to virtually hear from the lips of those ancient saints themselves in a form of second-hand mentoring.

In the cenobitic monasticism established in Egypt by Pachomius (292–348), the communal expression of *paideia* pioneered by Pythagoreans and Essenes found renewal within Christianity. Responsibility for the shaping of monastic character—which simply meant a life in search of perfection—was shifted from the one-to-one relationship of sage and student, to the structure of life governed by the rule. The classic form of Western monasticism in Benedict of Nursia's *Rule for Monks* (early sixth century) followed this essentially communal focus, without losing a concern for individual formation. Thus, in the prologue to the *Rule*, the individual monk is called to "return by the labor of obedience to Him from whom you had departed by the sloth of disobedience." The applicant to the monastery is to undergo a period of "testing of spirits" before being admitted to the novitiate, where "a senior is assigned to them who is skilled in winning souls to watch over them with the utmost care" (ch. 58).

The novice master provides the sort of hands-on mentoring in the monastic ethos and practice that reinforces the positive elements of what young monks could observe also (it was hoped) in the behavior of the entire community. Benedict was also aware of the need for personal attention when the framework of obedience to rule and abbot failed. Thus, the *Rule* exhorts the abbot to be solicitous toward the excommunicated (for faults), sending them sympathetic "brothers of mature years and wisdom" who might offer them counsel and support (ch. 27). In the final chapter of the *Rule*, Benedict acknowledges that he has provided only the "rudiments of the religious life," and for those "who would hasten to the perfection of that life," he offers the study of the Old and New Testaments, the writings of the "holy Fathers" (patristic authors), the *Conferences* of John Cassian, the *Lives of the Fathers*, and the *Rule of Saint Basil* (ch. 73). And in fact, the course of *lectio divina* within the long monastic tradition included the close and sustained reading of such spiritual authorities and the imitation of the examples they provided.

Mentoring in the Roman Catholic Tradition

THE LONG TRADITION

Catholic mentoring in the spiritual life—before and after the Protestant Reformation—continued to take place almost entirely within the frame of religious vows among men and women who, like ancient philosophers, chose to commit themselves to (what they regarded as) a higher and more difficult expression of Christian identity. Whether in Benedictine monasteries (male and female) and in the families of monks in the West that derived from the Benedictines (Cistercians, Trappists), or in male and female religious orders that sprang up in the Middle Ages and beyond—Dominicans, Franciscans, Carmelites, and many others—the basic pattern set by the monastic life continued.

From one perspective, such religious life was remarkably stable and predictable, with monks and mendicants passing through stages of postulancy, novitiate, simple vows, and solemn vows while living out their obedience to the order's rules and authority structure. From another perspective, those driven by the desire for unity with God entered upon an arduous journey of the soul that required careful guidance. The role of the individual "spiritual director" was therefore a key element in the mentoring process. Patriarchal arrangements obtained: male monks and mendicants often served as spiritual directors as well as confessors for women religious (as in the sixteenth century, John of the Cross was for Teresa of Avila, even though he was a follower of her reform movement). Among the many classics of mysticism written over this long span of time, several of them are noteworthy for adopting a mentoring stance toward the reader, leading him or her along on the path of mystical ascent: the anonymous *Cloud of Unknowing* (late fourteenth century), Teresa of Avila's *Way of Perfection*, and John of the Cross's *Ascent of Mount Carmel* (both late sixteenth century).

When the Council of Trent, seeking to reform the clergy who did not belong to religious orders, mandated the establishments of seminaries for the training of priests (session 23 in 1563), the model of spiritual formation in monasteries and religious orders was transposed to the preparation of diocesan clergy. Seminary life in many ways imitated the routine of monasteries. A formal position within Roman Catholic seminaries was therefore that of the spiritual director, whose responsibilities included conferences on the spiritual life. In addition to the official spiritual director, seminarians were encouraged to choose a personal director, who would serve both as confessor and as spiritual guide. Depending on the individual gifts of such directors, personal advice could range from the obtuse and purely formal to the personally engaging and psychologically discerning. Just as the monastery's novice master was to "test spirits," so in the Roman Catholic seminary, the spiritual director played a key role in helping the seminarian (and institution) to discern the authenticity of his vocation.

An unspoken premise of this system was that the seminarian's experience of spiritual direction would also serve to make a young priest a better confessor for lay Christians, and capable of offering spiritual direction to those who sought it. The mentoring found within seminaries, moreover, was assumed to be carried on after ordination in pastoral placements, where senior clergy—the priest or monsignor who served as pastor—was to provide both personal example and verbal instruction to the younger associates assigned to the parish. Sometimes this happened, sometimes it did not. But this "on the job" mentoring came as close as anything in the Roman Catholic tradition to what is currently understood as "professional mentoring," that is, dealing not only with personal spiritual progress but also with competence in ministerial practice.

The practices of spiritual mentoring within this long Catholic tradition were found almost exclusively within monasteries, religious houses, seminaries, and rectories. Laypeople had little access to such guidance, unless they made personal contact with such religious professionals or joined one of the "Third Order" sodalities that offered participation in the life of a religious organization.

Otherwise, laypeople depended on whatever counsel and advice could be delivered by their parish priests in the context of confession. Seldom did this become more than a hit-or-miss proposition. The content of spiritual instruction, moreover, remained largely monastic in form. Thus, although *The Imitation of Christ* by Thomas à Kempis (early fifteenth century) enjoyed an astonishingly wide readership—and in book 3 had the reader directly addressed as "my son" by Jesus—its message remained shaped by a "flee the world" disposition that ill fitted the lives of lay readers. What made Francis de Sales's masterpiece, *Introduction to the Devout Life* (1609), so remarkable was its wholehearted appreciation for the worldly circumstances of lay readers, and its effort to build a spiritual life in completely lay terms.

WHY MENTORING IS NEEDED

The commitment to "seek the face of God," to pursue a life of sanctity beyond that expected of ordinary discipleship, is inherently exceptional and perilous. It is exceptional: by no means did all Christians make such a commitment; thus the decision to become a monk or join a religious order was a choice for "the way of perfection," understood as bearing greater blessing and greater risk for those who chose it. For those who made the commitment, then and now (now less and less within the frame of a religious institution), it is the ultimate decision that measures all other choices. It is not like taking up a hobby or cultivating a certain craft. It is rather a religious commitment that utterly defines one's life. Since it is a matter of living one's life in a certain way, it is imperative that guidance come from someone who has made the same commitment earlier and has made significant progress along the same path.

The commitment is also perilous: seeking intimate communion with God is a dangerous pursuit. It is not like finding a friend or enjoying the company of other persons. God is not a person among other persons, or an object among other objects. The Living God is Spirit, the source and goal of all that exists. The journey is dangerous, first, then, because it deals with the Lord of all creation, and the Letter to the Hebrews reminds us that "it is a terrible thing to fall into the hands of the living God" (Heb 10:31); this is not a trivial enterprise but one dealing with ultimate reality. And since the "journey" is not one along material paths but through the very soul of the seeker, it is subject to all the perils that can befall a psyche that is reaching beyond its own capacity.

Mentoring in the Catholic tradition has therefore taken the form of a spiritual companionship and support during a long and lonely journey of the soul. The journey is long. It is not accomplished by reaching external marks of advancement. It is, indeed, never "accomplished" before death, and is incapable of being measured by any external marks. It is a life-long commitment to transformation of oneself according to the mind of Christ, to a renewal of one's mind and heart through the power of the Holy Spirit. The temptation to give up the quest out of fatigue and frustration is real; equally real is the temptation to cease questing out of the delusion that one *is* finished before death.

The journey is also inherently lonely. Not only do few undertake such a commitment, the process of transformation itself involves alienation from the comforts of the flesh, including the precious comfort of human companionship. The interior struggle is not easily shared with those not also engaged in the struggle—and this, even within a monastery or religious order. Even in such contexts, there are not many who understand or are even appreciative of the secret journey that the one who seeks God's presence has undertaken. The sense of being alone on such a perilous journey heightens the psychic dangers and increases the need for a spiritual guide.

The notion of progress is built into the image of a journey, so an obvious aspect of spiritual direction is identifying the stages of such progress as they were lived by the pioneers and trail markers of old, and helping adjust the perceptions and expectations of the one who is seeking to make a way through such spiritual stages. The classic stages of growth in the spiritual life are called the purgative way, the illuminative way, and the unitive way. The first represents the turning from vice and the cultivation of virtue; it involves what is usually thought of as asceticism: the disciplined cultivation of "a life worthy of God, who calls you into his own kingdom and glory" (1 Thess 2:12). Here, there is an emphasis on prayer, fasting, and almsgiving at a level more radical and absolute than the same practices as found among ordinary believers. The second signifies sporadic moments and states of spiritual insight or illumination, a more palpable "experience" of God. In this stage, more attention is given to the effects of "pray[ing] without ceasing" (1 Thess 5:17). The third points to the end point of the journey available in the present life, an enduring condition of unity with God that is not to be identified either with the way or purgation or illumination but that builds upon and subsumes those earlier stages.

Although the distinction between such stages seems clear enough, the actual movement through them is filled with uncertainty and ambiguity, making the discernment of a spiritual mentor critical. By no means, for example, does the purgative way ever end; the struggle to control the passions remains real throughout life. And that struggle raises all kinds of questions: When are fasting and other forms of fleshly mortification appropriate and when are they excessive? How does genuine humility manifest itself? How is religious obedience to be distinguished from will-lessness or masochism? The advanced stages of the spiritual quest raise even more questions: How can one distinguish between genuine divine visitations and self-generated visions? How can one follow the lead of such experiences and also be guided by religious obedience?

Spiritual mentoring is necessary above all because of the constant threat of delusion and self-deception in those engaged in such an exalted yet isolating quest. How easy it is to mistake states of dissociation arising from acute fasting with spiritual advancement, or periods of depression with the dark night of the soul, or erotic attraction with spiritual intimacy. Self-examination is not sufficient, for it can equally be compromised by fantasy and desire. The sane voice of another is required to cut through the tangle of self-delusion. The voice of sanity is especially valuable for those whose exercises have brought them to the brink of psychic exhaustion and confusion. The companion who has undertaken the same journey is best able to identify its dangers and wrong turnings, is best capable of reminding the one seeking sanctity that it is not a matter of spectacular works but of simple and ever-deepening faith, expressed most authentically not in flights of mystical exaltation but in loving kindness toward the neighbor.

The best of the mentoring tradition within the long Catholic tradition has combined a spirit of companionship arising from commitment to the same quest, with a tough-minded detachment that enables a true testing of the spirits. At its best, as exemplified by the experience of many we call saints, spiritual direction is one of the true (if seldom acknowledged) glories of a tradition that is too often identified with externals rather than with internal transformation.

But spiritual mentoring has by no means always been at its best, and it is important to remember the ways in which the practice of spiritual direction has itself been corrupted. There is no lack of stories recounting the ways in which spiritual directors manipulated those they advised, sometimes through authoritarian demands for obedience, sometimes through forms of persuasion that became sexually seductive, sometimes both. The breaking of boundaries that properly appalls us in the case of doctors and teachers and therapists is even more shocking—though seldom surprising—in the case of those whose help is sought in the most psychically demanding exercise of all: the quest of perfection.

The abuse of power displayed by confessors seducing those seeking repentance or by spiritual directors co-opting the freedom of choice properly belonging to those they direct, are all the more heinous because they are done in secret and under the cloak of the highest and best of human endeavors.

THE BREAKDOWN OF A TRADITION

Much of this essay has been cast in the past tense, because the tradition of spiritual mentoring within Catholicism has changed in fundamental ways, and its future is uncertain. To some extent, the alteration is one of the unintended consequences of the Second Vatican Council. The council's documents effected important shifts in focus. In contrast to the "flee the world" piety and intellectual stance that characterized the church in previous centuries, the council called for an engagement with the modern world. Rather than focus exclusively on clergy and religious, the council sought to empower laity within the church. In its earliest proclamation, the council called for the reform of the liturgy, making it the center of Catholic identity, and calling in particular for full participation by all in the Eucharist. The council advocated a more Scripture-based spirituality, at the same time approving of contemporary historical-critical approaches to the Bible. Empowerment of the laity, participation in public worship, the critical reading of Scripture, engagement with modernity: all these make an activist and communal form of Christian discipleship more attractive than an individual's quest for interior perfection. Asceticism, prayer, and contemplation were not proscribed, but neither were they highlighted.

The decades following the council saw the virtual collapse of the vast interlocking network of institutions that for centuries had been the natural setting for mentoring in the spiritual life. Monks and nuns left their houses and many fewer young people joined contemplative communities; religious orders as well found their numbers decimated; vocations to the priesthood almost disappeared and seminaries were forced to shut down. Those who remained in traditional forms of religious life were far fewer than before, and were aging as a group, without a younger cohort of eager men and women surging through the door seeking to be mentored in the spiritual life. The crisis of diminished numbers exacerbated a movement away from the contemplative to the active life: simply staffing all the ministries to which priests and religious were committed took all the energy available. The combination of the council's positive affirmation of lay and active discipleship, and the collapse of the patriarchal structures that made the transmission of wisdom from the old to the young intelligible, weakened the entire framework of spiritual mentoring as it had previously existed.

The weakening of institutional structures was accompanied by real changes in the understanding of the spiritual life. Three are particularly noteworthy. The Catholic charismatic movement, which began in the late 1960s, privileged the immediacy of powerful spiritual experience: speaking in tongues, prophesying, healing. The gift of the Holy Spirit energized many Catholics, leading them to form intentional communities based on such experiences. The need for the "discernment of spirits" in such settings was obvious: enthusiasm could and did lead to a variety of unhealthy expressions—as it did in the ancient church at Corinth. But the lack of an established structure for mentorship meant that centuries of wisdom concerning the spiritual life were not readily available; leaders of groups were often only months or weeks longer "in the Spirit" than newcomers. The desert fathers and Cassian would have known, for example, that an initial powerful experience is valuable only if it subsequently leads to a disciplined path of asceticism and prayer—real growth takes place after "the honeymoon period." By way of contrast, twentieth-century charismatic communities avidly sought new conversions to the movement because the initial experience of neophytes renewed and invigorated those whose own gifts had grown less exciting. Rather than dig deeper, the tendency in charismatic groups was to stay at the level of the surface.

A second development was a conception of discipleship that drew on the activist strain in the Second Vatican Council, manifested especially among those committed to a liberation understanding of the gospel. There is much that is positive in this prophetic understanding: the good news is translated into a passionate concern for social justice, and the rule of God is expressed through the liberating human from the structures of oppression and sin that keep them captive. Here, a concern for interior transformation is seen as less important than an active and external engagement with movements of social justice. Participating in actions of justice is seen as a more serious commitment to God than a life of conventional piety. Taken to an extreme, however, such a view of discipleship can exclude attention to asceticism and prayer: they are dismissed as narcissistic self-centeredness rather than a commitment to ameliorating social systems.

A third challenge to the classic understanding of the spiritual life as a quest for perfection was posed by a variety of therapeutic approaches to spirituality. The triumph of a psychological approach can be seen in the abandonment of language about sin and salvation in favor of language about sickness and health; in the perception of asceticism and self-abnegation as neurotic manifestations of an unhealthy masochism; in an emphasis on growth in self-esteem rather than stages of humility; in pursuing tranquility and peace more than an agonistic struggle with the passions; in rejecting the dark night of the soul in favor of constant comfort. The point of meditation is now to provide a rest for the spirit in a hectic world; the point of fasting—or dieting—is to have a healthier lifestyle.

The combination of institutional collapse and conceptual erosion means that the classic form of mentoring in the spiritual life has almost disappeared within Catholicism. Two important spiritual writers of the late twentieth century illustrate the change. Although the Trappist monk Thomas Merton drew attention because of his "turn to the world" in his later years—embracing a variety of spiritual traditions and adopting a prophetic stance toward an idolatrous culture—he was nevertheless formed by the most traditional forms of spiritual mentorship within the monastery, and passionately sought the path to perfection along classic lines. A student of the great mystics from the desert fathers through John of the Cross, his own spiritual writings (as in *Seeds of Contemplation* and *The New Man*) were fresh and engaging iterations of that long tradition. And he provided both fellow monks and a wide range of correspondents with spiritual counsel according to the same pattern. His engagement with modernity enlivened and broadened but did not fundamentally change his conviction that the point of life was the quest for holiness. He stood firmly within the long Catholic tradition of mentoring, despite—or perhaps because of—his prophetic stance toward contemporary culture. People became monks because of the example of Thomas Merton.

The profile of Henri Nouwen was quite different, although he was equally admired by many devotees for his popular spiritual writings. A priest and member of a religious order, he was not situated within a monastery, but led a life that can only be called itinerant: he moved frequently from one setting to another, sometimes occupying the role of a seminary professor, sometimes engaging an active social ministry (such as L'Arche), using the new experiences offered by those places as occasions for spiritual insight into his own spiritual journey. Although the classic shape of the spiritual life is still visible in many of his writings, his primary training in psychology deeply influenced his approach (see *The Wounded Healer* or *Intimacy*). Despite a charismatic presence that drew many of his readers to seek personal contact with him, Nouwen's awareness of his own brokenness made him reluctant to occupy the traditional role of a spiritual guide who offers himself for imitation. And it is difficult to imagine what such imitation might look like. He is the prototype of contemporary Catholic spiritual writers (such as Kathleen Norris) whose presence to others is primarily literary and whose vision of the spiritual journey is less face-to-face and more freelance and idiosyncratic (that is, less institutionally located and mediated) than in past generations. Matthew Fox's "creation spirituality," for example, engages many classics of spirituality within the Catholic tradition, but places them within an ecumenical eclecticism and highly personal "spiritual movement" that only with considerable effort can be seen as continuous with the longer Catholic tradition of spiritual mentoring.

The Catholic tradition is both long and remarkably resilient. It would be foolish to declare dead its long-standing commitment to spiritual mentoring; the Holy Spirit is always capable of breathing new life into dead bones and of bringing into existence new expressions of old values. But when in the first quarter of the twenty-first century we consider the magnificence of the tradition as it once existed, as well as its recent state of disarray and confusion, it is difficult to imagine what a revitalized future might be.